ILEX FOUNDATION SERIES 17

SINGING MOSES'S SONG

SINGING MOSES'S SONG

A PERFORMANCE-CRITICAL ANALYSIS OF DEUTERONOMY'S SONG OF MOSES

Keith A. Stone

Ilex Foundation
Boston, Massachusetts

Center for Hellenic Studies
Trustees for Harvard University
Washington, D.C.

Distributed by Harvard University Press
Cambridge, Massachusetts, and London, England

Singing Moses's Song: A Performance-Critical Analysis of Deuteronomy's Song of Moses
By Keith A. Stone

Published by Ilex Foundation, Boston, Massachusetts and The Center for Hellenic Studies, Trustees for Harvard University, Washington, D.C.

Distributed by Harvard University Press, Cambridge, Massachusetts and London, England

Production editor: Christopher Dadian
Cover design: Joni Godlove
Printed in the United States of America

Cover images: "Moses's Testament and Death" Luca Signorelli, 1481-1482. Fresco. From the cycle of the life of Moses Sistine Chapel, sixth compartment, south wall. Cappella Sistina, Vatican.

Library of Congress Cataloging-in-Publication Data

Names: Stone, Keith A., author.
Title: Singing Moses's song : a performance-critical analysis of
  Deuteronomy's song of Moses / Keith A. Stone.
Description: Boston, Massachusetts : Ilex Foundation ; Washington, D.C. :
  Center for Hellenic Studies, Trustees for Harvard University ; Cambridge,
  Massachusetts : Distributed by Harvard University Press, [2016] | Series:
  Ilex Foundation series ; 17 | "This book is a lightly revised version of
  my 2013 Harvard University PhD dissertation, completed in the Department
  of Near Eastern Languages and Civilizations"--Acknowledgments. | Ph. D.
  Harvard University 2013. | Includes bibliographical references.
Identifiers: LCCN 2016035523 | ISBN 9780674971172 (alk. paper)
Subjects: LCSH: Bible. Deuteronomy, XXXII, 1-43--Criticism, interpretation,
  etc. | Hebrew poetry, Biblical--History and criticism. | Performance
  poetry--Biblical teaching. | Bible. Deuteronomy--Criticism,
  interpretation, etc.
Classification: LCC BS1275.52 .S76 2016 | DDC 222/.1506--dc23
LC record available at https://lccn.loc.gov/2016035523

CONTENTS

Acknowledgments

THIS BOOK is a lightly revised version of my 2013 Harvard University PhD dissertation, completed in the Department of Near Eastern Languages and Civilizations. I would like to take this opportunity to offer my thanks once again to my advisors in that project – Professors Jo Ann Hackett, Gregory Nagy, and Jon D. Levenson. I would like to offer a double share of thanks to Gregory Nagy in his role as director of Harvard University's Center for Hellenic Studies, along with Zoie Lafis, administrative director of the CHS, for arranging the CHS post-doctoral fellowship that has allowed me time to prepare the manuscript for publication. Finally, I appreciate the gracious support of Niloo Fotouhi, executive director of the Ilex Foundation, and the congenial expertise of Christopher Dadian, Ilex's managing editor.

Chapter 1

Introduction

I FIRST BEGAN INVESTIGATING the Song of Moses (Deuteronomy 32.1–43[1]) as a performed piece in an oral poetics seminar led by Gregory Nagy, partway through the semester at a moment when I was searching for a text on which to base my final paper, hardly anticipating that it would become the "final paper" of my doctoral studies. I had rejected the Psalms as too obvious; after all, some of them feature explicit instructions for their performance in their title headings. I then turned to the major poems embedded in biblical narratives, among them the Blessing of Jacob in Genesis, the Song of the Sea in Exodus, the Oracles of Balaam in Numbers – until I reached the Song of Moses, in the book of Deuteronomy, which does not pretend simply to be the transcript of what was said once upon a time on a particular occasion[2] but is also accompanied by instructions more explicit (and much lengthier) than those of any psalm. Rather than being a drawback for my project, however, Deuteronomy's instructions for the Song make highly self-conscious reference to a tradition of performance – a tradition that the Deuteronomic[3] narrative claims, moreover, to be instituting. In providing an etiology, Deuteronomy practically admits that the Song was already established in a tradition of performance, much as is the case with stories of famous ancestors founding sanctuaries.[4] But it was not the pre-existing historical tradition of performing the Song that was of interest to me, in that seminar paper and now in this book-length study, so much as the performance that Deuteronomy wished to portray.

1. As a matter of convenience, I will cite the text of the Song of Moses using the abbreviation "SoM"; for example, "SoM 1–3" refers to Deuteronomy 32.1–3, the first three verses of the poem.

2. The four other poems to be found within Pentateuchal prose are: the Blessing of Jacob (Genesis 49.2–27), the Song of the Sea (Exodus 15.1–18), the Oracles of Balaam (Numbers 23.7–10, 18–24; 24.3–9, 15–24), and the Blessing of Moses (Deuteronomy 33.2–29). Outside of the Pentateuch, the major prose-embedded poems are the Song of Deborah (Judges 5.2–31), the Song of Hannah (1 Samuel 2.1–10), the Lament of David (2 Samuel 1.19–27), the Song of David (2 Samuel 22.2–51), the Last Words of David (2 Samuel 23.1–7), the Song of Asaph (1 Chronicles 16.8–36), the Psalm of Hezekiah (Isaiah 38.10–20), the Prayer of Jonah (Jonah 2.3–10), and the Song of the Three (Daniel 3 LXX).

3. Here I am using "Deuteronomic" simply to mean "of Deuteronomy." At a later point I will distinguish between "Deuteronomic" and "Deuteronomistic."

4. E.g. the book of Genesis attributes the beginning of cult at Shechem to the patriarch Abraham: "Abram traveled across the land as far as Shechem, as far as the oak of Mamre ... and he built there an altar to YHWH, who had appeared to him" (Genesis 12.6–7).

1

How, indeed, does Deuteronomy portray the Song? The Deuteronomic narrator marks off the text of the Song as a distinct unit, speaking immediately before and after it of "the words of this song" (דִּבְרֵי הַשִּׁירָה־הַזֹּאת), words that do in fact stand between these enclosing notices (31.30; 32.44). Deuteronomy labels it as a "song" (שִׁירָה: 31.19 [twice], 21, 22, 30; 32.44)[5] that is susceptible to being written (לכתוב: 31.19.22), to being taught (ללמד: 31.19, 22), to being placed in the Israelites' (collective, notional) mouth (לשים: 31.19), and to having its words spoken into the Israelites' ears (לדבר: 31.30; 32.44). Memory is key to its operation, for it is something that will not "be forgotten from the mouth" (להשכח: 31.21). Further, the Song is something that can respond or answer (לענות: 31.21), serving as an עֵד 'witness' against the Israelites (31.19, 21).[6] According to the Deuteronomic narrator, in sum, the Song's written transcript in 32.1–43 is evidently to function as the script for a repeated oral performance that takes on a life of its own when – becoming the subject of the phrase "to answer as a witness" (לַעֲנוֹת לְעֵד) – the Song accuses the very people who perform it.

According to the Song's self-description in SoM 1–3, the Song is an act of speaking (לדבר), represented by two nouns cognate with each other, אֵמֶר and אִמְרָה, both meaning 'speech' or 'word', as well as by the noun לֶקַח 'teaching', construed as something received (cf. the verb לקחת 'to take, to receive'). SoM 3a (the name of YHWH do I call out [שֵׁם יְהוָה אֶקְרָא]) indicates that the Song is also, at least in part, a proclamation of the divine name, presumably in a sense parallel to the second half of the line, in SoM 3b, which commands the ascribing of greatness or of great deeds to YHWH. Besides this form of praise, other kinds of utterance performed in the course of the Song's performance include questioning (SoM 6ab, 6cd, 30, 34, 37a–38b; without actually being given the label, these passages are nonetheless questions, while the one question that is explicitly commanded [in SoM 7c: שְׁאַל (ask!)] does not appear in the Song, although the response to it does, in SoM 8–18), announcing (להגיד; SoM 7c), speaking (לאמור; SoM 7d, 20ø, 26ø, 27b, 37ø, 40ø), misconstruing (לנכר; SoM 27b), asseverating (חַי אָנֹכִי לְעֹלָם [as I live forever]; SoM 40b), and giving a ringing cry (להרן; SoM 43a).

---

5. Within the Hebrew Bible, the singular of the relatively rare feminine noun שִׁירָה 'song' always indicates a song whose transcript is at hand in the text. Including the six occurrences in Deuteronomy listed above, it occurs seven other times: Exodus 15.1; Numbers 21.17; 2 Samuel 22.1 = Psalm 18.1; and Isaiah 5.1; 23.15. Although the masculine singular noun שִׁיר 'song' has this function of indicating a transcript once, in Isaiah 26.1: יוּשַׁר הַשִּׁיר־הַזֶּה (this song will be sung), it mostly occurs instead in more abstract locutions (cf. Psalm 69.31, 96.1; Amos 6.5).

6. Outside the near context of the Song, the verb לענות 'to answer' and the noun עֵד 'witness' appear together in Deuteronomy at 5.17/20 and 19.15–20, laws concerning the giving of (false) testimony. The instances of לענות in 21.7 and 25.9 function similarly, though without עֵד.

The Song of Moses Performed

I had thus found my performed (and to-be-performed) text. The thesis of that oral poetics paper was that the Song's performers – a category most synonymous with the audience of the book of Deuteronomy – were to occupy certain positions relative both to the performed text as well as to the tradition of performing it that Deuteronomy intended to create for them. To analyze these positions, I borrowed some of the insights of my teacher Gregory Nagy, insights that he developed in the course of his research on traditions of performing epic and lyric poetry in the ancient Greek-speaking world. While these particular insights are at points based on an analysis of the etymologies of ancient Greek technical terms for performance, they are also based on the nature of performance in a ritualized context informed by a founding myth – just such a context as is provided by Deuteronomy for the Song of Moses.[7] Thus, for example, a performer of Homeric epic is not to be understood as simply giving an impression of the characters that exist in the *Iliad* and the *Odyssey*; rather, in the performance, those characters reappear: "When a Homeric hero is quoted speaking dactylic hexameters, it is to be understood that heroes 'spoke' in dactylic hexameters, not that they are being *represented* as speaking that way."[8] Further, Homer himself – the paradigmatic, eponymous composer and performer of this body of traditional poetry – also becomes a character in the performance:

> when the rhapsode says 'tell me, Muses!' (*Iliad* II 484) or 'tell me, Muse!' (*Odyssey* i 1), this 'I' is not a *representation* of Homer: it *is* Homer. My argument is that the rhapsode is re-enacting Homer by performing Homer, that he *is* Homer so long as the mimesis stays in effect, so long as the performance lasts…. the rhapsode is a *recomposed performer*: he becomes recomposed into Homer every time he performs Homer.[9]

To adapt such a model of performance to the Song of Moses, then, who is its paradigmatic composer and performer? And who are the characters within the poem, appearing when it is performed?[10]

7. Nagy 1996; see also Nagy 1990.

8. Nagy 1996:61 [italics in original].

9. Nagy 1996:61 [italics in original]; on this and the previous point, see also Nagy 1996:220–21 and Nagy 2007:228–29.

10. Although he does not consider (here) the origin of re-performed characters (whether from tradition or from within the composition), Richard Schechner usefully describes the transformation that occurs in the moment of performance: "… performers are 'not themselves' and 'not not themselves.' … Performers link two realms of experience, the only two

The figure of Moses provides the obvious beginning point of the tradition of the Song's performance, as he is the one who writes down the Song and teaches it to the Israelites (31.22), subsequently performing it before them (31.30). His actions are the precedent for all other Israelite performances of the Song, which are to continue throughout their generations (31.21) in order that the Song may reach its intended addressees, a generation of Israelites living an unspecified time in the future.[11] These future Israelites will have been theretofore unappreciative performers of the Song, questioning YHWH's presence with them (31.17) – but it is through the Song, in fact, that YHWH will speak to them (31.19, 21).

It is important to look prior to Moses's involvement as well, for Moses does not seem to be the one who composes the Song, even though he is its first performer. Rather, YHWH himself seems to be taken as the composer,[12] insofar as he tells Moses to "write this song" (31.19) as if referring to something already in existence. It is reasonable to assume that, in the narrative imagination of Deuteronomy, YHWH presents Moses with the text of the Song in a way similar to his presentation of other texts, either in written form, as with the Decalogue (4.13), or in spoken form, as with everything else in the book of Deuteronomy that Moses relays from YHWH to the Israelites.[13] If he speaks the Song, or even sings it, YHWH can be understood as performing it, just as much as Moses, and, later, the Israelites also. However, Deuteronomy is not specific as to manner here, and it is enough for my present purposes that, at least as author and possibly also as performer, YHWH owns or intends the Song as a whole (and not simply the words that the character of YHWH speaks within the Song). Thus, in the tradition created by Deuteronomy for the Song, those who come later embody (or, more precisely, re-embody), in each moment of performance, both YHWH, who is the notional source of the tradition, and Moses, who is its notional first enactor.[14]

---

realms performance ever deals with: the world of contingent existence as ordinary objects and persons and the world of transcendent existence as magical implements, gods, demons, characters. It isn't that a performer stops being himself or herself when he or she becomes another – multiple selves coexist in an unresolved dialectical tension" (Schechner 1985:6). Such multiple selves are the focus of my analysis here.

11. The future, that is, relative to the narrative told in Deuteronomy 31.

12. I concur here with Fokkelman 1998:67. It is no coincidence that YHWH is the explicitly designated speaker of so much of the Song's contents (SoM 20–30, 34–35, 38, 39–42 – which amounts to eighteen of the Song's forty-three verses, or, counting another way, twenty-nine of its approximately sixty-nine couplets).

13. E.g. 1.42: "YHWH told me: 'Tell them: "You will not go up to battle – for I will not be among you – and you will not fall before your enemies."'"

14. This is by contrast to the Homeric case, in which the figure of Homer is both composer

These performers also embody the characters who exist within the composition of the Song. The figure of YHWH is the primary named character in the poem (e.g. SoM 19–20). Unspecified enemies are also said to speak at one point, if only hypothetically (SoM 27). There are indications of yet other characters in the Song's imperatives, interrogatives, and shifts in pronominal referents.[15] These additional characters or speaking voices include the earth and skies (who speak in SoM 4, having been commanded to do so in SoM 3b) and the figures of elders and ancestors in Israelite society (who begin speaking in SoM 8, having been invoked in SoM 7cd). Finally, there is the character who narrates the Song, saying "I" in its first few verses (SoM 1–3). Since it speaks of YHWH in the third person (SoM 3a), it is a human voice, and it is distinct from all the other human characters since it introduces them.[16] Further, although the surrounding parts of Deuteronomy make Moses the paradigmatic performer of the Song, the Song's "I" shows no signs, within the Song itself, of being Moses: this character does not name itself as Moses (or as anyone else), and it invokes as long past events that lie in Moses's future. To investigate the identity of this character, I turned to the Song's genre: does the kind of composition that the poem is imply anything about who or what its speaker might be? While I will delay a full discussion of the Song's genre until later in this chapter, here I will say that the Song is generically associated with the speech forms of prophets. In its context within Deuteronomy, the Song is more than simply one instance of prophetic speech or what a certain prophet said on a certain occasion in relating YHWH's words to those they concern. Rather, Deuteronomy treats the Song as a prophetic speech composed ahead of time by YHWH, a speech that includes YHWH's own words as well as those of their human deliverer. In other words, YHWH dictates, or quotes in advance, what a prophetic persona will say in quoting him. To sum up the preceding few pages (as well as the thesis of my original paper on the topic), those who perform the Song within the tradition defined by Deuteronomy embody not only YHWH and Moses as the founding figures of the tradition (as well as intervening performers who

---

and performer – unless the Muses are to be seen as the ultimate composers and the figure of Homer as the paradigmatic human performer. This latter possibility would be closer to the Deuteronomic case.

15. This kind of analysis is a common practice in biblical studies. For example, the call-and-response pattern in Psalm 24 is uncontroversially taken as a dialogue between attendants of the sanctuary and pilgrims arriving to worship; see e.g. Mowinckel 1962:1:177–78. With specific reference to the Song of Moses, Matthew Thiessen has used such features to create his own demarcation of the speaking voices (Theissen 2004:401–24).

16. This includes, by extension, YHWH's introduction of the enemies' hypothetical speech in SoM 27cd.

have also embodied YHWH and Moses previously) but also the characters who exist within the Song: a generic prophetic speaking voice, YHWH, Israelite ancestors, enemies, and even the skies and earth.

Deuteronomy's Use of Performance

As I went on to expand the seminar paper into a dissertation, I began investigating existing research on the Song of Moses, the use of performance-related methodologies in biblical studies, and how the performance dynamics I had observed in the Song might be understood in the context of Deuteronomy. On the last of these points, that of reconstructing the place of the Song and its performance within Deuteronomy, it is worth noting that Deuteronomy treats the text of the Song and the text of the law in a few parallel ways. Both are written by Moses (law: 31.9; Song: 31.19, 22) and taught by Moses to the people (law: 4.1, 5, 14; 5.31; 6.1;[17] Song: 31.19, 22). Both texts are to function as a witness against the people (law: 31.26; Song: 31.19, 21[18]). Further, like the Song, the words of the law are also to be recited on a regular basis. Constant and apparently daily verbal performance of the law is specified (6.6–7; 11.19), while concerning the Song it is commanded only that it should be a text that everybody knows (31.19, 21–22) – a fact that makes sense if Deuteronomy is seen as providing an etiology for the Song as an already-established item in ancient Israel's repertoire. It is in this context that I make my argument that, just as there are two senses in Deuteronomy to performing the law, both reciting its words and enacting its legal contents, so also performing the Song involves not just recitation but also enactment.

The Song also fits well into the context of Deuteronomy's emphasis on emotional and mental attitudes in the pursuit of obedience. By comparison to the rest of the Pentateuch, for example, Deuteronomy is remarkably concerned with remembering, forgetting, stubbornness, docility, and fear among the Israelites.[19] The creation of a performance whereby the Israel-

---

17. In 31.12, 13, the people are said to "learn" the law. The meanings of teaching and of learning are both conveyed in these passages by the verb ללמד.

18. Cf. also 31.28, where Moses evokes the opening lines of the Song along with the verb להעיד 'to call as witness'.

19. The root לזכר 'to remember' occurs fifteen times in Deuteronomy, compared to twenty-seven times in the rest of the Pentateuch. The root לשכח 'to forget' occurs fourteen times in Deuteronomy, compared to three times in the rest of the Pentateuch, none of which have the urgent sense of injunction present in Deuteronomy. Stiffness or hardening as a metaphor for recalcitrance (expressed with לקשות 'to be hard' or לאמץ 'to be strong' with reference to the heart, spirit, or neck) occurs six times in Deuteronomy, equal to the number of occurrences in the entire rest of the Pentateuch. The concept of circumcision of (the foreskin of) the heart

ites inhabit various other personas, taking on their emotions and historical perspectives, is a good match for Deuteronomy's overall program of training the Israelites in thought and feeling. Through the Song the Israelites take on: the anger and jealousy of YHWH as the Song's composer (cf. 31.16–17); the frustration of Moses, the mediator of the covenant they will violate (cf. 31.27, 29); the anticipation and inevitable disappointment of all participants in the tradition up to the point of the violation of the covenant; and from within the poem, the corresponding disappointment of the Israelite ancestors who experienced YHWH's generosity and whose descendants did not reciprocate; the anger and indignation of YHWH; and the ignorant arrogance of the enemies who take credit for their own success. The Song as a performed piece is thus at home in Deuteronomy as a whole,[20] both through its correspondence to Deuteronomy's interest in emotional and mental attitudes and also through its functional analogies with the law as portrayed in Deuteronomy.

Performance-Critical Methodology

As for performance-related methodologies in use in biblical studies, let me begin with performance studies in general, which, in the use of ritual and theater as models in analyzing cultural phenomena, is quite broad. The field began to gain recognition as such in the mid to late twentieth century, combining the methodological approaches of the social sciences with experience drawn from the performing arts. Notable names in the field's early development include the theorists Kenneth Burke,[21] Victor Turner,[22] and Erving Goffman,[23] and the experimental theater directors Jerzi Grotowski, Eugenio Barba, and Peter Brook, all active in the 1960s; Richard Schechner has also been directing since the 1960s, since becoming one of the more influential theorists and proponents.[24] The first institutionalized programs

occurs twice in Deuteronomy (10.16; 30.6); each of the Pentateuch's other nineteen mentions of circumcision refers solely to circumcision of the foreskin of the male member with no apparent extension to an emotional or mental state. The verbal root ירא 'fear' occurs thirty-seven times in Deuteronomy, compared to forty-three times in the rest of the Pentateuch. Some close synonyms of ירא do not occur at all in the rest of the Pentateuch (such as חתת 'be dismayed', twice in Deuteronomy, and ערץ 'tremble', four times in Deuteronomy).

20. In Chapter 2 I will discuss the Song's place in the editorial history of Deuteronomy, as well as the Deuteronomic characterization of Moses, particularly as a prophet, that informs the performance of the Song.

21. Burke 1945.

22. Turner 1957.

23. Goffman 1959.

24. See Schechner 1985 and Schechner 2003.

in performance studies appeared in the 1980s. "Performance studies" as a
rubric includes quite diverse approaches, e.g. cultural (whether anthropo-
logical or ethnographic); societal (whether psychological or more properly
sociological); linguistic and text-centered (speech act theory, citation); tax-
onomically analytical (distinguishing forms such as storytelling, dance,
musical, living-history); critical-theoretical (focusing on political, ethnic, or
gendered identities).[25] The particular approach that I am borrowing from
Nagy has its roots in the ethnographic work of Milman Parry and Albert
Lord on South Slavic oral song-making traditions in the 1930s (given definitive shape by Lord in his 1960 book *The Singer of Tales*[26]), also incorporating
the linguistic and text-centered strand mentioned above through attention
to the way the tradition makes reference to itself.

The approach I take here differs from most applications of performance-
related methodologies in biblical studies. A salient aspect of this difference
is that, in this study, the audience to the act of performance will seldom
be in view, the focus falling instead on the performers themselves in their
relationship to both the tradition and the particular composition they are
performing. By contrast, the tendency of studies that are explicitly labeled
as performance criticism of biblical texts has been to highlight the effect of
the performance on an audience, the performer being understood primarily as a member of the audience, as it were. Two recent studies exemplify
this tendency. In their 2009 book *Twice-Used Songs: Performance Criticism of the
Songs of Ancient Israel*, Terry Giles and William Doan examine poems that are
embedded in biblical narrative.[27] In summarizing their analysis of the Song
of Deborah in Judges 5, they write:

> "Then sang Deborah and Barak." With these words we are attuned
> to the singer in a performed "now," or present, that transports us
> through the past by means of direct presentation. The song itself,
> functioning as a parade or pageant, unfolds for spectators, making
> them (us) participants in a shared enactment of identity. The first-
> person "I" used throughout the song creates and sustains the
> immediacy of performance, granting the singer authority over time

25. For further introduction with extensive bibliography, see McKenzie 2005.
26. Lord 2000.
27. Giles and Doan 2009. They exclude prose-embedded poems that are not used as songs
in their present context, such as 1 Samuel 2.1–10, which, they point out, is cited as a prayer
(Giles and Doan 2009:18). I had the pleasure of presenting my initial paper on the Song of Moses to a session of the Performance Criticism of Biblical and Other Ancient Texts Consultation
graciously moderated by Terry Giles at the annual meeting of the Society of Biblical Literature
in Boston, November 23, 2008.

by establishing a spatial presence for the unfolding celebration…. The singer, by gathering the spectators-participants together, creates a space in which a demonstration of the Lord God of Israel's might and power can be celebrated and shared. The song is the performance structure for creating the show of celebration and involving the spectators as both spectators and participants in a complex exchange of direct contact.[28]

Their emphasis clearly falls on the way the audience is affected by the performance; even what is noteworthy about the singer's use of the first person is its effect on the audience – not, as in my analysis, its effect on the singer. Similarly, about the Song of Asaph in 1 Chronicles 16, Giles and Doan write:

Once again, the Chronicler's edits in 1 Chr 16:19 have the effect of drawing the audience into the work. He writes, "when you were few in number," (*bihyotekem*) instead of "when they were few in number" (*bihyotam*) in Psalm 105:12. In Chronicles the audience is thus addressed directly. The psalm's story of generations gone by becomes the audience's story in Chronicles.[29]

What counts for audience participation – on the subsequent page they call the audience of the Song of Asaph an "active audience" – is the fact of being actively addressed, in the second person, by contrast to being spoken about in the third person. This is an important kind of distinction and one that I use in my own analysis – the point being, however, that I use it for other purposes.

In their treatment of the Song of the Sea in Exodus 15, Giles and Doan make a remark that is sympathetic to the approach I use, noting the effect on the performer of taking on the speaking voice present in the Song of the Sea: "In verses 1–2, the phrases 'My strength,' 'my salvation,' 'my God,' 'my father's God,' 'whom I will praise,' and 'whom I exalt' immediately allow the song's performers to own and personify an intimate and personal connection with Yahweh."[30] The point remains, however, that Giles and Doan give a different focus to their analysis overall, for not only do they speak of the interaction between "performer[s]" and "spectator[s],"[31] but they also offer the following audience-centered characterization of the Song of the

28. Giles and Doan 2009:84.
29. Giles and Doan 2009:93. An earlier version of their chapter on the Song of Asaph is Giles and Doan 2008.
30. Giles and Doan 2009:54.
31. Giles and Doan 2009:56, 57.

Sea: "The function of the song is ... to draw the reader (or listener) into the
drama of the story by presenting a device whereby the reader (or listener)
can 'sing along' and so be part of the telling of the story."[32]

An earlier study by Doan and Giles illustrates the same tendency in another context. In their 2005 book *Prophets, Performance, and Power: Performance
Criticism of the Hebrew Bible*,[33] they make a case study of the Amos prophecies,
after first "[examining] the oral nature of prophetic presentation, [posit-
ing] performance as a type of orality, and then [seeking] to understand what
happens to orality when it appears in written texts."[34] For Doan and Giles,
the nature of this oral performance, whether the prophet's original oral
performance or the scribes' later oral performance based on written texts,
very much involves the interaction between performance and audience or
even solely the effect on the audience. Indeed, the performer is occasionally
elided altogether, as when they speak of "the centrality of the relationship
between dramatic activity and the spectator."[35] By contrast, the approach I
am taking emphasizes a different aspect of the phenomenon, which Doan
and Giles mention here too, in their discussion of scribal appropriation of
the original prophet:

> The scribes, who were creating text that still had to be spoken and
> performed for the majority of their audience, sought to capture the
> performative mind and imagination of the prophet. The prophet, in
> the act of performing as prophet, was the medium through which God
> appeared. The scribe, both as writer and speaker of the text, engaged
> in a kind of impersonation.[36]

This is in some respects analogous to what I quoted from Nagy above. In other words, the scribe is a recomposed performer, who becomes recomposed
into the prophet every time he performs the prophet. Even here, however,
Doan and Giles seem to be working with a model that puts an extra measure
of distance between the performing persona and the re-performed persona,
and not only because they are focusing on a shift in medium from the oral toward the written. For them, performers must "capture" and "impersonate"
those who came before; in my analysis I would say, rather, that the performer, acting within the tradition, in effect extends it. For a modern exercise
that falls somewhere between, or at least near, re-performance and imper-
sonation, see the 2002 collection edited by Philip Davies. As Davies notes in

32. Giles and Doan 2009:66.
33. Giles and Doan 2005.
34. Giles and Doan 2005:1.
35. Giles and Doan 2005:68.
36. Giles and Doan 2005:27.

the introduction, "this book is a collection of modern pseudepigrapha, in other words writings in the name of biblical personages composed by contemporary scholars."[37] In the book's "autobiographical" essays, the biblical personages in question speak retrospectively of what would be considered the future in relation to the biblical texts in which they appear, while in Deuteronomy Moses speaks prospectively of the future as judged by the narrative setting in which he appears. Nevertheless, the various authors' contributions provide, for me, a fascinating counterpoint to my observation in Deuteronomy of an attempt to make its Israelite recipients inhabit historical and emotional perspectives other than their own.

My present methodological focus on the performer rather than on the audience is justified by the primary source material, for Deuteronomy attempts to construct its Israelite audience as performers of the book itself, thus collapsing the roles of performer and spectator. If Deuteronomy's instructions are obeyed, its audience will not merely be exposed to the book's contents but will be made into performers of those contents. More than hearing the words of Deuteronomy's law pronounced by a designated member of their community every seventh year (31.10–11), all the Israelites are to learn the words by heart, repeating them in speech and in writing (6.6–9; 11.18–20) – all in addition to acting them out, or obeying them (e.g. 6.1, 17; 11.8). The giving of the Song of Moses forms a part of Deuteronomy's overall strategy by which the performer is transformed during the performance. In laying out its conception of the Song's history, both past and future, Deuteronomy draws attention to the Song as a "sacred drama" that permanently transforms those who participate in it and reinforces the Song's "power to transmute not just opinions but [also] ... the people who hold them."[38] Through the repeated performance, as the performer becomes the performed characters again and again,[39] the performer is transformed from the inside out.[40]

37. Davies 2002:11.

38. This is Clifford Geertz's description of Victor Turner's understanding of the transformative power of ritual (Geertz 1980:173).

39. In connection with "becoming the performed characters," I would like to draw attention to the language of being "occupied" in the following quotation: "To engage regularly with such literature – not merely to read the words but to declare them, to wrestle with them – is to occupy oneself with the tradition's project. The encounter with literature of such power encourages regularization of the attitudes to which it so ably gives voice" (Wettstein 1998). Note also the emphasis on tradition.

40. Cf. the formulation of Richard Schechner: "People use theater as a way to experiment with, act out, and ratify change. Transformations in theater occur in three different places, and at three different levels: 1) in the drama, that is, in the story; 2) in the performers whose special task it is to undergo a temporary *rearrangement* of their body/mind, what I call a 'trans-

The Song of Moses in Previous Research

Previous research on the Song of Moses has tended to overlook its aspect as a performed piece within a tradition of performance, mentioning it only in passing if at all. Of course, one unsurprising exception is provided by Giles and Doan, who note the impact of knowledge of the Song's origins: "In the story line, the song is God's song.... God composes and commissions the song.... Composition and commissioning are processes whereby the presence of the composer and commissioner is extended to audiences of the future."[41] Also: "In essence, the details of the commissioning become part of the narrative of the song."[42] Whereas I am focusing on the impact of this narrative on the Song's performers, Giles and Doan pay attention to the effect on those who hear the Song performed: "the Deuteronomic narrative writer wants to make sure that his audience is mindful of God's presence, and so he made Yahweh the author of the song about to be recited."[43]

In his 1990 commentary on the book of Deuteronomy, Patrick D. Miller points not to the Song's backstory as portrayed in Deuteronomy 31 but to the tradition of performance that extends into its narrative future:

> These closing chapters of Deuteronomy anticipate that tendency to
> fall away and make it clear that such inclination is already known
> to God. For this reason, the Lord gives to the people ahead of time a
> witness that will be both a reminder of what the Lord expected and
> self-incriminating testimony. Not only will the people hear their
> condemnation in the regular recitation of the law they have neglected
> to follow, they will declare their guilt in the words of the song Moses
> is to teach them. Like the reading of the law, the singing of the song
> has both a legal-judicial function and an educational one. It convicts
> as it instructs; it instructs as it convicts. Like the torah, it is to be
> written, taught, and put in the mouths of the people (v. 19). If it is sung
> regularly, like the law it will be not only a testimony after the fact but a
> warning beforehand.... In good times it will be a warning; in bad times
> of trouble and sorrow it will be a reminder and a confession.[44]

Miller observes three points of interest here: 1) that the act of performing the Song has meaning in relation to the performers themselves; 2) that this

---

portation' ...; 3) in the audience where changes may either be temporary (entertainment) or permanent (ritual)" (Schechner 2003:191 [italics in original]).

41. Giles and Doan 2009:108–9. Their discussion of the Song of Moses appears on pages 105–11.

42. Giles and Doan 2009:109 n. 11.

43. Giles and Doan 2009:109.

44. Miller 1990:225.

meaning is an educational one, having an educational effect; and 3) that the weight of this meaning shifts in counter-balance to the historical circumstances of the imagined future performers. For my analysis, the most important historical circumstance will be where exactly any given performer stands in the performance tradition relative to those who came before. Moses, for example, in his recitation of the Song, recalls only YHWH's previous act of composing and delivering the Song, whereas an Israelite of the future generation that questions YHWH's presence with them (Deuteronomy 31.17) bears the weight not just of YHWH's presence and of Moses's but of all the preceding generations of Israelites who performed the Song before them and now speak again in their re-enactment.

By far the greatest part of existing scholarship on the Song attempts to retrieve the poem's actual origins and circumstances of composition, in apparent dissatisfaction with the account offered in Deuteronomy 31.[45] Since, however, the historical facts under investigation here are those of the Deuteronomic account of the Song's origins and "latter end" (to borrow from SoM 20, 29), very little of this preceding work is relevant to the current project, with the exception of text criticism and proposals concerning the Song's genre. For the dynamics of traditional performance to operate, all that is necessary is that Deuteronomy describe the tradition for it to exist. As it happens, Deuteronomy describes the tradition's origins with YHWH, its initiation with Moses, its first step with Joshua and the rest of the generation that succeeds Moses, and its destiny with the generation that questions YHWH's presence. It matters in only a secondary fashion whether the composition that Deuteronomy identifies with that tradition was already in existence or was composed contemporaneously with Deuteronomy – or even whether a later composition has in the meantime been substituted in its place.

The Genre of the Song of Moses

As I just mentioned, the question of genre bears on a performance-critical analysis of the Song insofar as genre contributes to the characterization of

---

45. Paul Sanders summarizes and synthesizes the past and (nearly) current state of scholarship on the Song (Sanders 1996). In line with that scholarship, his goal is to offer more sound and, if possible, precise conclusions concerning the Song's actual origins. He categorizes previous attempts as based on possible historical allusions (especially the Song's unnamed "no-people" and "enemies"), linguistic features, theological traits, and genre. Sanders reconsiders the Song's linguistic features in particular and adds a line-by-line comparison of the Song to other (datable) biblical texts. In the end, Sanders rules out a post-exilic date for the Song. More recent notable studies include: Nigosian 1996; Nigosian1997; Fokkelman 1998; Britt 2000; Nigosian 2002; Nigosian 2003; Vogel 2003; Thiessen 2004; Keiser 2005; and Leuchter 2007, the last of which I will discuss in some detail below.

the voice that speaks using that genre, that voice being one of the characters within the poem who are embodied by the performers.[46] It has been customary for several decades to label the Song as a prophetic "covenant lawsuit" by genre, or רִיב / *rîḇ* 'contention'.[47] Thus, in my analysis, those who perform the Song would, in so doing, be adopting a prophetic voice. The "covenant lawsuit" designation follows a suggestion of Herbert Huffmon,[48] which was later reinforced by G. Ernest Wright.[49] Huffmon built on Hermann Gunkel's form-critical work regarding "prophetic" and specifically accusatory patterns in the Psalms,[50] pointing to Isaiah 1.2–3; Micah 6.1–8; and Jeremiah 2.4–13 within prophetic collections and mentioning the Song of Moses and Psalm 50 as well.[51] Of the Song, Huffmon writes: "Following the address to heaven and earth, Deut 32 continues in a manner very close to that of the 'lawsuit,'"[52] the apparent exception being "an appendix stating why Yahweh will remit the sentence ([SoM] 26–42)."[53] Wright is in general agreement with Huffmon concerning the Song's form, though finding the lawsuit to ex-

---

46. I am not pursuing the question of genre in order to extrapolate from it a *Sitz im Leben* and, from there, an indication of the Song's original historical context. On the results of such efforts, see Sanders 1996:84–96.

47. Fokkelman dismisses investigation into the Song's genre thus: "The reader who slowly and with concentration digests chapter 31 of Deuteronomy finds that it is not necessary any more to look for an original genre definition for the song. Everything (regarding character and function of the Song) has already been perfectly expressed there. ... [The writer] calls it עֵד, a warning and testimony for future generations, and that is what it is" (Fokkelman 1998:143). While I agree that Deuteronomy 31 adequately describes the Song's function, its character as prophetic speech is more fully indicated by considerations drawn from outside that chapter, as I will explore below.

48. Huffmon 1959.

49. Wright 1962. The primary difference between the positions of Huffmon and Wright is whether a setting for the lawsuit in the divine council is implied by the invocation of skies and earth (as Wright holds) or not (as Huffmon maintains); see Huffmon 1959:290–93 and Wright 1962:45–49.

50. Gunkel and Begrich, 1933. I quote the following outline description of the form as Huffmon extracts it from Gunkel (Huffmon 1959:285):
  I. A description of the scene of judgment
  II. The speech of the plaintiff
    A. Heaven and earth are appointed judges
    B. Summons to the defendant (or judges)
    C. Address in the second person to the defendant
      1. Accusation in question form to the defendant
      2. Refutation of the defendant's possible arguments
      3. Specific indictment

51. Huffmon 1959:286–89.

52. Huffmon 1959:288.

53. Huffmon 1959:289.

tend up through SoM 29 instead,[54] with SoM 30–43 being a "major instance of expansion" containing an "affirmation of faith and trust in the mercy of God to provide salvation for his people."[55] Given that even those who first gave this genre designation to the Song do not consider it to apply to the whole poem, it is remarkable that only a few objections have been raised to it. To those objections I now turn.

Matthew Thiessen argues instead that a hymnic form is primary, concluding that the Song is a covenant lawsuit embedded in a hymn.[56] In support of this conclusion, Thiessen adduces two lines of argument: first, that the number of speaking voices in the Song (discernible through shifts in grammatical person, imperatives, and interrogatives) is too great to be appropriate to a covenant lawsuit, in which only YHWH and the prophet should speak;[57] and second, that the majority of the Song's contents (including the non-lawsuit "appendix" or "expansion" noted by Huffmon and Wright) more closely resemble a hymn.[58] According to this conception, SoM 3 would be the first element, a call to worship or command to praise; SoM 4 would be the second, an introductory summary; SoM 8–14, 30–42 would be the central section of praise; and SoM 43, the renewed, or concluding, call to praise,[59] leaving SoM 1–2, 5–7, and 15–29 as the lawsuit. As a counterargument, I would observe that even according to Thiessen's own demarcation of the Song's speaking voices, the main section of the lawsuit (SoM 15–29) contains one voice too many. Thiessen picks out the voices of a choir, an officiator, and a priest or cultic prophet.[60] It seems that Thiessen's evidence leads, rather, to the conclusion that even in a modified form the prophetic lawsuit is recognizable. If this is so, however, why should it not remain recognizable when the number of speaking voices exceeds that expected by two or three?[61] This question of the extent of the lawsuit's recognizability extends to Thiessen's other claim (that the lawsuit form is embedded in a

54. The form as Wright sees it is: 1) call for the witnesses' attention (SoM 1–3); 2) introductory statement about the "case," whether by the "Divine Judge and Prosecutor" or his human representative (SoM 4–6); 3) "recital of the benevolent acts of the Suzerain" (SoM 7–14); 4) indictment (SoM 15–18); 5) sentence (SoM 19–29) (Wright 1962:52–53). According to Wright, SoM 2 constitutes a small expansion (Wright 1962:54).

55. Wright 1962:56.

56. Thiessen 2004:421.

57. Thiessen 2004:408–9, 414.

58. Thiessen 2004:420.

59. For this generic description of a hymn, Thiessen relies on Broyles 1999:13–15.

60. Thiessen 2004:417.

61. Incidentally, Thiessen ignores the voice of the enemies in SoM 27 (Thiessen 2004:408, 417).

hymn). Given that his reconsideration of the invocation of skies and earth both in the Song of Moses and in other biblical texts results in his affirming that its occurrence at the beginning of the Song is clearly the introductory feature of a prophetic lawsuit,[62] it might be fairer in terms of his analysis to say that the forms of a lawsuit and of a hymn are mutually embedded – that the prophetic tone colors the whole performance because of its distinct opening and its return at the center of the piece, and that the hymnic tone grows stronger throughout and leaves the final impression. In any case, the fact that a prophetic voice is primary at any point in the Song provides the bare minimum necessary for this part of my thesis, which is that Deuteronomy places a specifically prophetic speech in Moses's mouth and thus in the mouth of all those who come after him in the tradition.

Before moving on, I should note that Thiessen's observations raise the question of whether Deuteronomy meant the Song to be performed by multiple performers, in antiphony, or by a single performer. I emphasize a solitary performer for the following reasons. First, the Song opens with a singular voice, saying "I": "that I may speak," "the words of my mouth," "my teaching," "my utterance," and "I proclaim." Although not definitive, it corresponds to my second reason, which is that, whatever the actual performance history of the Song, it is Deuteronomy's account that controls. In Deuteronomy, the performance tradition has its origins in acts of individuals, from YHWH the composer, whose individual intent lies behind each of the several voices in the Song to Moses the paradigmatic performer; even the Song itself is portrayed as a singular speaking entity: "this song will answer as a witness" (31.21).

Dwight Daniels has taken issue in absolute terms with the existence of the covenant lawsuit as a genre.[63] He proceeds by examining what are supposed to be the main occurrences of the genre and argues that they each more closely resemble another form entirely.[64] Although he does not discuss the Song of Moses at all, Daniels's argument does not bode well for it remaining a lawsuit, given that even Huffmon and Wright consider the Song to be a modified instance of the genre (which is not to say that an ancient genre of speech may not be attested now in only a single exemplar). For my present purposes it is more important to know what kind of persona the Song's speaking voice represents – what genre of persona, as it were – than it is to know which particular genre of speech is being used. Therefore, since Daniels's observations offer no contribution to positively identifying the Song's genre (nor to ruling out its being some other genre of prophetic

---

62. Thiessen 2004:406.
63. Daniels 1987.
64. Isaiah 1.2–3, 8–20; Jeremiah 2.4–13; Micah 6.1–8; Hosea 4.1–3 (Daniels 1987:343–53).

speech), let me continue for a moment to one last objection to designating the Song as a covenant lawsuit.

George Mendenhall objected to Wright's treatment of the Song, particularly to the claim that the Song is a timeless liturgy (instead of a response to a discrete historical event), as well as to Wright's linking of the invocation of skies and earth to the concept of the divine council.[65] As it happens, Mendenhall adduces little evidence in support of his objections. It is just as well, however, for what is more relevant for this project is the genre designation he offers for the Song instead, which is that of a prophetic oracle. He does not go into detail on this point either, beyond to say: "As a prophetic oracle there are virtually no remaining serious problems of form or content."[66] Here I will use Klaus Koch's description of prophetic judgment oracles as a point of comparison:[67]

1) a call to attention and "messenger formula" (כֹּה אָמַר יְהוָה [thus says YHWH]);
2) a description of the situation requiring judgment;
3) a transition marked by לָכֵן (therefore) and/or a repetition of the messenger formula or the typical phrase נְאֻם יְהוָה (a saying of YHWH);
4) YHWH's judgment speech; and often
5) a restatement or further development of the situation requiring judgment, introduced by כִּי 'for'.

The Song displays a similar structure:

1) general appeal to skies and earth (SoM 1–3), followed by direct address to those whom the judgment concerns (SoM 6–7);[68]
2) the situation requiring judgment, which is the juxtaposition of YHWH's past beneficence with the Israelites' ingratitude and faithlessness (SoM 8–18);
3) transition: וַיֵּרְא יְהוָה ... וַיֹּאמֶר (SoM 19a, 20ø; YHWH saw ... and he said);
4) YHWH's judgment speech (SoM 20a–25); the judgment speech includes a restatement, introduced by כִּי, of the situation requiring judgment: כִּי דוֹר תַּהְפֻּכֹת הֵמָּה בָּנִים לֹא־אֵמֻן בָּם (SoM 20cd; for they are a generation of reversings, children with no reliability in them).[69]

Although this correspondence, like the proposals of Huffmon and Wright,

---

65. Mendenhall 1975.
66. Mendenhall 1975:175.
67. Koch 1969:191–94, 207–8.
68. The messenger formula does not appear here since the next element, the description of the situation requiring judgment, is spoken in a human voice.
69. כִּי introduces the statement in SoM 22 as well: כִּי־אֵשׁ קָדְחָה בְאַפִּי (for the fire of my anger is kindled). YHWH's anger may also represent a summary of the situation requiring judgment.

does not include the last half of the Song, it nevertheless provides an alternative genre designation for the Song, if the rubric of covenant lawsuit is found wanting. It should be noted that this genre is also associated with prophetic speech.

In order to sum up this section on the Song's genre, I observe that both of the positive suggestions that have been made concern modes of prophetic speech, whether a lawsuit or an oracle. I include here Thiessen's proposal that the prophetic lawsuit has been adapted (and combined with a hymn), given that the form was adapted in a way that left it recognizable – and was presumably adapted because of those very characteristics. The Song's performers thus hear themselves speaking as a prophet during their performance – though not as any specific, named prophet, since the Song was given to Moses, Deuteronomy's prophet, only in order to pass it on to others. It is following this line of argumentation that I distinguish a generic prophetic persona as one of the characters within the Song that its performers embody.[70]

The Text of the Song of Moses

As I have already mentioned, the earliest recoverable state of the Song's actual history of performance is not at issue here, nor is the earliest recoverable state of the Song's text. Rather, the usefulness of text criticism for this investigation is, when necessary, to recover the state of the Song's text as it was when used by Deuteronomy. Although a comparison of the Masoretic Hebrew and Septuagint Greek text traditions reveals quite a number of variants between them that affect the demarcation of speaking voices within the Song, none of these differences in demarcation present a problem for relating the Song to its context in Deuteronomy. In Chapter 3 below I address the fact of these variants by presenting the MT and LXX (as exemplified by the Leningradensis and Vaticanus manuscripts) side by side. Since the Hebrew version of Deuteronomy is my primary focus, I will limit my discussion of the LXX to pointing out the differences in speaking voice. For example, in the MT, the speech of the elders runs from SoM 8 through SoM 18, with the Song's prophetic persona breaking in at SoM 14e, 15b and taking over at SoM 17d–18; in the LXX, the elders speak through the end of SoM 17, with the deity breaking in at SoM 16 and the prophetic persona taking over at SoM 18.

---

70. Since it is the *rîb* designation that appears most often in the scholarly literature on the Song, I will interact primarily with that definition in the rest of my analysis.

I have adopted one emendation to the MT, at SoM 8.[71] The MT reads יַצֵּב גְּבֻלֹת עַמִּים לְמִסְפַּר בְּנֵי יִשְׂרָאֵל (he set up the boundaries of the peoples according to the number of the sons of Israel), whereas two manuscripts from the Dead Sea, 4QDt[q] and 4QDt[j], at this point have readings of בני אל [...] (sons of El/g[od]) and בני אלהים (sons of god) respectively. This latter reading is supported obliquely by the LXX ἀγγέλων θεοῦ (messengers of god). The difference between בני ישראל and בני אלהים does not affect the demarcation of speaking voices; I adopt it, rather, because בני אלהים apparently reflects the text of the Song as it was incorporated into Deuteronomy. As I will discuss at length in Chapter 4 below, the reading with בני אלהים seems to have been borrowed and elaborated at Deuteronomy 4.19 and 29.25 in particular (as well as in such passages as 2.5 and others to be discussed below), in connection with the theme of YHWH determining the relationships between individual peoples, territories, and divine beings.[72]

71. For a full discussion, see Sanders 1996:156–58 and the literature cited there, particularly Skehan 1959.

72. I have not adopted an emendation at SoM 43, where the MT seems also to have been modified for apologetic reasons, for in this case the alternative reading is not a better match with the rest of Deuteronomy than the MT reading. For a detailed text-critical discussion of SoM 43, see Sanders 1996:248–56.

Chapter 2

Preliminary Considerations in Deuteronomy

I N THE PREVIOUS CHAPTER I dealt with such disparate introductory issues as previous scholarship on the Song of Moses, especially regarding its genre, and the particular performance-critical methodology that I am employing in this study. In this chapter I address two matters relating to the Song's setting within Deuteronomy. First, the exilic date of its incorporation, as a quoted text, into the book. While ascertaining the historical circumstances of any given performer in a performance tradition is not necessary to understand (or to describe) the levels of re-enactment that can occur during any given hypothetical performance, such knowledge does help locate the performer at a specific point within the performance tradition, in cases where historiography and history overlap. An exilic date for the Song's incorporation into Deuteronomy means that the intended performers of the Song according to Deuteronomy's narrative – those Israelites who have experienced YHWH's wrath and abandonment (31.17) – correspond to those who have had such experiences in historical fact. The second topic to be investigated in this chapter is Deuteronomy's portrayal of Moses and of prophethood in general, since both Moses and the idea of a prophet as historiographic figures are re-embodied in the performance of the Song. Deuteronomy's Moses is re-embodied by the performer as a founder of the tradition of performance, and Deuteronomy's ideal "prophetic persona" is re-embodied as a character within the Song (insofar as the Song is recognizable as a prophetic genre of speech).

Deuteronomy's Incorporation
of the Song of Moses

Although theories of Deuteronomy's formation abound, in all the Song is considered a secondary – if not tertiary – addition or appendix to the more original parts of the book,[1] which at the bare minimum are taken to include chapters 12–26 and sometimes as much as chapters 1–28. With regard to Deuteronomy 31, it is generally agreed that 31.16–22 constitute the Song's earliest introduction, mentioning it directly and reflecting much of its vocabulary and thematic content. Another introduction to the Song appears

---

1. So e.g. Nelson 2002:4; Mayes 1979:40, 382.

in 31.24–30, also mentioning it directly amid striking parallels to its content – the difference being that this second introduction fuses the Song and the torah (which appears earlier in the chapter, at 31.9–13) into a single authoritative textual entity by speaking of them in very similar terms. Both are written (31.9, 19, 22, 24), delivered to Levites and elders (31.9, 25, 28) as well as to the whole people (31.11–12, 30) at an assembly (31.12, 28, 30), delivered orally (31.11, 28, 30), to be taught or learned (both expressed by the verb ללמד; 31.12–13, 19, 22), and to function as witness against Israel (31.19, 26, 28).[2] Although these two introductions, especially the first, are all that is strictly necessary to create the performance history of the Song that is the object of my study, the relationship of the Song and its introductions to the remainder of Deuteronomy 31 and to the rest of the book has importance in two respects. First, the Deuteronomic/Deuteronomistic context of the Song's performance history means that, for those figures who participate in that history, it is their portrayals in Deuteronomy that are operative – Deuteronomy's portrayals of YHWH, of Moses, of Joshua, of Israelite generations of past, present, and future. In the case of Moses, for example (as I will discuss later in this chapter), this distinction matters in connection with his status in Deuteronomy as prophet par excellence.[3] Second, if the authors of Deuteronomy preserve the command for all Israelites to learn and repeat the Song, then in what ways, if at all, does their work show the signs of their own mastery of the Song's lessons? I will discuss that topic in Chapter 4 below.

As for the place of the Song within Deuteronomy as a whole, I take as my starting point the 1975 article of Jon D. Levenson, "Who Inserted the Book of the Torah?"[4] Combining Hans Walter Wolff's hypothesis of a frame around the core of Deuteronomy (Dtn)[5] with Frank Moore Cross's hypothesis of two redactions of the Deuteronomistic History (Dtr),[6] Levenson proceeded, by a method of lexical comparison, to confirm the compositional unity of Wolff's frame[7] (also defining it more precisely, drawing on Norbert Lohfink's observations[8]) as well as to demonstrate its further compositional unity with

2. James W. Watts lists most of these similarities as well (Watts 1992:67).

3. By contrast, Watts explores the opposite direction of influence, namely, the way that the Song contributes to the characterization of these figures – particularly Moses and YHWH – as they are already present in the narrative of Deuteronomy as well as of the Pentateuch.

4. Levenson 1975.

5. Wolff points in particular to 4.29–31 and 30.1–10 (Wolff 1961:183). Levenson concludes that the Dtr$_2$ frame is comprised of 4.1–40; 29.21–28; 30.1–20; 31.16–32.44 (Levenson 1975:221).

6. Cross 1973:275.

7. Levenson 1975:212–15.

8. Lohfink 1964.

Cross's second (exilic) redaction of the Deuteronomistic History (Dtr$_2$).[9] Along the way, Levenson noted numerous lexical parallels between Deuteronomy's Dtr$_2$ frame and the Song of Moses, which is not of a piece with the frame but is rather a discrete text embedded within it[10] (as indicated by the unusual fact, already mentioned, of being given two separate narrative introductions[11]). From this, Levenson concluded that the authors of the frame not only incorporated the Song into "Deuteronomy"[12] but also drew much of their inspiration from it:

> The Song of Moses exerted not only an influence of a literary nature on the exilic hand, evident in his recomposition of the covenant at Moab, but also a profound theological influence over the entirety of his bracket. The exilic frame to Dtn is the sermon for which the Song of Moses is the text.[13]

Moreover, Levenson maintained that it was specifically the authors of Dtr$_2$, not of Dtr$_1$, who incorporated the core of the book into the larger work that now, in fact, goes by its name (i.e. the Deuteronomistic History), in light of the fact that that "book of the law" is situated in such a way as to interrupt the narrative of Dtr$_1$,[14] whereas, by contrast, Dtr$_2$ provides a self-conscious frame for it. Levenson then confirmed the results of his literary analysis by noting several theological disjunctions between the Deuteronomic core and Dtr$_1$,[15] one of which – the role of the king – resonates sympathetically with the viewpoint of Dtr$_2$ instead.[16]

Levenson's research in this area has importance for this project both because it provides a concrete beginning into an investigation of Deuteronomy's own re-performance, as it were, of the Song (which is the topic of Chapter 4, below) as well as because it offers a clear and defensible theory of the delimitation of sources and of the editing of Deuteronomy 31–32, where the Song's place in a future history of performance is created. On the second point, the contents of Deuteronomy 31–32 may be briefly outlined as follows, following Levenson's schematization:[17]

9. Levenson 1975:219–21.
10. Levenson 1975:215–17, 222.
11. Levenson 1975:212, 222.
12. Levenson 1975:221; cf. 212.
13. Levenson 1975:217.
14. Levenson 1975:219, 223.
15. Levenson 1975:224–31.
16. Levenson 1975:231–32.
17. Levenson 1975:210–12.

31.1–8: Dtr$_1$, account of succession to Joshua (continuing from 3.28)

31.9–13: Dtn, concluding the Moab covenant (continued in 32.45–47)

31.14–15: JE, account of succession to Joshua (continued in 31.23)

31.16–22: Dtr$_2$, the Song's original introduction

31.23: JE, account of succession to Joshua (continuing from 31.14–15)

31.24–29: Dtr$_2$, partly parallel to Dtn in 31.9–13 but becoming distinct at 31.26b[18]

31.30: [Dtr$_2$, opening notice of Moses's recitation of the Song[19]]

32.1–43: Song

32.44: [Dtr$_2$, closing notice of Moses's recitation]

32.45–47: Dtn, concluding the Moab covenant (continuing from 31.9–13)

Integral to Levenson's proposal is the distinction of Deuteronomy 4 from Deuteronomy 1–3 (which appear as one speech in the narrative of Deuteronomy) in order to assign only Deuteronomy 4 to the hand of Dtr$_2$; as mentioned above, in this regard Levenson builds on the earlier work of Norbert Lohfink. Nathan MacDonald has called into question the thematic arguments on which he considers this distinction to be primarily based, by offering in return a set of thematic links between the two parts of Moses's speech.[20] While also acknowledging that the case for isolating Deuteronomy 4 has likewise been grounded on that chapter's "recognized links to other secondary material in the Deuteronomistic History,"[21] MacDonald limits his response on this front to noting that assigning Deuteronomy 4 to a later

18. Levenson 1975:211: "Vv. 24–26a is a parallel account, but with v. 26b …, we begin to hear a different note, one which extends to the end of the chapter and into the next. That note is the conviction that Israel will inevitably abandon the covenant and thus incur justified punishment. A passage originally dealing with the deposition of the text of the covenant at Moab has been rewritten to introduce the song in 32:1–43, whose keynote it stresses from v. 26b on."

19. Levenson does not directly discuss 31.30 and 32.44, except to include them under the rubric of the Song (Levenson 1975:221). These two verses show a strong affinity with Dtr$_2$, insofar it is the only (other) source in this chapter to speak of the Song and to use the phrase עַד תֻּמָּם (to completion); further, all the lexical items that these two verses share with Dtn are found also in Dtr$_2$: the verb לדבר 'to speak'; בְּאָזְנֵי / בְּאָזְנֵיהֶם (in the ears of / in their ears); the root קהל, in the verb להקהיל 'to assemble' and in the noun קָהֵל 'assembly'; and the direct object phrase אֶת־דִּבְרֵי / אֶת־כָּל־דִּבְרֵי (the words of / all the words of). For these reasons, I label 31.30 and 32.44 as belonging to Dtr$_2$.

20. MacDonald 2006.

21. MacDonald 2006:208.

period of deuteronomistic activity leaves the original form of the Deuter-onomistic History in an unsatisfactory condition, the most salient aspect of which would be that Deuteronomy 1–3 do not make a good introduction to the book's central material.[22] According to Levenson's proposal, however, this awkward transition would never have been a problem since "Deuter-onomy" was not part of the Deuteronomistic History until Dtr$_2$ included it: "It is hardly surprising to find Dtr 2 interrupting Dtr 1. What is surprising is that Dtr 1 is interrupted also by Dtn, for nothing in Deut 1:6–3:28 gives a hint that a long paraenetic address and then a law code are about to be recited.... The suggestion thus arises that Dtr 1 did not include Dtn, or, to phrase the issue differently, that Dtr 2 not only framed Dtn but also introduced it into the history."[23]

Levenson's entire proposal concerning the redactional stages of Deu-teronomy, based as it is on literary evidence, remains sound.[24] Regarding Deuteronomy 31–32 specifically, it is either adopted outright in the literature,[25] or something like it or compatible with it is employed as non-controversial.[26] There is, however, one challenge to Levenson's proposal that I will address here, since it also deals specifically with the Song's func-tion in Deuteronomy and the date of its incorporation into the book. In his 2007 article "Why Is the Song of Moses in the Book of Deuteronomy?," Mark Leuchter offers several arguments for dating the moment of the Song's first incorporation into the text of (what would later become known as) Deu-teronomy to the (pre-exilic) era of Josiah, rather than to the exile.[27] I will address each of Leuchter's arguments here, beginning with the two that are broadest in scope.

The fact that, according to Deuteronomy, the Song is, specifically, to be taught (31.19, 22) suggests to Leuchter a correspondence with a Josianic-era critique of Solomon in Deuteronomistic texts.[28] To make this connection, Leuchter refers to David Carr, whose argument he summarizes as noting that a text's being taught (by Moses, to the people) "is a characteristic of the

22. MacDonald 2006:209.

23. Levenson 1975:223.

24. Cf. the literature cited by MacDonald 2006:206 n. 13.

25. Sanders 1996:348–52.

26. For example, although treating all D-related material in Deuteronomy 31 as an undif-ferentiated block (as is appropriate to the purposes of his analysis), Joel S. Baden also isolates 31.14–15, 23 from the context, identifying these verses specifically as E, rather than as "JE" (Baden 2009:185–88). Similarly, Watts follows Driver's opinion that a "late Deuteronomic" re-dactor took 31.16–22 from a separate source, rather than, as in Levenson's proposal, simply composing it (Watts 1992:79, citing Driver 1906:lxxvi).

27. Leuchter 2007.

28. Leuchter 2007:300–301.

Deuteronomistic literature that presented itself as an alternative to older modes of Wisdom instruction associated with Solomon's reign."[29] The point Carr is making here, however, has rather to do with (as he construes it) the hitherto unacknowledged breadth of materials (that is, what Carr would consider educational materials) included in what even some biblical texts associate with Solomonic modes of wisdom, not with a distinction between Solomonic and other kinds of wisdom.[30]

Leuchter also adduces the Song's genre, that of the prophetic *rîḇ*, in support of a Josianic date for its inclusion in Deuteronomy.[31] Since the Josianic era witnessed both reflection on the role of the prophet as well as the editing of many prophetic textual traditions (in coordination with the editing of the Deuteronomistic History), the editorial choice of placing a distinctly prophetic-sounding poem in the mouth of Deuteronomy's Moses would be most at home in that same period. The point is well taken, but it provides only broad, circumstantial evidence.

Two other pieces of Leuchter's argument deal with Deuteronomy 32.45–47, which immediately follow the text of the Song and its closing citation in Deuteronomy. Leuchter considers Jeremiah 43.1 to be an allusion to Deuteronomy 32.45, functioning to equate the entire foregoing Jeremianic corpus with what it considered to be the entire Deuteronomic corpus, that is, ending at Deuteronomy 32.45.[32] First of all, the fact of allusion, when it is proven, proves only that one text preceded another, not how much time has passed between them. A text alluded to by an exilic text, as Leuchter knows Jeremiah 43.1 to be, may itself be exilic in date, or it may be pre-exilic; what it cannot be is post-exilic. Second, according to the very hypothesis of Levenson with which Leuchter takes issue, Deuteronomy 32.45 was present as the conclusion to the Moab covenant in a pre-exilic edition of Deuteronomy, an edition that, however, did not yet include the Song. That is, even if the Jeremianic allusion to Deuteronomy 32.45 proved what Leuchter says it does about the date of an edition of Deuteronomy that ended there, it would not also prove that that edition contained the Song.

Leuchter also draws 32.47 into view, characterizing it as displaying a sympathetic appropriation of Mesopotamian legal conventions, to be ex-

29. Leuchter 2007:300–301, referring to Carr 2005. Although Leuchter cites pages 133–35 in Carr, it is pages 132–33 that deal with the topic at hand.

30. By contrast, Steven Weitzman understands the Song's taught nature within the context of last-words tradition found throughout the Ancient Near East (Weitzman 1997:37–58, esp. 42–45, which is based on his earlier article "Lessons from the Dying: The Narrative Role of Deuteronomy 32" (Weitzman 1994).

31. Leuchter 2007:301–2.

32. Leuchter 2007:305–6.

pected in the Josianic era (and in the period of Neo-Assyrian hegemony more broadly), whereas "texts associated with the exile are more clearly marked by an overt resistance to Mesopotamian culture."[33] To this I would respond that, although this point too is well taken, it is no argument against the hypothesis that a text that existed in a pre-exilic – Josianic, even – edition of Deuteronomy continued to appear in an exilic edition that only then contained the Song.

The frequent allusions to the Song in Jeremiah's early prophecies provide Leuchter with another avenue of approach to a pre-exilic date for the Song's presence in Deuteronomy. Following the observations and conclusions of William L. Holladay, Leuchter takes the fact that allusions to the Song "[appear] alongside dramatic references to the Deuteronomic legislation" as evidence supporting his thesis.[34] Ultimately, however, the very thesis of Leuchter's article undermines the relevance of these allusions: "The prophet [Jeremiah] invokes The Song against his Levitical Shilonite kinsmen not simply because it was part of the Deuteronomic corpus of this day, but because it was somehow associated with them and with northern Levitical tradition before its interpolation into Deuteronomy."[35] If Jeremiah was using the Song to exhort the Shilonite Levites "to join the Josianic cause"[36] as represented by a pre-exilic edition of Deuteronomy,[37] then that is reason enough, it would seem to me, for Jeremiah to mention both the Song and Deuteronomic legislation in the same breath, without the Song necessarily already being part of Deuteronomy.

Finally, coordinating observations made by Bernard M. Levinson and James W. Watts, Leuchter offers the intriguing proposal that the Decalogue and the Song of Moses stood at either end of a pre-exilic edition of Deuteronomy, framing the legal core and lending to it their authority within the Israelite culture of the time.[38] Crediting Levinson, Leuchter says: "the Decalogue is invoked to base the ensuing Deuteronomic innovations in a recognized and ancient tradition,"[39] and from Watts he draws the following quotation: "by equating the song with the law, Deuteronomy 31 was enlisting the song's popularity to support the promulgation of deuteronomic law."[40]

33. Leuchter 2007:302.
34. Leuchter 2007:304. Leuchter refers to William L. Holladay 2004:73–74 (Leuchter 2007:305 n. 55).
35. Leuchter 2007:314.
36. Leuchter 2007:314.
37. Leuchter 2007:313.
38. Leuchter 2007:310–12.
39. Leuchter 2007:311 n. 81, citing Levinson 2000: 279–82.
40. Leuchter 2007:314 n. 97, citing Watts 1993:358.

According to Leuchter, the outer limits of this composition would have been 4.44 at the beginning and 32.47 at the end of Deuteronomy, as indicated by the clustering of certain "shared terminology" around the two touchstone texts (including a few occurrences in the intervening material but in no case appearing before 4.44 or after 32.47).[41] Simply put, however, quite a few of the specified words and phrases do appear outside these limits – primarily in Deuteronomy 4, though also in chapters 1–3, and in one case in chapter 34. For example, the phrase הַיּוֹם, in the sense of "today" and to which Leuchter points in 5.3 and 32.46,[42] occurs with the same sense not only in 1.10, 39; 2.18, which belong to the pre-exilic Dtr₁ (not to mention the more specific phrase הַיּוֹם הַזֶּה [this day] in 2.22, 25, and, in the distinctive usage עַד הַיּוֹם הַזֶּה [to this day], in 3.14[43]), but also in 4.4, 8, 26, 39, 40, which belong to the exilic frame of Dtr₂, and even in 34.6, in the phrase עַד הַיּוֹם הַזֶּה (to this day).[44] While Leuchter also appeals to וְלִבְנֵיהֶם (and to their children) in 5.26/29 (which he cites as 5.25) and בְּנֵיכֶם (your children) in 32.46,[45] comparable phrases occur outside the indicated limits: וּבְנֵיכֶם (and your children) in 1.39; לְבָנֶיךָ וְלִבְנֵי בָנֶיךָ (to your children and to your children's children) in 4.9; בְּנֵיהֶם (their children) in 4.10; בָּנִים וּבְנֵי בָנִים (children and children's children) in 4.25; and וּלְבָנֶיךָ (and for your children) in 4.40.[46] As for the prolonging of days in the land of possession, which Leuchter notes in 5.30/33 (cited as 5.29) and in 32.47,[47] the relevant terminology appears also in 4.26, 40.[48] Finally, while the parallel is not exact, Deuteronomy 4.10 (הַקְהֶל־לִי אֶת־הָעָם וְאַשְׁמִעֵם אֶת־דְּבָרָי) [assemble the people to me that I may cause them to hear my words]) contains much of what Leuchter

---

41. Leuchter 2007:310.

42. Leuchter 2007:310–11.

43. On this phrase, see Geoghegan 2003.

44. It would be possible to argue, in favor of Leuchter's position, that הַיּוֹם (today) and עַד הַיּוֹם הַזֶּה (to this day) are distinct usages; on the other hand, Geoghegan, upon whose analysis Leuchter relies elsewhere, attributes עַד הַיּוֹם הַזֶּה in Deuteronomy 34.6 to a pre-exilic redaction (Geogheghan 2003:226).

45. Leuchter 2007:311.

46. Cf. the interest in Caleb's children in Deuteronomy 1.36: בָּנָיו (his children).

47. Leuchter 2007:311. Deuteronomy 5.30/33: וְהַאֲרַכְתֶּם יָמִים בָּאָרֶץ אֲשֶׁר תִּירָשׁוּן (that you may lengthen days in the land that you will possess); Deuteronomy 32.47: תַּאֲרִיכוּ יָמִים עַל־הָאֲדָמָה אֲשֶׁר אַתֶּם עֹבְרִים אֶת־הַיַּרְדֵּן שָׁמָּה לְרִשְׁתָּהּ (you will lengthen days on the soil towards which you are crossing the Jordan to possess). Note the interchangeability of אֶרֶץ 'land' and אֲדָמָה 'soil'.

48. Deuteronomy 4.26: אָבֹד תֹּאבֵדוּן מַהֵר מֵעַל הָאָרֶץ אֲשֶׁר אַתֶּם עֹבְרִים אֶת־הַיַּרְדֵּן שָׁמָּה לְרִשְׁתָּהּ לֹא־תַאֲרִיכֻן יָמִים עָלֶיהָ (you actually will perish quickly from the land towards which you are crossing the Jordan to possess – you will not lengthen days upon it); Deuteronomy 4.40: לְמַעַן תַּאֲרִיךְ יָמִים עַל־הָאֲדָמָה אֲשֶׁר יְהוָה אֱלֹהֶיךָ נֹתֵן לְךָ (in order that you may lengthen days upon the soil that YHWH your god is giving you). Note again the interchangeability of אֶרֶץ 'land' and אֲדָמָה 'soil'. The latter example features the verb לתת 'to give', rather than the verb לרשת 'to possess', which occurs in the former as well as in the two verses quoted in the preceding footnote.

points to in 5.19/22 (cited as 5.18: הַדְּבָרִים הָאֵלֶּה [these words]; אֶל־כָּל־קְהַלְכֶם [to your whole assembly]) and in 32.45 (כָּל־הַדְּבָרִים הָאֵלֶּה [all these words]; אֶל־כָּל־יִשְׂרָאֵל [to all Israel]).[49]

Levenson's argument that Deuteronomy's legal core was first "inserted" into "Deuteronomy" by the same authors (Dtr$_2$) who composed the frame around it – a frame that shows the marked literary influence of the Song – does not stand or fall with the corollary suggestion that the Song also first entered Deuteronomy at the same time, nor is it antithetical to the possibility that the Song was known to those who composed earlier parts of the Deuteronomistic History (Dtr$_1$) or to those who composed the legal core itself. For Leuchter's insights do demonstrate that the Song would have been at home in the pre-exilic period and perhaps even, more specifically, during the reign of Josiah – without, however, requiring that the Song was comprised within Deuteronomy at the time. My observations in Chapter 4 below, concerning the great familiarity with the Song shown by Deuteronomy outside of the exilic frame, will contribute, in a way, to the theses of both Levenson and Leuchter. If the legal core, or the "Book of the Torah," does indeed show this familiarity, then Leuchter's case for the pre-exilic proximity of Deuteronomy and the Song is strengthened – although even then not to the point of requiring their compositional unity – as is Levenson's conclusion that it was the exilic authors of the frame who inserted the law code, insofar as both the frame they composed and the law code they inserted display the distinctive influence of the Song.[50]

Deuteronomy's Moses and Deuteronomy's Prophet

The other salient feature of Deuteronomy's manner of adopting the Song is that it sets up the Song as specifically Mosaic and prophetic in nature. Therefore, to perform the Song in a way informed by Deuteronomy is to do something characteristically Mosaic and prophetic, a fact that has ramifications for the following chapter's analysis of the performance of the Song. The Mosaic aspect is primary; Deuteronomy creates it not just through Moses being the Song's first performer – and the only one whose performance is recounted in the book – but even more so through showing Moses's words

---

49. Leuchter 2007:310.

50. Some of the examples in Chapter 4, below, will involve Dtr$_1$ texts; however, the most impressive cases involve passages from the law code – or, more properly, its exhortatory preface in Deuteronomy 5–11.

throughout the book as anticipating the Song in many ways. The Song's prophetic resonance within Deuteronomy's narrative also arises through its connection to Moses, as well as through certain resemblances between the Song and the description of future prophetic activity as found in Deuteronomy 18. Not only so, but even considered independently, apart from the context provided by Deuteronomy, the Song is a recognizably prophetic composition (as discussed above) on account of its genre. The goal of the rest of this chapter will be to highlight some of the ways in which earlier parts of Deuteronomy anticipate the Song with the purpose of fleshing out the portraits of Moses and of what a prophet is in general – personas that the Song's performers then re-enact.

Although Mosaic anticipations of the Song are found from the beginning of the book, the most effective of these features appear immediately preceding it in the narrative, in Moses's speech in Deuteronomy 31.24–29. The most outstanding example is Moses's command in 31.28, which the Song's opening line echoes in several ways: 1) two Hiphil imperatives, with their complements, that resemble each other in terms of rhythm and vowel sequence (31.28: הַקְהִילוּ אֵלַי [assemble to me!]; SoM 1: הַאֲזִינוּ הַשָּׁמַיִם [give ear, o skies!]);[51] 2) the following of that imperative with morphologically identical forms of the same verb, meaning "so that I may speak" (31.28: וַאֲדַבְּרָה; SoM 1: וַאֲדַבֵּרָה);[52] 3) the root אזן (31.28: בְּאָזְנֵיהֶם [in their ears]; SoM 1: הַאֲזִינוּ [give ear!]); and 4) the invocation of skies and earth as a pair, which, in combination with the first-person context of Moses calling them as witnesses against the Israelites, is also anticipated by virtually identical phrasing in 4.26 and 30.19.[53] Thus the Song's very first words identify it as typical of Mosaic speech in the book of Deuteronomy. So too does Moses's use of the root שחת 'destroy, become corrupt' in 31.29 in connection with the Israelites' corruption as manifested in their idolatrous practices. Moses employs this vocabulary not just immediately before the Song but also much earlier in the book: he uses it also in 4.16, 25, 31; 9.12, 26; and 10.10, either for the Israelites' idolatry or for the punishment (as a consequence thereof) that Moses describes YHWH as threatening and, later, relenting from.[54] The occurrence of the root שחת

---

51. 31.28: *haqhîlû ʾēlay*; SoM 1: *haʾazînû haššāmayim*. Note particularly the vowel sequence *a-î-û-a* and that the accent falls on the second and last of these in each case.

52. The only slight difference is the lengthened vowel in the form in the Song, which comes at the end of its phrase.

53. 4.26; 30.19: הַעִידֹתִי בָכֶם הַיּוֹם אֶת־הַשָּׁמַיִם וְאֶת־הָאָרֶץ (today I call the skies and earth as witnesses against/concerning you); 31.28: וְאָעִידָה בָּם אֶת־הַשָּׁמַיִם וְאֶת־הָאָרֶץ (that I may call the skies and earth as witnesses against/concerning them).

54. The root שחת 'destroy, become corrupt' also appears in 20.19, 20 in Moses's instruction on the treatment of trees during a siege.

(at SoM 5) in a poem that condemns Israelite idolatry can only be heard, in its present context in Deuteronomy, as recalling Moses's earlier accounts, including his use of it in 31.29. So too with other elements from the same verse of Moses's last speech before the Song: The phrase בְּאַחֲרִית הַיָּמִים (31.29: at the end of days), referring to evil events the Israelites will experience, is recalled in SoM 20b, 29b, along with the same phrase in 4.30 and the similar one in 8.16. The verb להכעיס 'to vex' (31.29), referring to the Israelites' angering of YHWH, is recalled in SoM 16b, 19b, 21b, along with its identical occurrences in 4.25 and 9.18.

It is not only elements recurring from Moses's speech in 31.24–29 that evince the Song's Mosaic character within the book of Deuteronomy. I present other notable instances here in list form:

1) The image of the Israelites being carried by YHWH in the wilderness, whether as children of a human parent, as in 1.31, or as nestlings of an eagle, appearing in SoM 10–11 as a variation on the theme.

2) The language of apportionment and inheritance, which Moses uses throughout Deuteronomy with reference to the relationship between individual nations, gods, and territories (the verb לחלק 'to apportion' in 4.19 and 29.25; the noun נַחֲלָה 'inheritance' in 4.20, 21, 38; 9.26, 29; 12.9; 15.4; 19.10, 14; 20.16; 21.23; 24.4; 25.19; 26.1; and the verb להנחיל 'to cause to inherit' in 12.10; 19.3; 31.7), as well as with reference to the relationship between Israel's individual tribes and their territories (the verb להנחיל 'to cause to inherit' in 1.38; 3.28; the noun נַחֲלָה 'inheritance' in 29.7) or the lack thereof in the case of the Levites (the nouns נַחֲלָה 'inheritance' and חֵלֶק 'portion'] in 10.9; 12.12; 14.27, 29; 18.1, 2[55]) – all this language is recapitulated in SoM 8–9, in להנחיל, חֵלֶק, and נַחֲלָה, though with reference only to Israel, its land, and its god.[56]

3) Moses's instruction in 6.20–25 on the manner in which Israelites are to answer their descendants' questions, which is echoed by the command in SoM 7 for the Israelites to ask questions of their ancestors.

4) Satiety as a point of crisis that may lead to apostasy, which appears in Moses's words at 6.10–15; 8.7–19; and 11.10–17 and reappears in the Song at SoM 13–18.

5) Moses's many variations on the phrase אֲשֶׁר לֹא לָדַעַת (which [someone] does not know) at 1.39; 8.3, 16; 11.2, 28; 13.3, 7, 14; 28.33, 36, 64; 29.25;

---

55. נַחֲלָה appears without חֵלֶק in 18.2.

56. In 21.16, להנחיל refers to a human father giving inheritances to his sons, a use that ties into the previous point, where YHWH treats the Israelites as his children.

and 31.13, which make the parallel phrases [אֲשֶׁר] לֹא יְדָעוּם (which they did not know) and [אֲשֶׁר] לֹא שְׂעָרוּם אֲבֹתֵיכֶם (which your fathers did not dread) in SoM 17b, d sound very Mosaic indeed.

6) Several instances of the motif of effacing the memory of a nation that has offended against YHWH, at 9.14 (YHWH's sentiments as recounted by Moses); 12.3; 25.19; and 29.19,[57] which find their culmination in the motif's reappearance in SoM 26.

7) Finally, the Song's anxiety over the correct interpretation of military victory – who is able to bring it about, and who is responsible for it when it has occurred (SoM 27, 30, 39) – echoes Moses's numerous exhortations on the subject during other moments of decision (1.20–30, 41–44; 2.4–5, 9, 12, 19, 21–22, 24–25, 30–33, 36; 3.2–3, 22; 4.38–39; 7.2, 17–24; 9.1–3; 11.2–7, 23, 25; 12.29; 20.3–4; 21.10; 23.15; 28.7, 25; 31.3–5).

Although within the Song the aforementioned elements are spoken by characters other than Moses – in the sense that, although Moses performs the Song, he is not a character within it – their presence on Moses's lips in earlier parts of Deuteronomy nonetheless suffices to render their reappearance in the Song a recapitulation of Mosaic speech. Through this resemblance to Mosaic speech (in the form reported by Deuteronomy), the Song obtains at least a nominal claim to being prophetic speech as well, since Deuteronomy describes Moses as occupying a prophetic role in Israelite history, as being even the measure of a prophet (18.15, 18).[58] Deuteronomy constructs the Song as prophetic speech in a more detailed fashion, however, for Deuteronomy 18 does not just name Moses as the paradigm of a prophet but also gives a description that is matched or echoed by the Song at several points, one effect of which is to align a performer of the Song with the idea of a prophet raised up by YHWH.[59] This alignment operates through

57. In 29.19 Moses speaks not of a nation per se but of "a man, woman, family, or tribe" that thinks to act without consequence (29.17–18).

58. 18.15: נָבִיא מִקִּרְבְּךָ מֵאַחֶיךָ כָּמֹנִי יָקִים לְךָ יְהוָה אֱלֹהֶיךָ (a prophet from among you, from your brothers, like me will YHWH your god raise up / institute for you); 18.18: נָבִיא אָקִים לָהֶם מִקֶּרֶב אֲחֵיהֶם כָּמוֹךָ (a prophet will I raise up / institute for them, from among their brothers, like you.) Cf. 34.10: לֹא־קָם נָבִיא עוֹד בְּיִשְׂרָאֵל כְּמֹשֶׁה (there has still not arisen / been instituted a prophet in Israel like Moses).

59. For Weitzman too, the Song's prophetic quality flows from its association with Moses, but not because Moses is a prophet in Deuteronomy or because the Song shows any correspondence to the prophetic role described in Deuteronomy 18 (nor because it is a genre employed by prophets); rather, Weitzman says, the fact that it predicts the future requires it to be prophecy: "Once the song was attributed to Moses, it was almost inevitable that it was understood as a prophecy, since it refers to events after Moses' death" (Weitzman 1997:40).

parallels involving, for example, the motif of putting words "in the mouth" of a prophet (18.18: וְנָתַתִּי דְבָרַי בְּפִיו [I will put my words in his mouth]) and in the mouth of succeeding generations of Israelites (31.19: שִׂימָהּ בְּפִיהֶם [put it (the Song) in their mouth]). Correspondingly, the prophetic role requires speaking in YHWH's name (18.19, 20, 22: לְדַבֵּר בִּשְׁמִי / בְּשֵׁם יְהֹוָה [to speak in my name / in the name of YHWH]), while performers of the Song will invoke his name (SoM 3: כִּי שֵׁם יְהֹוָה אֶקְרָא [for it's YHWH's name I proclaim]). These two resemblances of phrasing reflect the situational similarity between the prophetic role and that occupied by the Song and its performers. The voice of YHWH is no longer heard directly, but the categories of both prophet and Song-performer, which I am arguing overlap, speak in his place (18.16; 31.19) in a voice that must be heard (18.15, 19; SoM 1). Deuteronomy 18's placement of the origin of prophetic speech at Horeb provides a further link to the Song as represented in Deuteronomy 31, for both narratives feature an assembly (קָהָל; 18.16 and 31.30; cf. 31.12, 28) at which prophetic speech supersedes law.[60]

---

60. I note here a few other minor parallels, two relying on the near context of the law of the prophet in Deuteronomy 18: the opposition in 18.9, 12–14 between being תָּמִים 'perfect' and committing תּוֹעֵבֹת 'abominations' in the manner of the nations previously inhabiting the land and the similar opposition in SoM 4, 16–17 between YHWH's "perfect" deeds and the "abominations" that are the objects of Israel's worship (notably, defined also as זָרִים 'foreign'); also, the fact that the law of the prophet and the performance of the Song find their relevance once Israel has entered the land (18.9; 31.16). Finally, note the use of rhetorical questions beginning with אֵיכָה 'how?' in 18.21 and SoM 30ab.

Chapter 3
The Song of Moses Speaker by Speaker

The Song's Performers in Deuteronomy's History

IN THE PERFORMANCE HISTORY that Deuteronomy envisions for the Song, YHWH plays the most important role. As author, he is the originating member in the chain of re-performances of the Song; everyone who sings the Song in a manner informed by this tradition is re-enacting YHWH through the words that he composed. The same kind of phenomenon is observable in other cases, by which I mean the sense in which Shakespeare can be heard in performances of his plays, the sense in which Homer can be heard in all the words of the *Iliad*[1] and the *Odyssey*, and the sense in which David can be heard in recitations of the psalms attributed to him. With certain of David's psalms, in fact, added titles have even made it possible to imagine the particular circumstances under which David composed them.[2] A description of the circumstances under which it originated is also available for the Song, which has, instead of a short superscription, a much longer introduction in Deuteronomy 31. Additionally, Shakespeare, Homer, and David were also known as performers of their compositions, not just authors, whereas this is less clear for YHWH. Nevertheless, some actual performance on his part is implicit in the introduction to the Song. It is reasonable to assume that, in the narrative imagination of Deuteronomy, YHWH presents Moses with the Song in a manner similar to his presenting other texts, either in written form, as with the Decalogue,[3] or in spoken form, as with everything (including the Decalogue[4]) in the book of Deuteronomy that Moses relays from YHWH to the Israelites. Deuteronomy 9.10 adds a graphic touch to the depiction of the performed nature of written texts, mentioning "stone tablets written with the finger of God." Therefore, although in 31.19 YHWH refers in lapidary fashion to "this song" without remarking on exactly how the Song came to be, it is consistent with Deuteronomy's narrative overall to

---

1. As I will discuss the merging of performed and performing personas below, here let me note that the *Iliad*'s Homeric composing persona merges itself with the voice of Achilles, particularly in the moments when Achilles's closest companion Patroklos is being addressed. See Martin 1989.

2. Cf. the superscriptions to Psalms 3, 7, 18, 34, 51, 52, 54, 56, 57, 59, 60, 63, 142, for a recent treatment of which see Johnson 2009.

3. Deuteronomy 4.13; 5.22; 9.10; 10.2, 4.

4. Deuteronomy 5.4–5.

say that YHWH must have performed the Song in some manner – whether writing, speaking, or even perhaps singing – in order for there to be something present for "this song" to refer to. Given that in Deuteronomy the other texts of YHWH's that Moses writes out were first spoken by YHWH, not written, some sort of oral delivery seems more likely in the case of the Song. Subsequent performers, therefore, recall YHWH not just in his moments of composing the Song but also in his moments of writing or sounding it out in order to transmit it to Moses and thereby to future Israelites.

Moses is the second member of the tradition of performing the Song as envisioned by Deuteronomy. While YHWH is evoked by subsequent performers due both to his authorship as well as to his (somewhat ambiguous) role as very first performer of the Song, Moses is evoked insofar as he is the Song's first recipient, its first teacher, its first human performer, and its first (or only) writer.

Given, therefore, the respective places of YHWH and of Moses in the performance history of the Song, their personas resonate in all subsequent performances. But what about each of them resonates? Because the performance of the Song is a product of Deuteronomy and its unique goals, it is first of all the Deuteronomic YHWH and the Deuteronomic Moses who are embodied by the performers. Therefore, I will focus on the characters of YHWH and of Moses as they appear in Deuteronomy and for the most part leave aside other texts that depict them, although such a farther-reaching analysis would find its place in a larger, canonical context.[5]

Deuteronomy does not mention specifically many more people who would have taken part in the tradition of performing the Song and who would thus, in addition to YHWH and Moses, also be invoked by later performers. Joshua is the only individual specified (31.14, 32.44); the precise nature of his role, however, is obscured by the preeminence of Moses, so long as Moses is alive. On the one hand, although Joshua is clearly present, it is primarily Moses whom YHWH addresses in the matter of the Song, and it is Moses who carries out the divine commands (e.g. 31.16, 22, 30). On the other hand, YHWH's command to Moses in 31.19 is formulated in the plural: כִּתְבוּ לָכֶם (write for yourselves), thus leaving room for Joshua, and 32.44 says that Joshua (called Hoshea there) had already joined Moses in the first recitation of the Song. As successor to Moses, Joshua is both first performer

5. The need for this circumscription arises also from the practical concern of suitably defining this project. For not only does Deuteronomy provide enough material on its own for me adequately to illustrate the kind of analysis I am proposing, but including other Pentateuchal texts, for example, would require a more thorough consideration of the vexed question of the relationship of Deuteronomy to those texts (i.e. whether Deuteronomy is meant to replace or to supplement them).

along with him and the first imitator who comes after him. Those who come later in the tradition imitate him in both of these capacities.

In addition to Joshua, there is also categorical mention of the "Isra-elites" (31.22), the "Levites" (31.25), "elders" and "officials" (31.28), the "entire Israelite assembly" (31.30), and the "people" (32.44), some of which obviously overlap. After this point, however, given where the narrative of Deuteronomy ends, the list of members of the performance tradition can only broaden out vaguely to future Israelite generations. According to the rest of the introductory material in Deuteronomy 31, the Song will be performed by Israelites at least through such time as: 1) the Israelites en-ter the land, become prosperous, and begin worshipping the gods of the land rather than YHWH (31.16, 20; cf. 31.27, 29); 2) YHWH, in his resulting anger, brings disaster on the Israelites (31.17, 21; cf. 31.29); and 3) the Is-raelites doubt thereupon that YHWH is with them anymore (31.17).[6] This chain of events is presented as beginning immediately after Moses's death (31.16), but nothing suggests that it will be completed quickly; the divine-ly-ordained disasters are to take place at a future time described vaguely as "the end of days" (31.29), after which the Song will function to witness against the (equally vaguely described) "descendants" of the Israelite na-tion (31.21). The Song, too, speaks in terms of generations (SoM 5, 7, 20) and of a hearkening back from the present time to the nation's beginnings long ago (SoM 7). On the whole, the book of Deuteronomy does likewise.[7] Thus, in positing a history of the Song's transmission that extends across such an indeterminate time (a history of oral transmission being equivalent to a history of performance), Deuteronomy assumes that quite a number of Israelites will have learned the Song by performing it. As is the case for all etiologies, Deuteronomy takes a well-established fact and posits an event or process that led up to and finally resulted in it. From the point of view, then, of the apparent intended real-life addressees of the book of Deuteronomy in the seventh century BCE who knew the Song so well (as well as, potentially, from the point of view of the actual recipients of Deuteronomy throughout its reception history), all of their Israelite forebears had taken part in the transmission of the Song, following on from YHWH's giving of the Song to Moses and from Moses's paradigmatic act of recitation, with the whole pro-

6. This sequence is summarized in 31.21 with the simple note that the Song "will not be forgotten from the mouth of their descendants."

7. E.g. Deuteronomy 2.14; 6.2, 20. Cf. also the "until this day" statements in 2.22; 3.14; 10.8; 11.4; 34.6. Within the narrative context of Deuteronomy, the intervening time must be long enough to allow for the Israelites to occupy the land, begin to co-exist peacefully with neighboring nations, and establish both YHWH's centralized cult and a (hereditary) kingship (12.10–11; 17.14–20).

cess informed by the intentions and purposes stated in Deuteronomy 31. Additionally, just as any given recipients of Deuteronomy in this chain can thus imagine themselves as the latest performers of the Song to date, so can they imagine any of the previous generations of performers as the latest performers of the Song in their own time.

If I were conducting my analysis in a larger context, I would also consider the evocation of any Israelite figure who was understood to have lived before the time of the first compositional stage of Deuteronomy to include the Song of Moses and after the last days of Moses's life, whenever that was understood to be. For example, one might imagine that seventh-century Israelites understood David as an ancestor who lived after the time of Moses and thus also as a one-time performer of the Song, as someone who knew it and sang it, having received it from his older relatives and having also passed it on to his younger ones. The persona of David, therefore – in addition to YHWH, Moses, Joshua, and so on – would also resonate in performances of the Song that took place after what was understood to be his lifetime. So too would Solomon, who fits so well into the paradigm offered by the Song of prosperity followed by – or at least coupled with – lack of complete loyalty to YHWH; Ahaz, who was confronted by enemies and who was rescued (though most ostensibly by Assyria rather than by YHWH); and Hezekiah, who also faced a military threat and who according to the narrative in Kings was rescued by YHWH. These re-performed personas produce some of the more poignant resonances that exist in the performance tradition, insofar as their own life circumstances, as understood by the tradition, relate directly to the themes of the Song, but there are many others.

A performance tradition includes not only those who perform and who have previously performed but also those who are present and who have previously been present at performances.[8] The narrative of Deuteronomy indicates that Moses (along with Joshua) was present at the very first performance of the Song (assuming that YHWH presented it in some manner orally) and that "Levites," "elders" and "officials," and "the entire Israelite assembly" were present when Moses (and Joshua) delivered the Song in Deuteronomy 32. Further, since the Song was written into the deposited copy of the torah (as the latter half of Deuteronomy 31 seems to presume), we can number the future hearers of the commanded septennial torah reading (31.10–13) among the members of the tradition whom Deuteronomy envisions as present at performances of the Song.

There are two corollaries of significance for this kind of performance-based analysis. First, all who are present at a performance of the Song know

8. In fact, members of a tradition often perform for or at least in front of each other.

that they are re-enacting previous auditors in the performance tradition – in much the same way that performers of the Song know that they are re-enacting the performers who came before them. Those who are present at any particular performance of the Song can put themselves, for example, in the place of Moses (and Joshua), first receiving the Song from YHWH, or in the place of the elders, receiving it from Moses (and Joshua). The second corollary is that the Song's auditors, in the very act of hearing the Song, evoke the characters who are directly addressed within the Song. More precisely, perhaps, the Song's auditors are invoked by the Song's performers in the roles of the characters who are directly addressed within the Song. These characters are the sky and earth, the Israelites in general, and the nations. To sum it all up, then, just as the Song's performers re-enact the Song's previous performers as well as the characters who speak within the Song, so are the Song's auditors cast in the roles of the Song's previous auditors as well as of the characters who are addressed within the Song.

The Song's Speaking Parts

Having outlined the figures external to the Song, I will now list the characters who are part of the composition itself, in the order in which they appear.

— The prophetic persona of the Song speaks of YHWH in the third person, speaks to the Israelites in the second person (singular and plural) as well as of them in the third person, and speaks to "the nations" in the second person, in the final verse of the Song (SoM 1–3, 5–7, 14e, 15b, 17d–20ø, 31, 36–37ø, 38cd, 43). At one point, this voice includes itself in a group that has YHWH as its god (SoM 3b), by employing the first person plural. Although the Song speaks here and there in tones of wisdom (e.g. SoM 2) and of hymnic praise (e.g. SoM 43), it is primarily a prophetic voice, insofar as features of prophetic speech, whether lawsuit or oracle, are so prominent within the Song.

— The skies and the earth speak of YHWH in the third person (SoM 4).

— The Israelite elders speak of YHWH in the third person and also of the Israelites and/or the enemies in the third person (SoM 8–14d, 15a, 15c–17c, 30cd, 32–33).

— YHWH speaks of Israel and of his enemies in the third person (SoM 20b–27c, 28–30b, 34–35, 37a–38b, 39–42). YHWH is never addressed directly in the second person.

— The enemies speak in the Song only by virtue of being quoted, in a hypothetical manner, by YHWH (SoM 27cd). They are a self-aware group, using the first person plural, and speak of YHWII in thc third person.

Along with those who speak, I include as implicit characters those who are directly addressed by the speakers: the sky and earth (SoM 1, 3), the nations (SoM 43), and Israelites in general, who are the addressees of every remaining occurrence of the second person. The sky and earth, as noted above, respond when they are addressed and are thus also speakers. The nations, who are addressed at the end of the Song in an apparently apostrophizing manner, do not respond. The Israelites do not respond to any specific instance of being addressed, although they are addressed at various points throughout and are thus the primary addressees of the Song.[9]

Notes on Presentation

In the analysis below, I will refer to "the performers," plural, and to "the performer," singular – without, however, meaning to specify some situations of performance in which only one person is performing and others in which more than one person is performing.[10] Similarly, I will refer to "those present at a performance of the Song" and "someone present at a performance of the Song." My analysis is based on an assumption that performing the Song is fundamentally an individual action,[11] corresponding not only to the fact that the greatest part of the Song's first-person language is singular

9. The prose introduction to the Song labels (future) Israelites as the primary recipients: "When much evil and distress finds them, this song will answer/sing in their presence as a witness" (31.21).

10. Similarly, I will refer to "those present at a performance of the Song" and "someone present at a performance of the Song."

11. As mentioned above, Matthew Thiessen proposes that the Song was performed by a group, with speaking parts assigned to various members, including "a priest or cultic prophet" for the voice of YHWH, a "director of the liturgy" for most of the second-person addresses (which he takes to be addressed to the "congregation" present at the performance), "the choir" for "the responses, whether to the officiator's questions and commands or the speeches of YHWH," and possibly "the elders of the congregation" for the voice that responds to "the director's imperative that Israel ask its father and elders to relate the history of YHWH's dealings with the people" (Theissen 2004:416, 418). Thiessen's reconstruction of a group performance is related to the hymnic form he argues is most prominent in the Song and thereby to a cultic, liturgical setting. Although I focus on individual performance (for reasons given above, in the sentence to which this note is appended), my analysis and Thiessen's are not mutually exclusive. Note, for example, that Deuteronomy commands both communal and individual recitation of torah.

rather than plural[12] but also to the fact that the Deuteronomic Israelite is, to a remarkable degree, a self-consciously individual member of the tradition and of the collective.[13] Therefore, when I use "performer," I am referring to any given instance of an individual performing the Song, and when I use "performers," I am referring simply to an aggregation of such instances, understood as discrete in place and particularly in time. I will also use "the Song" and "the prophetic persona" interchangeably with "the performer" and "the performers." When I use the name "Moses," I will not mean any of the preceding but the character of Moses as he appears elsewhere in Deuteronomy and particularly in Deuteronomy 31 (most pertinently as the first recipient, performer, and teacher of the Song).

In this chapter, I present the Song as it appears in Codex Leningradensis (accompanied only by such text-critical comments as bear on questions pertaining to a performance-critical analysis of the Song).[14] I present the Song piece by piece, delineating the pieces according to what I perceive to be changes in speaking voice. While focusing on this Hebrew text of the Song, below it I also give corresponding pieces of the Song as it appears in Codex Vaticanus (again with relevant text-critical commentary and underscoring divergences between these Greek and Hebrew texts).[15] Selections from the Hebrew text will appear first, followed by their translation, which will be followed by selections from the Greek text and their translation. Even though the speakers change at different points in the Greek Song, I divide it according to the Hebrew, the better to show what is at stake in my analysis. However, an appendix to the chapter contains the entire text of the Song according to Vaticanus with the speaking voices demarcated according to the indications proper to that text.

What I am setting out to accomplish in this chapter can be compared to listening to a piece of music over and over again, each time picking out a different instrument or voice. I will be replaying the Song of Moses speech by speech, or section by section, with the sections divided according to the

12. One may object that the singular of the third person frequently represents a collective, as in SoM 10: "he found him in a land of wilderness" ("him" referring to the Israelite nation, introduced in the preceding verse by the eponym "Jacob") – and why, then, should not the first person singular also represent a collective? However, it is not so clear in the case of the first person singular which group would be represented by it, especially when it stands in contrast to the first person plural in SoM 3: "for it's YHWH's name I proclaim; give grandeur to our god."

13. I am thinking particularly of Deuteronomy 6, which pictures the individual's role in preserving and promulgating tradition (see 6.7–9), and of Deuteronomy 13, which emphasizes individual responsibility in policing other members of one's community.

14. I take this text from Elliger 1997.

15. This text I take from Brooke and McLean 1911.

voice that is carrying the melody at any given time. At the beginning of each speech, I place two lines of text that note, in the first line, the voices that belong to the performance history of the Song and, in the second line, the voices that exist within the Song. The first line remains the same for each speech, since the same potential history of performance stands behind every potential performance of the Song. According to Deuteronomy's vision, every (eventual) performer of the Song will have at their disposal within the performance tradition YHWH as the Song's composer or authorizer; Moses, the Song's first human performer and an ancestor who recounts YHWH's past great deeds; Joshua, not only involved in the Song's first performance and an ancestor who can recount YHWH's deeds, but also the prototype of a younger generation who receives the Song and passes it on; those assembled on the plains of Moab, who share with Joshua the position of having seen YH-WH's deeds and of receiving the Song in order to pass it on but who are not defined, as Joshua is, as individuals. Deuteronomy creates as a given the first few steps in the Song's history by thus portraying these acts of delivering and of receiving the Song, explicitly leaving the rest (Deuteronomy 31.19–21) to the historiographical imagination, up through the point when the generation experiencing "much evil and distress" will have received the Song and perform it with understanding. To reflect Deuteronomy's vision of an ongoing tradition with a definite if undetermined end point – or, at least, point of crisis – I use not only ellipsis points in the first line of notation but also the place-holding terms "subsequent performers" and "present performers"; for Deuteronomy, although the paradigmatic "present performers" belong to that future generation that will ask "Is it not because my god is not with me that these evils have found me?" (31.17), it remains true that each generation after Moses constitutes, for a time, the Song's "present performers." For example, in analyzing the case of Joshua and those assembled in Deuteronomy 31 (leaving aside for the moment Joshua's participation in Moses's first performance of the Song), the categories of "subsequent performers" and "present performers" overlap completely in referring to Joshua and the assembly; once Joshua's generation begins to perform the Song (having heard it during the events recounted in Deuteronomy 31–32), there is no one who performed it both subsequent to Moses and prior to them with reference to their "present" at that point in the (future) history constructed by Deuteronomy. Next, from the point of view of the generation following Joshua's, Joshua's generation intervenes as "subsequent performers," coming after Moses's initial performance and before their own performance in their "present." Thus, whichever generation may be viewed at a given time as "present performers," all previous performances of the Song are available to be re-enacted by them, including Moses's as well as YHWH's initial act of composition.

While the first line of notation concerns re-enactment in performance, the second concerns enactment in performance. The second line shows the layering of the speaking voices within the Song, with the leading voice always found in the rightmost position. Because the Song is a recognizably prophetic composition, there is always a prophetic persona speaking. At times this prophetic persona may quote another voice, such as that of YHWH, and that voice may quote yet another voice, as the character of YHWH in fact does.

It is as if Deuteronomy has constructed the Song as a stage, upon which an Israelite then enters. The first line of notation represents those who have performed on this stage before: this Israelite person's parents and grandparents; relatively unrelated Israelites of the past, such as priests, prophets, kings, and officials – all the way back to those assembled on the plains of Moab, including Joshua and finally Moses. Even YHWH, although he might not have occupied this stage himself, is nonetheless present in the history of performance as the ultimate composer of the drama. In this metaphor, the second line of notation represents the masks, or personas, that the performing Israelite notionally wears during the Song. Given that the Song is, generically, a prophetic-sounding composition, the first mask the performer puts on is that of a prophetic persona; this mask stays on throughout the whole Song while being most clearly visible when addressing the Israelite community directly with second person forms. When it comes time for the persona that is delivering this prophetic *rîb* or oracle to quote, for example, what the elders say in response to SoM 7, the performer adds a mask, so to speak, representing the persona of the elders who speak of Israel with third person forms, and when the prophetic persona briefly breaks into the elders' speech, the performer removes the mask of the elders momentarily, addressing the Israelite community directly again. In passages where the performer alternates quickly between two voices, wearing one mask while holding another still in hand and about to put it back on, the enacted voices merge in a way that is distinct from the operation of the performance tradition and of quotation within the composition. These latter produce a layering effect, the present performer re-enacting the performances of preceding generations re-enacting the performances of yet preceding generations and so on, at the same time as enacting a prophetic persona enacting, for example, YHWH as a character enacting, for a further example, the enemies as characters. On the other hand, the quick alternation of the enacted personas within the composition produces, rather, an effect of fusion, reinforced in the case of the Song by such facts as the alternating voices telling a single narrative and re-using the same terminology (both of which are features of the elders' speech into which the prophetic persona is interposed).

Finally, if the Song is a stage, then this chapter can also be compared to the work of a photographer at the performance. As my analysis proceeds, I will focus at times on one or another of the masks, or personas, being worn. At others I will adjust the focus of the performance-critical lens so as to bring the Song's previous performers into focus.

SoM 1–3

YHWH as composer: Moses's recitation: subsequent performers ... present performers ⇒ Song's prophetic voice

1 הַאֲזִינוּ הַשָּׁמַיִם וַאֲדַבֵּרָה וְתִשְׁמַע הָאָרֶץ אִמְרֵי־פִי

2 יַעֲרֹף כַּמָּטָר לִקְחִי תִּזַּל כַּטַּל אִמְרָתִי
כִּשְׂעִירִם עֲלֵי־דֶשֶׁא וְכִרְבִיבִים עֲלֵי־עֵשֶׂב

3 כִּי שֵׁם יְהוָה אֶקְרָא הָבוּ גֹדֶל לֵאלֹהֵינוּ

1 Give ear, O skies, that I may speak, and may the earth hear the
   utterances of my mouth.

2 May my teaching drop like rain, may my utterance drip like dew,
   like late rains upon grass, like early rains upon shrubbery.

3 For it's YHWH's name I proclaim. Ascribe grandeur to our god!

1 πρόσεχε οὐρανέ, καὶ λαλήσω· καὶ ἀκουέτω ἡ γῆ ῥήματα ἐκ στόματός
   μου.

2 προσδοκάσθω ὡς ὑετὸς τὸ ἀπόφθεγμά μου, καὶ καταβήτω ὡς δρόσος τὰ
   ῥήματά μου·
   ὡσεὶ ὄμβρος ἐπ' ἄγρωστιν, καὶ ὡσεὶ νιφετὸς ἐπὶ χόρτον.

3 ὅτι τὸ ὄνομα κυρίου ἐκάλεσα· δότε μεγαλωσύνην τῷ θεῷ ἡμῶν.

1 Give heed, O sky, and I will speak, and let the earth hear the utterances
   of my mouth.

2 Let my saying be awaited as rain and let my utterances descend like
   dew,
   like heavy rain on field grasses and like snow on pasturage.

3 For the Lord's name have I invoked. Ascribe greatness to our god!

Speaker(s): The identity of the voice that begins speaking in SoM 1 presents a small puzzle, especially if the Song is considered apart from its specific context in Deuteronomy. This voice says "I" (five times in these three verses), though without naming itself. An examination of the voice's other characteristics leads to one relatively sure conclusion, however: it is human. It begins by speaking as a prophet does, employing what is gener-ally considered to be a recognizable feature of the *rîḇ* or prophetic lawsuit. It continues by adding didactic elements, speaking as a wise teacher in the Israelite wisdom tradition; in SoM 2, it mentions "my teaching" and "my ut-terance" and compares them to the natural world, arguing for the reception of the life-giving teaching that the Song contains or represents. Then, in SoM 3, the voice speaks of YHWH in the third person, meaning that YHWH is ruled out as a possible speaker here. This, then, is a human voice, and, in-sofar as it is not tied to a named individual or corporate identity, it functions in some ways analogously to the lyric "I." As I have indicated in the introduc-tion to this chapter, I am labeling it the (prophetic) voice of the Song.

Fokkelman offers four possibilities for the identity of the Song's "I," without deciding between them or fleshing out the implications for each: 1) "the lyrical 'I', i.e. a character with primarily literary and semiotic status from the world evoked by this poetry"; 2) YHWH (by virtue of being named the author of the Song in Deuteronomy 31); 3) Moses (who is connected to the Song in Deuteronomy 31 in a way that Fokkelman does not specify); and 4) "the person [or persons, presumably, if this poem was composed over time within a performance tradition] who actually wrote the poem."[16] The first three of these also figure in my discussion. The fourth does not, however, because of having been lost to tradition and replaced by YHWH. Despite his protestations, Fokkelman does not investigate what it might mean that that the characters of Moses and YHWH, as depicted by the book of Deuteronomy, speak as characters in the Song.[17] With a single exception, "Moses" becomes a cipher for the lyric "I," as "God" simply stands for the divine voice.[18] Fok-kelman finds the construct of the actual author useful as the speaking voice of SoM 31.[19]

Addressee(s): The sky and the earth are addressed in the Song's first three verses. This is especially clear in the case of the sky, since the very first word הַאֲזִינוּ (give ear!) is an imperative directed to the sky; there is nothing to suggest that the addressee has changed by the time we get to the imperative הָבוּ (ascribe!) in SoM 3. The earth is equally addressed in these verses, given not only the parallelism between "sky" and "earth" in SoM 1 but also the parallelism between their verbs הַאֲזִינוּ and תִּשְׁמַע, which are parallel both in meaning and – although תִּשְׁמַע is not an imperative form – in volitivity.[20]

---

16. Fokkelman 1998:67.
17. Fokkelman 1998:67.
18. Fokkelman 1998:70.
19. Fokkelman 1998:112.

20. "According to IE [Ibn Ezra], הבו refers to heavens and earth and not to the audience that the prophet is addressing. The poet, I believe, had in mind the heavens and the earth in a figurative sense, viz., the people" (Levy 1930:60).

Discussion: Here I will first discuss the various resonances of the speaking voice in SoM 1–3, before doing the same for the addressees.

At the most conspicuous level of the Song, a human speaker addresses the earth and sky in the opening verses. This address is taken by many as the first feature of the *rîḇ* genre, regardless of the fact that the generic picture is complicated immediately afterward by the presence of wisdom elements in SoM 2 and of hymnic elements in SoM 3. The *rîḇ* genre predominates, however, given that such a prominent feature of it – the invocation of the earth and sky to hear – comes first, setting the tone for the rest of the Song, and also given that at least half of the rest of the Song also appears to be a *rîḇ*. By thus speaking in a prophetic mode, the performer necessarily acts out a characteristically prophetic voice[21] (although not the voice of a particular, named prophet[22]). By keeping the Song alive through oral performance, successive generations of Israelites become prophets, at least while they are performing the manifestly prophetic composition that the Song is.

Yet, to perform the Song is not just to sing it anew and isolated each time but also to participate in the tradition of handing it down – and in so doing to re-enact those who have handed it down before, including the first author. That is, even though it has been determined that the "I" of these verses must belong to a human character, the words it speaks do belong to YHWH, by virtue of his authorship of the Song;[23] it is, indeed, only because of YHWH's complaint as framed by the book of Deuteronomy that this prophetic speech has been composed at all. In these verses, the performers speak as YHWH did in composing them. The performers enact YHWH first sounding out the human, prophetic voice that announces his own divine complaint; they enact him first sounding out the voice of a wise human teacher, commanding that his own divine teaching be received (SoM 2); they enact him first sounding out the voice of a human hymnist, invoking his own divine name and commanding his own praise (SoM 3).

Just as the words of the Song belong to YHWH, whom Deuteronomy 31

---

21. Although I argue that they are less prominent in the Song overall, the same can be said for these verses about a wise voice (SoM 2) and a hymning voice (SoM 3).

22. Similarly, the voice of the Israelite elders (which begins speaking in SoM 8) is a generic voice, rather than having the names of any specific elders attached to it by the Song (or even by the context in Deuteronomy 31). The enemies (SoM 27cd) and the Israelite voice (SoM 31) are also generic, in the sense of being non-specific, although not in the sense of employing a recognizable genre.

23. Accordingly, of the fifty-three occurrences of the first person in the Song, forty-four are spoken by YHWH, while only six are spoken by the prophetic persona (all in the first three verses), two by the Israelite voice in SoM 31 (both plural), and one by the enemies (also plural).

presents as their first composer, so also do they belong to Moses on account of his place in the Song's performance history. Throughout Deuteronomy, Moses is the paradigmatic deliverer of YHWH's words, a fact that holds true for the Song as well. Everyone who performs the Song within Deuteronomic tradition recalls the recitation of Moses, the Song's first human performer, on the plains of Moab to the congregation of Israel. Further, each performer re-enacts Moses as prophet, for not only has Moses done something typically prophetic in delivering the divine message in the form of a *rîb*, but Moses is Deuteronomy's prophet par excellence. While the Song is already, in and of itself, a prophetic composition, Deuteronomy then attaches the Song to its construction of Moses as prophet.

As noted above, Fokkelman dismisses an investigation into the Song's genre, maintaining that Deuteronomy 31 provides enough information on this score in naming it an עֵד 'witness' and in describing the conditions of its performance.[24] However, the עֵד is not a genre with recognized features (recognized by biblical scholars, at least), so the label itself does not tell us much. Further, Deuteronomy 31's description of it is not detailed. Given that 31.28 makes a connection between the label עֵד and the invocation of sky and earth in SoM 1 through the use of the root עוד, along with several striking parallels to SoM 1 to be discussed in the next paragraph, it is possible that עֵד is Deuteronomy's name for what we are calling the prophetic *rîb* 'lawsuit'. On the other hand, I agree with the spirit of Fokkelman's comment, insofar as I suggest that Deuteronomy is creating a ritual sui generis for the Song of Moses.

Deuteronomy makes the Song's opening words belong to Moses in one further way. These words are his not just because of his prior performance of them and not just because of his identification as a prophet but also because of the similarity of the Song's opening words to the command that, in the narrative of Deuteronomy, Moses has just issued, in 31.28:[25] ... הַקְהִילוּ (gather [them] ... that וַאֲדַבְּרָה בְאָזְנֵיהֶם אֵת הַדְּבָרִים הָאֵלֶּה וְאָעִידָה בָּם אֶת־הַשָּׁמַיִם וְאֶת־הָאָרֶץ I may speak these words in their ears, that I may call the skies and earth to witness against/concerning them). The commands in 31.28, just quoted, and in SoM 1 (הַאֲזִינוּ) are both formulated with a plural Hiphil imperative followed by a singular Qal cohortative, and in fact the cohortative form is the same in each: וַאֲדַבְּרָה.[26] The root אזן that appears in 31.28 in the phrase בְאָזְנֵיהֶם (in

24. Fokkelman 1998:143.

25. 31.28 is similar to SoM 1 because it is in fact modeled on it, but I describe the similarity synchronically in order to highlight the impression given by performing the Song informed by its narrative context.

26. The form in 31.28, not coming at the end of a poetic line, does not exhibit the pausal

their ears) reappears in the first word of the Song as הַאֲזִינוּ '(give ear!). The skies and the earth appear provide a further link, first in a purpose clause in 31.28 ("that I may call [them] to witness") and then in its fulfillment in SoM 1, where they are actually invoked.

As indicated by the resonances of the phrase אִמְרֵי־פִי (the utterances of my mouth) in SoM 1b, the performer's voice is a voice of both authority and docility. Insofar as "my mouth" is Moses's mouth, the performer impersonates a human authority within the Israelite community while singing the Song. Insofar as "my mouth" is YHWH's authorial mouth, the performer speaks from a position of even higher authority – though of course also at a greater distance from the words, given that YHWH appears only as an object of the words in SoM 1–3 and is not, in that sense, their primary speaker. Conversely, "my mouth" reminds performers that their words were placed in their mouth by someone else: by YHWH, ultimately, by Moses, and even by Israelites of intervening generations, who previously enacted the authoritative voices of YHWH and Moses. Further, the words having been placed there, it would seem to be only by virtue of divine fiat that they have not been subsequently forgotten: "this song will answer/sing in their presence as a witness, for it will not be forgotten from the mouth of their progeny" (31.21).[27] "My mouth" thus connotes both the mastery of tradition and being mastered by tradition.

The concern of the Song at the end of this opening speech is recognition of two facts, namely, that YHWH's name is worthy of being called on and that YHWH has done great things. By calling for the construction of a tradition of performance in which the Israelites enact the Song's voice and its concerns, Deuteronomy puts the Israelites in the position of recognizing YHWH properly;[28] within the narrative of Deuteronomy 31, it is YHWH, as the Song's author, who puts the Israelite performers in this position.

The fact that the "I" of these verses uses a first-person plural pronominal suffix for the word אֱלֹהֵינוּ (our god) indicates that this "I" perceives itself as belonging to a group that has YHWH as its god. The question is whether

---

vowel: וָאֲדַבְּרָה. Note that the imperative to assemble also appears in YHWH's reported command to Moses in 4.10: הַקְהֶל־לִי אֶת־הָעָם וְאַשְׁמִעֵם אֶת־דְּבָרַי (gather the people to me that I [YHWH] make make them hear my words). Within the context of Deuteronomy as a whole, this resonance strengthens the effect of the overlapping of the voices of YHWH and Moses that reaches its highest pitch in the Song.

27. Cf. 31.19: "set it in their mouth, in order that this song may be my witness among/ against the Israelites." This is not a fiat, but it does reveal the divine intention.

28. Deuteronomy is everywhere concerned that the Israelites recognize what YHWH has done for them (e.g. 10.21).

its addressees, here the sky and the earth, are included in this group, such that the "I" is addressing them as fellow members. Or are the sky and earth outsiders to the group that the "I" belongs to? There is no way to decide between these readings, since each makes sense. On the one hand, it seems almost natural that the sky and earth would not belong to any group that humans belong to, especially if the speaking voice's Israelite identity is highlighted;[29] they are certainly not members of Israel. On the other hand, if we consider the "I" in its role as prophetic persona, we might hypothesize that it and the heavens and the earth are all members of the divine council, the prophetic persona being a privileged witness who then delivers to humans the messages or reports from the divine council.

Moreover, it is possible that these Israelite and heavenly-courtier identities would overlap in the performance tradition. Even if it is as a participant in the divine council that the Song calls YHWH "our god" (i.e. the god at the head of the divine council), it is nonetheless true that every Israelite is to take on, through performing the Song, this prophetic role of witness in the divine council. Merging in this way with the "we" of the divine council, the "we" of Israel comes to exist in a broader, more cosmic framework, which ultimately fits nicely with Deuteronomy's insistence elsewhere that Israel has a relationship with the god who directs all other divine figures (4.19; 10.17).

Fokkelman proposes a solution based on simple addition (the singular first person of אֶקְרָא [I proclaim] plus the plural second person of הָבוּ [ascribe!] yields the plural first person of אלֹהֵינוּ [our god]), but this amounts to circular reasoning, since he summarizes his solution by saying that the 1cp suffix proves that the addressees are included in the speaker's group.[30] Sanders proposes three potential addressees for הָבוּ – "the celestials (cf. v. 1), earthlings in general, or the Israelites" – but equivocates, saying that "in all likelihood the poet addresses every possible listener."[31] If the sky and the earth comprise a merism here, then "every possible listener" is correct. I prefer to understand them more specifically, however, in part because the imagery that follows their invocation appertains to meteorological and terrestrial phenomena. Also, the parallel imperative to the גּוֹיִם 'nations' in SoM 43 is followed by concerns that appertain to the Israelite people as distinct from other peoples. Finally, it is important that the addressees of הָבוּ, who

---

29. If we highlight the voice of the performers themselves, in their persona as the imagined and actual ultimate addressees of the book of Deuteronomy, then we may compare this usage of the first person plural to 13.3, 7, 14; 26.3, 6–9, 15, in which a hypothetical or idealized member of the Israelite people speaks.

30. Fokkelman 1998:69–70.

31. Sanders 1996:141.

speak in SoM 4, be not too specifically Israelite, since there is an Israelite perspective alluded to in the Song that clearly needs to receive the kind of orthodox instruction that is offered in SoM 4.

Since the addressees of SoM 1–3 are the heavens and the earth, all those who are present at a performance of the Song and thus in a way addressed by it can construe themselves as occupying the audience-like role of the heavens and the earth. That role is evidently characterized by being attentive to the Song (SoM 1), being the metaphorical enablers of its message (SoM 2), and being knowledgeable about YHWH's great deeds (SoM 3).[32] In SoM 4, for which see below, that role will include proclaiming YHWH's greatness. If the "we" defined by the first-person plural possessive pronoun of אֱלֹהֵינוּ (our god) in SoM 3 is a strictly Israelite group, then those who are addressed by the Song this point are placed, if only momentarily and rhetorically, on the outside of Israel looking in.[33]

In addition to taking on the roles of those addressed within the composition (that is, the heavens and the earth), the hearers of the Song may also compare themselves to those who are addressed as part of the tradition of the Song's performance. The figure of Moses has priority in this category (along with Joshua), being the first to receive the Song from YHWH. As the performer assumes the persona of Moses as prophetic and authoritative giver of the Song, those who hear the Song step into Moses's role as receiver of the Song, a figure to whom the Song is entrusted for others. The Song's hearers also inhabit the role of the assembly to whom Moses delivers the Song, who are themselves receiving it in order to pass it on to others, all of which is also true of the generations of Israelites intervening between the Song's first rendition and the time of any given Israelite performer.

To sum up, in these opening verses, performers of the Song enact all previous performing members of the Song's performance history, most notably (for Deuteronomy) YHWH as author and Moses (and Joshua) as first deliverer; they also enact the Song's prophet-like speaking voice, which is beginning a prophetic *rîḇ* in addressing the sky and earth. Hearers of the Song within the tradition are put in the position of all previous receivers of the Song, which in Deuteronomy's world most notably includes Moses (and Joshua) and the people assembled to hear it at the end of Deuteronomy 31; hearers are also put in the position of the sky and earth, the direct addressees of SoM 1–3.

32. As it happens, these characteristics are similar to what Deuteronomy prescribes for the Israelites in e.g. 4.1, 3; 5.1, 24; 6.7–9; 10.21.

33. Cf. the external point of view encouraged in Deuteronomy 4.7–8: "For what other great nation has its gods so near to it as YHWH our god is whenever we call to him? Or what other great nation has statutes and ordinances as righteous as all this torah that I am setting before you today?"

SoM 4

YHWH as composer: Moses's recitation: subsequent performers ... present performers ⇒
Song's prophetic voice: heavens and earth

4   הַצּוּר תָּמִים פָּעֳלוֹ כִּי כָל־דְּרָכָיו מִשְׁפָּט
אֵל אֱמוּנָה וְאֵין עָוֶל צַדִּיק וְיָשָׁר הוּא

4   "The rock, whose action is full of integrity! – for all his ways are justice.
A god of trustworthiness without iniquity, righteous and
straighforward is he."

4   θεός, ἀληθινὰ τὰ ἔργα αὐτοῦ, καὶ πᾶσαι αἱ ὁδοὶ αὐτοῦ κρίσεις·
θεὸς πιστός, καὶ οὐκ ἔστιν ἀδικία· δίκαιος καὶ ὅσιος κύριος.

4   "As for <u>God</u> – his works are true, and all his ways are judgments.
A god to be trusted, and there is no injustice; just and holy is <u>the Lord</u>."

Speaker(s): In this verse, a voice responds to the command הָבוּ גֹדֶל (ascribe greatness!) in SoM 3 by giving an account of YHWH's qualities. The general principle, as expressed by Watts, is that "imperative exhortations to praise ... mark some inset hymns."[34] In the present case, Michael Knowles states it as a hypothesis: SoM 4 "may [be interpreted] ... as an antiphonal response to the exhortation" in SoM 3.[35] Thiessen agrees that SoM 4 is spoken by a different voice than the one that pronounces SoM 1–3.[36] Both Thiessen and Knowles appeal to the imperative וְהָב as evidence of the shift; neither says why they think the response stops at the end of SoM 4. For my rationale, see below at SoM 5–7. Although the earth and sky are not explicitly named as the speakers, it is most straightforward to understand the imperative of SoM 3, to which the speakers of SoM 4 are responding, as continuing the volitive force of the verbs in SoM 1, where the earth and sky are definitely addressed. Whereas the speaker of SoM 3 refers to YHWH by name, the speakers of SoM 4 employ an epithet: הַצּוּר (the rock).

The content of the declarations made in this verse bears on the question of the group to which the earth and sky belong, posed above in the discussion of אֱלֹהֵינוּ (our god). Does the voice of the earth and sky have anything in common with the other voices that resound in the Song? Since they speak with perfect orthodoxy, they do not clearly belong to the same group as the enemies, who are explicitly said to speak incorrectly of YHWH in SoM 27. The orthodox speech of the heavens and earth would also seem to have

---

34. Watts 1993:347.
35. Knowles 1989:310 n. 7.
36. Thiessen 2004:409, 417.

little in common with the generation of the Israelites who, as described in the Song, act corruptly, forsake YHWH, give their worship to others, and are encouraged by the Song to bring YHWH's actions to mind and to understand them correctly. The Israelite ancestors, however, speak correctly about YHWH (SoM 8–17), as does the Song's prophetic persona – and, of course, YHWH himself.[37] Whether the heavens and earth as speakers of SoM 4 belong to their own separate group or to a group that includes the prophetic persona and/or the elders of Israel and/or YHWH, all these voices are aligned in the Song by virtue of speaking correctly about YHWH.

Addressee(s): Although the statements in SoM 4 contain no second-person forms, they are spoken in direct response to the speaker of SoM 1–3.

LXX: Nothing in Vaticanus indicates a difference in speakers from Leningradensis. However, the two manuscripts differ in the way they characterize both YHWH and, as will be seen below, the other recipients of Israel's worship. Throughout the Song, Vaticanus reads θεός 'god' wherever צור 'rock' in Leningradensis applies metaphorically to deity (SoM 4a, 15, 18, 30, 31 [twice], and via a relative pronoun in SoM 37).[38] Here, the Greek leaves no room for a word meaning "rock" to be understood as the name of Israel's deity, unlike the Hebrew; instead, the question of a divine name is answered, if it is at all, by the repetition of κύριος 'lord' at the end of the verse.

Additionally, the Greek constructs the verbless clause in SoM 4d not with a pronoun (which would have more closely matched the Hebrew הוא 'he, that one') but with the noun κύριος 'lord', which is Vaticanus's usual representation of the Tetragrammaton throughout the Song.

Discussion: The statements made in SoM 4 offer a counterpoint and a response to SoM 3: a response insofar as SoM 4b–d can be understood as explaining YHWH's greatness, as called for in SoM 3b, and a counterpoint insofar as צור 'rock' in SoM 4a seems to be used as an alternative to the name of YHWH as proclaimed in SoM 3a.

While in SoM 3, YHWH as the composer of the Song employs the voice of the performers to proclaim his own name (שֵׁם יְהוָה אֶקְרָא [YHWH's name do I proclaim]) and to ask for his own greatness to be recognized (הָבוּ גֹדֶל לֵאלֹהֵינוּ [ascribe greatness to our god!]), in SoM 4 he puts into the mouth of the performers words that elaborate on these themes. Throughout the Song, YHWH

---

37. In this connection, note that the rhythm and vowels of the phrase הַצּוּר תָּמִים פָּעֳלוֹ (haṣṣūr tāmîm pōʿolô [the rock whose action is full of integrity]), here spoken by the heavens and the earth, are echoed in the phrases צור יְשֻׁעָתוֹ (ṣūr yᵊšuʿāṯô [the rock of his salvation]) spoken by the elders in SoM 15d and צור חָסָיוּ בוֹ (ṣūr ḥāsāyū ḇô [the rock in whom they took refuge]) spoken by YHWH in SoM 37b.

38. The only occurrence of צור 'rock' elsewhere in Deuteronomy has a literal sense (8.15); correspondingly, the Greek word there is πέτρα.

as composer is a didactic figure, insofar as it is ultimately he who teaches the Israelites the proper words to say and what is true about him and about Israel.

Moses as first reciter is also a didactic figure in SoM 4 (even if he is more of a teaching assistant), which accords very well with his role as portrayed in Deuteronomy; he knows of YHWH's provision for the Israelites from a rock (see Deuteronomy 8.15[39]), and his recitation of YHWH's deeds of greatness in fact occupies huge portions of the text of Deuteronomy. Constructing a situation in which the Israelite performers take on the didactic concerns of YHWH and Moses, Deuteronomy thereby encourages them also to be receptive to its message.

Little about SoM 4 resonates with the prophetic nature of the performance. Although it is typical for the prophet to call on natural phenomena at the beginning of a *rîḇ*, it is not typical for them to respond.[40] As for the natural phenomena themselves, it is a question whether we should ascribe agency to the heavens and the earth in Deuteronomy, a book that elsewhere polemicizes against the worship of heavenly bodies; 17.13 lists the sun, moon, and "the entire host of the heavens" alongside the "other gods" whose worhsip is punishable by death. Two facts counter this possible objection. First, the entities whose worship is prohibited in 17.13 seem to be distinct from the sky proper, merely residing there, whereas the sky and the earth are a much more generic pair. That is, the heavens are the domain in which one finds other deities, and the earth is the domain in which one finds other nations. SoM 4 thus seems to suggest that heavenly bodies do exist and that their proper allegiance is to YHWH, given that the sky itself proclaims YHWH's greatness. Second, Deuteronomy ascribes agency of some sort to other, and to just as certainly inanimate, entities such as "this song" (31.19) and "this book of the torah" (31.26), so why not also to the earth and sky?

When performers speak in SoM 4 through the personas of the earth and sky, then, they are taken far outside the drama unfolding between YHWH and his people – or, stated in the opposite way, they are brought in as unrelated parties. The performers are made to testify to YHWH's integrity, justness, and lack of iniquity from a distant – one might even say objective – point of view and to name him by an appellation that reflects yet another

---

39. Fokkelman, too, notes that "the reciter employed by the author, Moses, can certainly agree" with צור 'rock' as a fitting metaphor for YHWH and his beneficence (Fokkelman 1998:70).

40. On the other hand, if we allow that a prophet may have the function of reporting the deity's words as heard in the divine council, we may also hypothesize the reporting of other words uttered there, such as those spoken by heaven and earth.

natural phenomenon: "the rock."[41] In that sense, the performers are here delivering what they asked for in SoM 3.

SoM 5–7

YHWH as composer: Moses's recitation: subsequent performers ... present performers ⇒ Song's prophetic voice

שִׁחֵת לוֹ לֹא בָּנָיו מוּמָם[42] דּוֹר עִקֵּשׁ וּפְתַלְתֹּל   5

הֲ־לַיהוָה תִּגְמְלוּ־זֹאת עַם נָבָל וְלֹא חָכָם   6

הֲלוֹא־הוּא אָבִיךָ קָּנֶךָ הוּא עָשְׂךָ וַיְכֹנְנֶךָ

זְכֹר יְמוֹת עוֹלָם בִּינוּ שְׁנוֹת דּוֹר־וָדוֹר   7

שְׁאַל אָבִיךָ וְיַגֵּדְךָ זְקֵנֶיךָ וְיֹאמְרוּ לָךְ

5   It went corrupt on him – not his children at all, a crooked and perverse generation.

6   Is it YHWH that you requite with this, O people that is foolish and not wise?
     Isn't he your father and acquirer? He's the one who made you and established you.

7   Remember the days of old, think on the years of generation upon generation.
     Ask your father that he may tell you, your elders that they may say (it) to you.

41. On צוּר 'rock' as an epithet for YHWH, see Knowles: "Whether ṣûr thus qualifies as a divine name in its own right cannot be concluded on the basis of these [biblical, primarily psalmic] parallels alone, but its metaphoric equivalence is unquestionable" (Knowles 1989:308). Besides appearing once elsewhere in Deuteronomy as a common noun (8.15), צוּר appears frequently in the Psalms as an epithet for YHWH. It occurs seven times in the Song as a divine appellation and once as a common noun.

42. מוּמָם is an important crux. Sanders understands it as מוּם 'blemish' plus the adverbial suffix ־ָם, appealing to the fact that מוּם belongs to a similar semantic grouping as the roots שׁחת 'destroy, become corrupt' and תמם 'be perfect, complete', which occur close together both here (including תָּמִים 'full of integrity' in SoM 4) as well as in Leviticus 22.19–25, which concerns the acceptability of sacrificial animals; similarly, מוּם and a noun from the root עול (unattested as such in biblical Hebrew but having to do with acting wrongly or unjustly; see SoM 4 again) appear close together here as well as in Job 11.14–15 (Sanders 1996:147–48). Sanders's observations demonstrate that the word מוּם 'blemish' would be at home at this point in the Song, but they fall short of proving that this particular word must be מוּם. With Salvador Carillo Alday and James Boston, I parse the final mem as an enclitic, reading מְאוּמָה 'at all' with a quiescent aleph, and understand the word to be functioning adverbially (as it does in 1 Samuel 21.3; Carillo Alday 1970:14–15; Boston 1996:34–36). This allows it to relate to the Song's preoccupation, evident elsewhere, with the degree to which – if "at all" – Israel shows itself as belonging to YHWH. Finally, the similarities in sound and meaning between the phrase לֹא בָּנָיו מוּמָם (not his children at all) that contains מוּמָם here and the phrase בָּנִים לֹא־אֵמֻן בָּם (children with no reliability in them) in SoM 20d provide another argument in favor of the final mem of מוּמָם being an enclitic particle rather than the third person masculine singular suffix.

5   <u>ἡμάρτοσαν</u>, <u>οὐκ αὐτῷ</u> τέκνα, <u>μωμητά</u>· γενεὰ σκολιὰ καὶ διεστραμμένη.

6   ταῦτα κυρίῳ ἀνταποδίδοτε οὕτω, λαὸς μωρὸς καὶ οὐχὶ σοφός ;

     οὐκ αὐτὸς οὗτός σου πατὴρ ἐκτήσατό σε, καὶ ἐποίησέν σε.[43]

7   <u>μνήσθητε</u> ἡμέρας αἰῶνος, σύνετε ἔτη γενεῶν γενεαῖς.

     ἐπερώτησον τὸν πατέρα σου καὶ ἀναγγελεῖ σοι· τοὺς πρεσβυτέρους σου

       καὶ ἐροῦσίν σοι.

5   <u>They failed</u>, <u>not</u> children <u>to him</u>, <u>blamable ones</u>, a crooked and twisted
       generation.

6   Do you thus requite the Lord with these things, dull and unwise
       nation?

     Did not he, this your father, acquire you? He also made you.

7   <u>Remember</u> the days of old, observe the years of a generation of
       generations.

     Consult your father and he will tell you, your elders and they will speak
       to you.

Speaker(s): There are no changes in pronominal reference and no imperatives that would indicate a change in speaker. SoM 5, however, does not continue the topic of YHWH's greatness that was called for in SoM 3 and proclaimed in SoM 4; rather, the verse focuses on the corruption of the Israelites (albeit in leading up to another proclamation of YHWH's greatness, beginning in SoM 8). I understand the earth and sky to have stopped speaking and the prophetic speaking voice of the Song to pick up again in SoM 5, continuing through the end of SoM 7. Another approach to the same recognition of a change in speaker here is to work backwards from SoM 7, where it is more clear that the Song is speaking: if in SoM 7 the voice of the Song introduces characters who begin speaking in SoM 8, and in SoM 3 introduces characters who begin speaking in SoM 4, then the Song's voice must resume at some point in between. SoM 5 is the most likely point for this to occur. Either way, the adjectives נָבָל 'foolish' and חָכָם 'wise' in SoM 6 and the verbs זְכֹר (remember!) and בִּינוּ (think on!) and in SoM 7 strengthen the link to the speaker of the Song's opening speech, as does the idea of listening to the discourse of one's elders, especially one's father, insofar as these details accord with the presence of wisdom motifs also in SoM 1–3.

Even though the change in topic from SoM 4 to SoM 5 is decisive in the context of the poem, it is worth noting that SoM 5–7 would make good sense as spoken by witnesses to a covenant, which Deuteronomy 31 evidently considers the heavens and the earth to be (31.28). Most basically, these three verses attest to the Israelites' failure to uphold their side of the covenant.

---

43. Many other manuscripts add καὶ ἔκτισέν σε (and he founded you) at the end of this line, corresponding to וַיְכֹנְנֶךָ (he established you), although Vaticanus omits the phrase.

More specifically, the language of kinship – YHWH as father and the Israelites as sons – reflects the predominant metaphor used for the relationship
between suzerain and vassal. Further, since covenants are meant to have
validity for subsequent generations, it makes sense for the witnesses to refer
the present-day Israelites to the Israelites with whom the covenant was first
made. (The rest of the book of Deuteronomy takes another approach, insist-
ing that the covenant was in fact made with the present-day Israelites; see
5.3.) Finally, קָנֶךָ (your acquirer), עָשְׂךָ (he made you), and וַיְכֹנְנֶךָ (he established
you) at the end of SoM 6 can be understood as allusions to the suzerain's
gracious acts on behalf of the vassal (as can גֹּדֶל 'greatness' in SoM 3; Deuteronomy uses the word this way in 3.21–24; 9.26–29; and 11.1–7, although not
in 5.24).

Addressee(s): The addressees are not specified until SoM 6, where the
second person first appears, in both singular and plural; the Israelites are
addressed, although not by name. While according to the Song more than
one nation can be foolish and unwise, there is only one nation of whom
YHWH is also called the "father" and "acquirer."

LXX: The readings of Vaticanus in SoM 5a, an exceptionally difficult passage in the Hebrew, differ in a number of details from those of Leningradensis:
1) the subject of the verb is plural (as if reflecting שִׁחֲתוּ [they became corrupt]
rather than שִׁחֵת [he/it became corrupt]); 2) it shows the opposite order of
what are two near-homonyms in Hebrew (translating לֹא לוֹ [not to/for him]
rather than לוֹ לֹא [to/for him not]); 3) correspondingly, it shows no third
masculine singular possession modifying the following word (as if from בָּנִים
[children] rather than בָּנָיו [his children]); and 4) μωμητά 'blamable', a plural
adjective, does not match either reading proposed for מוּמָם, although semantically it is closer to the noun מוּם 'blemish'; the similarity in sound may have
facilitated this translation. Also, as μωμητά is plural because of its relationship to τέκνα 'children', the ם- ending, when understood as a pronominal
suffix (where מוּמָם would mean "their blemish"), is plural because of its relationship to בָּנָיו. It is as if the translators were working with a Hebrew text
that read מוּמִים (blemishes). This would be the only attestation in biblical
Hebrew of a plural form of the noun מוּם (or of an unattested adjective of the
same formation).

To sum up, the *Vorlage* of SoM 5a seems to have been: שִׁחֲתוּ לֹא לוֹ בָּנִים
מוּמִים (they became corrupt, not children to him, blemishes). Beyond SoM 5,
Vaticanus has a plural form for the first verb in SoM 7 (μνήσθητε [remem-
ber!]), unlike Leningradensis's singular form (זְכֹר [remember!]), although the
subsequent verb is plural according to both manuscripts (σύνετε [observe!]
and בִּינוּ [think on!]). Nevertheless, Vaticanus also mixes singular and plural

second person forms in these verses. None of these divergences, however, have an appreciable affect on the identity or timing of speaking voices.

Discussion: The first half of SoM 5 has a particular resonance with the voices of the Deuteronomic characters of YHWH and of Moses in as they appear in 9.8–10.5. The motif of Israel's failure to be YHWH's sons recalls the moment at Horeb when YHWH seems to disown Israel, when he says: שִׁחֵת עַמְּךָ אֲשֶׁר הוֹצֵאתָ מִמִּצְרָיִם (9.12; your [= Moses's] people, whom you brought out of Egypt, have become corrupt) and וְאֶעֱשֶׂה אוֹתְךָ לְגוֹי (9.14; let me make you [Moses] into a nation). YHWH repudiates his involvement with Israel by saying that they are Moses's people, proposing to destroy them and start over again with Moses. At that point Moses takes on responsibility for the people by interceding on their behalf (9.18, 25–29) and countering that they really do belong to YHWH – given that YHWH has, "by [his] greatness" (בְּגָדְלֶךָ), redeemed them from Egypt (9.26; compare SoM 3) – and prays that YHWH "not destroy" those whom Moses, bringing the matter full circle, calls "your [= YHWH's] people" (9.26; אַל־תַּשְׁחֵת עַמְּךָ).

When the voice of Moses as past performer is thus brought into focus, in the Song it is heard offering a rebuke to the Israelites. The voice of Moses describes their actions using the word that YHWH used before (שִׁחֵת [it became corrupt], in 9.12) and declares that the Israelites are not acting as if they belong to YHWH: לֹא בָּנָיו מוּמָם (not his children at all). Whereas in Deuteronomy 9 Moses reminded YHWH of his relationship with Israel and called on him to return to it, in the Song the voice of Moses reminds the Israelites of their relationship with YHWH. What remains the same between these two recitations is that YHWH's past beneficence is appealed to. In 9.26 YHWH is said to have redeemed the Israelites and brought them out of Egypt; in SoM 6 YHWH is said to have created, made, and established them. In SoM 5–7 the performers of the Song are made to assume the voice of Moses, to allude to an episode in which Moses interceded on their behalf, and also to accuse themselves in that very same voice.

On the other hand, when YHWH's voice as composer is brought into focus, we hear in SoM 5 a more straightforward re-enactment of the moment of disowning in Deuteronomy 9. Hearing YHWH's voice in SoM 6 results in pronominal irony, effectively remaking the third-person references to the deity (which are in an emphatic syntactical position) into first-person speech: "Is it *I* whom you requite with this ...? Aren't *I* your father and acquirer? *I* am the one who made you and established you."

There is a difference between the identity of the אָבִיךָ (your father) that appears in SoM 6 and the אָבִיךָ (your father) that appears in SoM 7. The former is parallel with קֹנֶךָ (your acquirer) – namely, YHWH – while the latter is

parallel with זְקֵנֶיךָ (your elders), who are the forebears of the Israelite performers of the Song. This concept of the human אָב, as ancestor, in addition to
being evoked in the moment of performance by virtue of representing past
performers of the Song, is specifically treated as another person to be inter-
rogated and who will respond – through the performer's own mouth, no less
– in the words of the Song starting in SoM 8. Note the multivalence of these
ancestors when the Levites, elders, and officials of 31.24, 28 are thought of as
filling the role: as recipients and addressees of the Song, they are being prepared to function as the source of knowledge that they are in the Song (in
SoM 8–14d, 15a, 15c–17c); as performers of the Song in their own right, they
are enjoined by SoM 7 to ask their own ancestors for a recitation of YHWH's
great and generous acts. This second point works well with Deuteronomy's
notion that it is not addressing the generation of Israelites who originally
witnessed YHWH's actions but the generation after that (e.g. 1.35, 5.3). As
for the divine אָב, the description of YHWH as acquiring Israel rather than
creating Israel matches what is described in SoM 8–9, where, without comment on whether YHWH was involved in creating or constituting the nation
of Israel, the elders describe YHWH's action as one of having assigned Israel
to himself.

SoM 7cd adds to the overlaying of personae, mixing up who is speaking
with who is supposed to be hearing: Who is doing the asking? Who will do
the telling? The speaking voice within the composition is the prophetic persona (which, in the narrative of Deuteronomy 31, is the same as Moses). With
Moses as the speaker, the most obvious (or at least the most immediate) addressee is the group of assembled levitical priests, elders, and officials. The
second most obvious addressee is the customary addressee of the second-
person (whether plural or singular) in Deuteronomy, that is, the nation of
Israel, for whom, in fact, the Song is ultimately given. Are the Israelites at
large – Moses's hearers in the book of Deuteronomy – being commanded
to interrogate their own ancestors? However, YHWH's instructions regarding the Song also makes the present-day members of the nation of Israel
into the primary speaking voice; to whom, then, would they be speaking?
Are they speaking (with Moses) to the primeval assembly, speaking just as
knowledgeably as he of their faults and asking them to recite what they
learned from their own forebears? Or should Moses be included among the
group of addressees indicated by "your father … your elders"? After all, in
the post-exilic world of Deuteronomy's final composition, Moses is long
dead. Even within the narrative, at the time of the giving of the Song in the
narrative of Deuteronomy 31, Moses cannot help but be aware of the near-

ness of his death (31.14); in fact, according to 31.16, he is already about to join his ancestors (הִנְּךָ שֹׁכֵב עִם־אֲבֹתֶיךָ). Or, are the Israelites speaking to members of their group who lived after the time of Moses, Joshua, and the elders but before their own time, perhaps to the Israelites on account of whose sin "much evil and distress" has found them (31.17), again with knowledge of their faults? Are they speaking to other members of their group in their own present? Are they speaking to themselves? Within a tradition of continuous performance, all of these are true at once. In a chorus of voices, the Israelite performers of these verses are made to announce their own corruption (SoM 5), to ask exasperated rhetorical questions of themselves (SoM 6a, cd), to call themselves foolish (SoM 6b), and to ask their ancestors to help them recall the nation's past experience (SoM 7).

SoM 8–14d

YHWH as composer: Moses's recitation: subsequent performers … present performers ⇒ Song's prophetic voice: elders

בְּהַנְחֵל עֶלְיוֹן גּוֹיִם בְּהַפְרִידוֹ בְּנֵי אָדָם	8
יַצֵּב גְּבֻלֹת עַמִּים לְמִסְפַּר בְּנֵי יִשְׂרָאֵל	
כִּי חֵלֶק יְהוָֹה עַמּוֹ יַעֲקֹב חֶבֶל נַחֲלָתוֹ	9
יִמְצָאֵהוּ בְּאֶרֶץ מִדְבָּר וּבְתֹהוּ יְלֵל יְשִׁמֹן	10
יְסֹבְבֶנְהוּ יְבוֹנְנֵהוּ יִצְּרֶנְהוּ כְּאִישׁוֹן עֵינוֹ	
כְּנֶשֶׁר יָעִיר קִנּוֹ עַל־גּוֹזָלָיו יְרַחֵף	11
יִפְרֹשׂ כְּנָפָיו יִקָּחֵהוּ יִשָּׂאֵהוּ עַל־אֶבְרָתוֹ	
יְהוָה בָּדָד יַנְחֶנּוּ וְאֵין עִמּוֹ אֵל נֵכָר	12
יַרְכִּבֵהוּ עַל־בָּמֳתֵי אָרֶץ וַיֹּאכַל תְּנוּבֹת שָׂדָי	13
וַיֵּנִקֵהוּ דְבַשׁ מִסֶּלַע וְשֶׁמֶן מֵחַלְמִישׁ צוּר	
חֶמְאַת בָּקָר וַחֲלֵב צֹאן עִם־חֵלֶב כָּרִים וְאֵילִים	14a–d
בְּנֵי־בָשָׁן וְעַתּוּדִים עִם־חֵלֶב כִּלְיוֹת חִטָּה	

8   "When the high one made the nations [into] inheritances, when he distributed the sons of men,
       he set up the boundaries of the peoples according to the number of the sons of Israel.
9   For his people are YHWH's allotment, Jacob the boundary-rope of his inheritance.
10   He found him in a land of wilderness and in a howling, desert emptiness.
       He enclosed him, he took thought for him, he guarded him as the pupil of his eye.

11   Like an eagle, he stirred up his nest, over his young ones he hovered.
     He spread his wings, he picked him up, he carried him on his pinions.
12   Yʜwʜ alone led him, and there was with him no foreign god.
13   He made him ride on the heights of the land, and he ate the produce of
          the field.
     He suckled him with honey from the cliff and with oil from the flint of
          the rock,
14a–d with curd of cattle and milk of flock, alongside fat of lambs and rams,
     ones from Bashan and beliers, with kidney fat of wheat."

8   ὅτε διεμέριζεν ὁ ὕψιστος ἔθνη, ὡς διέσπειρεν υἱοὺς Αδάμ,
     ἔστησεν ὅρια ἐθνῶν κατὰ ἀριθμὸν ἀγγέλων θεοῦ.
9   καὶ ἐγενήθη μερὶς κυρίου λαὸς αὐτοῦ Ιακώβ, σχοίνισμα κληρονομίας
     αὐτοῦ Ισραήλ.
10   αὐτάρκησεν⁴⁴ αὐτὸν ἐν τῇ ἐρήμῳ, ἐν δίψει καύματος, ἐν γῇ ἀνύδρῳ·
     ἐκύκλωσεν αὐτὸν καὶ ἐπαίδευσεν αὐτόν, καὶ διεφύλαξεν αὐτὸν ὡς
     κόραν ὀφθαλμοῦ.
11   ὡς ἀετὸς σκεπάσαι νοσσιὰν αὐτοῦ, καὶ ἐπὶ τοῖς νοσσοῖς αὐτοῦ
     ἐπεπόθησεν,
     διεὶς τὰς πτέρυγας αὐτοῦ ἐδέξατο αὐτούς, καὶ ἀνέλαβεν αὐτοὺς ἐπὶ τῶν
     μεταφρένων αὐτοῦ.
12   κύριος μόνος ἦγεν αὐτούς, οὐκ ἦν μετ' αὐτῶν θεὸς ἀλλότριος.
13   ἀνεβίβασεν αὐτοὺς ἐπὶ τὴν ἰσχὺν τῆς γῆς, ἐψώμισεν αὐτοὺς γενήματα
     ἀγρῶν·
     ἐθήλασαν μέλι ἐκ πέτρας, καὶ ἔλαιον ἐκ στερεᾶς πέτρας·
14a–d βούτυρον βοῶν καὶ γάλα προβάτων μετὰ στέατος ἀρνῶν καὶ κριῶν,
     υἱῶν ταύρων καὶ τράγων μετὰ στέατος νεφρῶν πυροῦ,

8   "When the most high divided the peoples, when he spread out the sons
          of Adam,
     he set up the boundaries of the peoples according to the number of the
          angels of God.
9   And his nation Jacob became his portion, Israel the allotment of his
          inheritance.
10   He made him self-sufficient in the desert in a thirst of burning, in a
          waterless land.
     He encircled him and taught him, and closely he guarded him as the
          pupil of his eye.

44. "MT begins with ימצאהו 'he found him (in a desert land),' but LXX avoids the notion
that God found Israel, as though she had been lost; rather by taking direction from verbs in
the second stich, ἐκύκλωσεν, ἐπαίδευσεν, διεφύλαξεν, which all speak of divine solicitude for
his people and of active care, the translator found a new word, αὐτάρκησεν, a denominative
creation from the adjective αὐτάρκής 'sufficient,' thus "he made self-sufficient." In a desert
land God enabled his people to survive" (Wevers 1995:514).

11   Like an eagle would shelter its nest, for his nestlings he longed.
        Spreading apart his wings, he received <u>them</u>, and he took <u>them</u> up onto
            his back.
12   The Lord alone led <u>them</u>. There was with <u>them</u> no foreign god.
13   He made <u>them</u> ride on the strength of the land, and <u>he hand-fed</u> them
            with produce of the fields.
        They sucked honey from rock and oil from solid rock,
14a–d   butter of oxen and milk of sheep, with fat of lambs and of rams,
        sons of bulls and of goats, with kidney fat of wheat."

Speaker(s): In SoM 7, the Song commanded its hearers to ask their ancestors to relate their knowledge of the past: "Ask your father that he may tell you, your elders that they may say (it) to you." These imperatives (and the corresponding jussives, even more so[45]) anticipate the change in speaker between SoM 7 and SoM 8, which is formally marked by a shift in pronominal reference to the third person: whereas the voice that has just been speaking in SoM 7 addresses the Israelites directly, the voice in SoM 8 does not do so. Therefore, I understand that the ancestors begin to speak in SoM 8. Their voice, which I label above with the rubric "elders" (drawn from זְקֵנֶיךָ in SoM 7), keeps speaking through SoM 14d and reappears in SoM 15a, 15c–17c, recognizable by the return of third-person pronouns for Israel and the Israelites, in alternation with the prophetic persona's direct address.

Addressee(s): The elders, since they do not use the second person, do not address anyone specifically. However, since their voice appears in response to the injunction in SoM 7, they may be understood as directing their words to the descendants of theirs who made the request that they speak. In the future narrative imagined by Deuteronomy 31, these descendants are the progeny who will one day construct a false hypothesis about divine involvement in their circumstances (31.17), who will have been taught the Song by their ancestors, and who will therefore be performers of the Song (31.19, 21).

LXX: In place of the Polel of the root בין 'to take thought for' in SoM 10, Vaticanus has ἐπαίδευσεν (he taught, educated); elsewhere in Deuteronomy, the verb παιδεύω 'to educate' corresponds to the Piel of the root יסר 'discipline' (4.36; 8.5; 21.18; 22.18). This verb reinforces the Song's image of YHWH as parent, especially given the occurrences of παιδεύω in 8.5 and 21.18, which have to do with parental discipline of children. By contrast, a form of διδάσκω 'to teach' or μανθάνω 'to learn' would have introduced into the poem a teacherly role for YHWH; see, for example, the translations of ללמד in 31.12, 13, 19, 22.

---

45. It is not the imperatives but the (equally volitive) jussive forms וְיַגֵּד (let him announce) and וְיֹאמְרוּ (let them say) that are the verbs of speech here.

Throughout SoM 11c–13, the Greek has plural pronouns where the Hebrew refers to Israel in the singular, as if picking up the plural from the metaphorical "nestlings" in SoM 11b, whereas the Hebrew returns immediately to the singular in SoM 11c.[46] In SoM 12b, the singular pronoun in עִמּוֹ (with him) may refer to YHWH or to Israel; by contrast, the Greek has a plural: μετ' αὐτῶν (with them), which must refer to the Israelites. In the Greek of SoM 13b, YHWH is the subject of ἐψώμισεν αὐτούς (he fed them); in the MT, the corresponding verb is וַיֹּאכַל (he ate), and Israel is the subject.

Discussion: The elders have a distinct voice insofar as they speak of both YHWH and his people in the third person; the voice of the Song itself most often speaks to the Israelites in the second person rather than of them in the third person. Further, the elders use the third-person singular almost exclusively when discussing the nation, except for the plural forms in the two couplets in SoM 16–17b.[47] The elders do not use "I" or "we."

In these verses, the elders respond to a request for their knowledge. In SoM 7, the recipient-performers of the Song are commanded (and command themselves): זְכֹר יְמוֹת עוֹלָם בִּינוּ שְׁנוֹת דּוֹר־וָדוֹר (remember the days of old, think on the years of generation upon generation), and when they perform SoM 8–14d (and SoM 15a, 15c–17c), both they and their ancestors, whom they are enacting, obey that command. The voice of the elders that they perform answers from a position of knowledge: they speak of time long past, before the nation was created even, and of events that have to do with its creation and subsequent history (SoM 8). Beginning in SoM 9, they show knowledge of YHWH's perspective, describing it in the third person. While their account is thus framed somewhat objectively, it is focused on YHWH. In the elders' voice, the performers tell of the unique relationship that exists between YHWH and the people (SoM 9; see also SoM 12) and of the affectionate and parental manner in which YHWH remedies the people's initial situation of destitution (SoM 10–11), listing the details of YHWH's generous provision (SoM 13–14).[48] YHWH's generosity is so great, in fact, that there is an extra

---

46. In the Hebrew Song, the elders continue to refer to Israel with singular pronouns up through the moment when the specific deeds of unfaithfulness begin to be described; then it switches from the eponymous singular ancestor to the plural. The shift from Israelite enjoyment of YHWH's beneficence to forgetfulness occurs as early as SoM 15a (depending on exactly how negative are the connotations of וַיִּבְעָט [he kicked]) and definitely by SoM 15c (וַיִּטֹּשׁ [he forsook]), whereas the shift to the plural occurs at the earliest in SoM 16a (יַקְנִאֻהוּ [they made him jealous], where the Masoretes vocalize the ambiguous consonants as a plural verb) and definitely by SoM 17a (יִזְבְּחוּ [they sacrificed]).

47. See also the metaphor of nestlings in SoM 11, which exhibits the plural.

48. Note that וַיֵּנִקֵהוּ [he suckled him], as well, perhaps, as the milk imagery חֶמְאָה 'curd' and חָלָב 'milk', can be understood to elaborate the motif of YHWH's parenthood.

colon in SoM 14.[49] The elders' speech thus constitutes an Israelite voice that is aware of the connection between YHWH and Israel and of the beneficence that characterizes their relationship on the divine side.

That SoM 8 is the place where a voice starts speaking, that it recites a narrative in a poetic manner, and that it locates this narrative far in the past by means of the preposition ‫ב‬ plus verbs representing primordial events – these three facts suggest that SoM 8 could be the introit of an "epic" recitation of the nation's history. If it is the case that an epic narrative known to ancient Israelites was inserted in the Song beginning at SoM 8, then the voice of the elders is marked by more than the imperatives and jussives in SoM 7 and the shift from second-person to third-person pronouns in SoM 8. The fact of quoting a recognizable text would thus be another way in which the elders possess a voice that is distinct within the Song and, further, would heighten the contrast of their voice with that of the Song's prophetic persona throughout SoM 14–17, where they alternate in quick succession. Passages in the Song that might be continuations of such a recognizable epic are SoM 32–33 and 37a–38b, at least insofar as these passages speak of Israel in the third person and reprise two major features of the elders' speech in SoM 8–17, namely, floral and faunal imagery and the relationship between the Israelites and the other recipients of their worship.

It is a jarring fact in the narrative world constructed in Deuteronomy 31 that the Song is composed to tell about events that lie in the future from the point of view of YHWH, of Moses, and of Moses's immediate audience (Levites, elders, officials) but in the past from the point of view of the Song itself and of the elders whose voice is being performed within it. From the point of view of the performers, Moses's voice can be identified with that of the elders insofar as Moses himself is an ancestor. On the other hand, as already mentioned, Moses lived before the events described in the second half of the elders' speech and knows about these events only because YHWH knows about them (even if they do fit in with what he knows firsthand – which, of course, YHWH also knows – about the "make" or "manner" of the Israelites [Deuteronomy 31.21, 27, 29]).

The elders introduce two related images of YHWH as a solicitous parent: an eagle watching over its nestlings (SoM 11) and a mother nursing a child (SoM 13cd). The elders are themselves parental figures, and by speaking in their voice at this point in the Song a performer would find himself or herself not only taking on a parental persona (that of the elders) but also sympathetically describing YHWH's actions with parental imagery.

---

49. Or, in the words of Fokkelman: "This strophe has been stuffed like a sausage. In the same way, Israel is stuffed with delicacies" (Fokkelman 1998:89).

SoM 14e

YHWH as composer: Moses's recitation: subsequent performers ... present performers ⇒
Song's prophetic voice

וְדַם־עֵנָב תִּשְׁתֶּה־חָמֶר 14e

14e   And for wine you drank the blood of grapes.

14e   καὶ αἷμα σταφυλῆς ἔπιεν οἶνον.

14e   And for wine <u>he drank</u> the blood of grape bunches.

Speaker(s): The second person singular form of the verb לשתות 'to drink'
indicates the voice of the Song interrupting the elders, addressing the nation of Israel directly. Sanders's comments on this line come close to my
own concerns: "The form תשתה can be retained even though the use of
the second person comes as a surprise. One may be inclined to adopt the
third person of the LXX but the LXX often eliminated such variation in the
Hebrew text. Driver and Budde rightly suggested that the poet here inten-
tionally addressed the listeners in a more direct way. He wanted to raise
their attention."[50] According to my delineation of personae, there are four
successive switches from one colon to the next in SoM 14e–15c, following
the second- and third-person pronominal references. This alternation corresponds with the heightening of the polemical tone, making for a fitting
prelude to the first explicit appearance of the divine voice in SoM 20, which
itself takes a very polemical stance toward the Israelites.

Addressee(s): The Israelite people is here addressed with the second
person singular; in reciting this line, the performers address themselves.

LXX: The Greek does not shift to second-person address in SoM 14e.
Rather, the elders' speech lasts uninterrupted through the end of SoM 15,
where – again, only in the Greek – YHWH begins speaking.

Discussion: Earlier (in SoM 7), the Song introduced the elders, by calling on the present-day Israelites to interrogate their ancestors; now the
Song shows itself to be allied with the elders, with the result that the two
main voices in the poem so far recount – by turns, in quick succession – a
single narrative accusation of the Israelites. Insofar as both of these voices
are enacted by anyone (by any Israelite) who is performing the Song, the
performer is thus accusing himself or herself from two points of view at virtually the same time. According to Deuteronomy 31, the voice of the elders
has a historical reality outside the Song as well, such that the performers are
accusing themselves not just as the characters of the elders within the poem
but also as their own elders who actually handed down the poem to them.

50. Sanders 1996:175. Sanders is referring to Driver 1906:360 and Budde 1920:23.

SoM 15a

YHWH as composer: Moses's recitation: subsequent performers ... present performers ⇒ Song's prophetic voice: elders

וַיִּשְׁמַן יְשֻׁרוּן וַיִּבְעָט   15a

15a   "Yeshurun grew fat and kicked."

15a   καὶ ἔφαγεν Ἰακώβ καὶ ἐνεπλήσθη, καὶ ἀπελάκτισεν ὁ ἠγαπημένος,

15a   And Jacob ate and was filled full, and the beloved one kicked.

Speaker(s): With the return to the third person, the elders take over again from the voice of the Song's prophetic persona.

Addressee(s): Though the elders do not use the second person, they may still be understood as directing their speech to their descendants, in response to SoM 7.

LXX: The Greek continues to refer to Israel in the third person, as it does all throughout SoM 8–15.

Discussion: The elders whom the performers are quoting in the Song's prophetic voice begin to reveal a polemical tone in their historical account through their use of the trope of fatness.[51] The previous verse exhibited an irregularity of form, insofar as it has one colon too many. SoM 15a evinces a related ambivalence or moment of turning at the level of vocabulary and semantics. It begins positively: the beneficiary of YHWH's generosity does in fact prosper: וַיִּשְׁמַן (he became fat).[52] What's more, this beneficiary is called by a name (יְשֻׁרוּן, from the root ישׁר, having to do with being straight or upright) that alludes to his uprightness[53] – which is also a quality of YHWH, in SoM 4, where he is said to be יָשָׁר 'upright'. The next word, however, the verb וַיִּבְעָט, shows that something is amiss with Israel's prosperity. Usually translated "he kicked [out]," it conveys rebelliousness and at the very least a failure to accept YHWH's patronage calmly.[54] It is at this point that the voice

51. Alternatively, we could say that the polemical perspective evoked by the Song's prophetic persona (who is, fundamentally, the narrator of the poem) in SoM 5–6 begins to break through. Or yet again, we could say that the polemical perspective of YHWH begins to break through, since YHWH is the ultimate composer of the Song.

52. Sanders is of the opinion that וַיִּשְׁמַן (he grew fat) itself has a negative connotation in this verse, noting the root's occurrences in Isaiah 6.10; Jeremiah 5.28; Ezekiel 34.16; and Nehemiah 9.25 in negative contexts (Sanders 1996:179 n. 433). Since each of these contexts is ironic, however, the verb itself (and adjectives formed from it) does not have a necessarily negative connotation. There are straightforwardly positive uses of the root שׁמן 'fat' as well, e.g. Genesis 49.20; Numbers 13.20; Judges 3.29; Isaiah 30.23.

53. According to Sanders, this epithet is used in an ironic sense (Sanders 1996:180); Fokkelman labels it sarcastic (Fokkelman 1998:89).

54. The root בעט occurs only here and in 1 Samuel 2.29, where it has a negative connotation

being performed by Israelite singers of the Song – the voice of their own forebears – begins to turn against them.

SoM 15b

YHWH as composer: Moses's recitation: subsequent performers ... present performers ⇒ Song's prophetic voice

שָׁמַנְתָּ עָבִיתָ כָּשִׂיתָ   15b

15b   You grew fat, you became thick, you were over-fed.

15b   ἐλιπάνθη, ἐπαχύνθη, ἐπλατύνθη·

15b   He grew fat, he thickened, he widened.

Speaker(s): The second person directed toward Israel indicates that the prophetic persona is now speaking.

Addressee(s): The Israelite nation is addressed by the second-person singular verbs, which is to say that the performers address themselves.

LXX: In Vaticanus, the verbs continue referring to Israel in the third person, so there is no change in speaking voice. These three verbs form part of the speech of the elders that runs through the end of SoM 15.

Discussion: Breaking from the quotation of the elders' persona, in SoM 15b the performers' focus switches back momentarily to the Song's prophetic persona, in the guise of which they address "you [nation of Israel]" – meaning themselves and all those who are present to witness the performance. Behind this voice, of course, stands YHWH, as composer, speaking directly through and to the Israelites about the particular manner in which they will receive his (still future) generosity in the land.

---

and is also associated with being or becoming fat. In 1 Samuel 2.29, weightiness (the root כבד, understood as honor) and fatness (the root ברא) are positive qualities that only become inappropriate when their possessor is competing with YHWH: "Why do you kick [בעט] at my sacrifice and my offering, which I have commanded for my dwelling-place, and honor [כבד] your sons more than me by getting fat [ברא] on the first part of every offering of my people Israel?" Fokkelman gives the verb יִבְעָט in SoM 15a the meaning "to feast, to gorge oneself," by virtue of parallelism with the verbs of fatness in the near context, regarding the evidence of cognates as relatively flimsy: "The dictionaries (Ges.-B., BDB, KBL, and HAL) and the commentaries chose either 'kick back' [recalcitrantly], which is almost impossible to document, or 'despise' with an eye to cognates in rabbinical Hebrew, Jewish Aramaic, an Syriac, i.e. from material originating a thousand years later" (Fokkelman 1981–1993:4:139; see his further discussion at 4:569–70). Even according to Fokkelman's reading, however, the verb וַיִּבְעָט signals that something is amiss with Israel's prosperity, if only because it is emphasized by such a glut of synonyms in this line and in the next.

SoM 15c–17c

YHWH as composer: Moses's recitation: subsequent performers … present performers ⇒
Song's prophetic voice: elders

וַיִּטֹּשׁ אֱלוֹהַ עָשָׂהוּ וַיְנַבֵּל צוּר יְשֻׁעָתוֹ 15cd

יַקְנִאֻהוּ בְּזָרִים בְּתוֹעֵבֹת יַכְעִיסֻהוּ 16

יִזְבְּחוּ לַשֵּׁדִים לֹא אֱלֹהַ אֱלֹהִים לֹא יְדָעוּם 17a–c

חֲדָשִׁים מִקָּרֹב בָּאוּ

15cd   "He forsook the god[55] who made him, and scorned the rock of his
salvation.

16   They made him jealous with foreign things, with loathsome things
they vexed him.

17a–c   They sacrificed to spirits who were not divine, gods they had not
experienced,

new ones, recently arrived."

15cd   καὶ ἐνκατέλιπεν τὸν θεὸν τὸν ποιήσαντα αὐτόν, καὶ ἀπέστη ἀπὸ <u>θεοῦ</u>
σωτῆρος αὐτοῦ.

16   παρώξυνάν <u>με</u> ἐπ' ἀλλοτρίοις, ἐν βδελύγμασιν <u>αὐτῶν</u> παρεπίκρανάν[56]
<u>με</u>·

17a–c   ἔθυσαν δαιμονίοις <u>καὶ</u> οὐ θεῷ, θεοῖς οἷς οὐκ ᾔδεισαν·
καινοὶ πρόσφατοι ἥκασιν,

15cd   And he left behind the god who made him, and abandoned <u>God</u>, his
savior."

55. אֱלוֹהַ is much more frequently (as a percentage of its total occurrences in the biblical
corpus) used as a proper noun, translatable by "God," than are the related words אֵל and אֱלֹהִים.
Each of these also makes appearances as a common noun, however, and אֱלוֹהַ is no exception;
e.g. Habakkuk 1.11; Isaiah 44.8; Daniel 11.37–39. In the Song, אֵל and אֱלֹהִים seem to be used as
common nouns; for אֵל, see SoM 4c, 12c, 18b, 21a; for אֱלֹהִים, see SoM 3b, 17b, 37a, 39b. While אֵל
and אֱלֹהִים could, in some of these cases, be functioning as proper nouns, the presence in all of
them of pronominal suffixes, relative clauses, or other modifiers indicates that they are more
likely to be common nouns. In SoM 15cd, both אֱלוֹהַ and its parallel term צוּר 'rock' are used with
modifying constructions. Note that all eight occurrences of the Tetragrammaton in the Song
are syntactically unmodified. Finally, אֱלוֹהַ seems to be used as a common noun also in SoM 17a,
denoting a category distinct from that represented by שֵׁדִים 'spirits'.

56. παρεπίκραναν, while intelligible as a form of παρεπικραίνω = ἐπικραίνω 'bring to
fulfilment, fulfil, accomplish' (from κραίνω, with a similar meaning), is evidently rather
a form of παραπικραίνω 'embitter, provoke' (from πικραίνω 'make sharp or bitter'), since
such a meaning best matches the Hebrew. Πικραίνω is semantically opposed to γλυκαίνω 'to
sweeten'; thus a metaphor other than anger is being used here to indicate the shift in YHWH's
attitude. This use of the metaphor of taste is related to the fact that, although YHWH fed the
Israelites with good things (SoM 13–14), they became a vine that produced bitter-tasting fruit
(SoM 32–33).

16   They irritated <u>me</u> with foreign things, with <u>their</u> abominations they
            embittered <u>me</u>.

17a–c   They sacrificed to spirits <u>and</u> not to God, to gods they had not
            experienced.

        New and recent they have come.

Speaker(s): The elders' voice – again recognizable by the use of the third person and by the continuity with the train of thought that began in SoM 8 – sounds out here for the last time in the Song.[57] The elders again employ a large number of third-person masculine singular pronominal object suffixes, as they did in SoM 10, 13; however, while in SoM 10, 13, and 15 they refer to Israel, in SoM 16 these pronouns refer to YHWH.

Addressee(s): The elders' account contains no second-person forms. Since they are delivering it in response to SoM 7, however, they are in a larger sense addressing their descendants.

LXX: In SoM 15cd, the voice of the elders continues, referring to Israel as "him." In SoM 16, however, the performers assume – for the first time in the Greek Song – YHWH's voice, who speaks of how "they," the Israelites, have behaved with regard to "me." In SoM 17, the first-person object pronouns disappear, while "they" remain the subject of the verbs, therefore it is the elders who resume speaking, as they have already (in the Greek Song) referred to the Israelites with third-person plural pronouns (SoM 11–13).[58]

Discussion: This speech has many of the same performative resonances as the elders' earlier speeches, for which see the discussions above at SoM 8–14d, 15a. I have already observed that the speeches of the elders and of the Song's prophetic voice, although they are distinct on the basis of their differing pronominal referents, show a tendency to merge or at least to reinforce each other, insofar as they tell the same accusatory narrative and alternate in quick succession. This convergence is especially clear in a line such as SoM 15ab: the elders pronounce the first half and the Song finishes it, both voices speaking only of the theme of the Israelites' growing fat. Similarly, in SoM 15cd, the elders reprise two lexemes from SoM 6: the root נבל, which the Song applied as an adjective to Israel in the phrase עַם נָבָל (foolish people) and which the elders use as the verb וַיְנַבֵּל (he scorned), with Israel as the subject; and the verb לַעֲשׂוֹת 'to make', which in both verses has YHWH

---

57. An Israelite voice that uses third-person pronouns speaks in SoM 31, but there is no reason to assign it specifically to the elders. These pronouns refer to Israel's enemies (not to the Israelites themselves, as is the case in the elders' speeches in SoM 8–17), and, further, this voice also uses first-plural pronouns, which the elders do not do at the points where it is clear they are speaking.

58. So has the Song itself, once, in the verb ἡμάρτοσαν (they erred) in SoM 5a.

as its subject and Israel as its object, referring to YHWH's act of creating the people.[59]

SoM 17d–20ø

YHWH as composer: Moses's recitation: subsequent performers … present performers ⇒ Song's prophetic voice

לֹא שְׂעָרוּם אֲבֹתֵיכֶם	17d
צוּר יְלָדְךָ תֶּשִׁי וַתִּשְׁכַּח אֵל מְחֹלְלֶךָ	18
וַיַּרְא יְהוָה וַיִּנְאָץ מִכַּעַס בָּנָיו וּבְנֹתָיו	19
וַיֹּאמֶר	20ø[60]

17d   – whom your fathers did not dread.

18   The rock that begot you you neglected, and you forgot the god who was in labor with you.

19   YHWH saw and felt contempt because of the vexation of his sons and daughters,

20ø   and he said:

17d   οὓς οὐκ εἴδησαν οἱ πατέρες αὐτῶν.

59. The voice of YHWH reprises the first of these, the root נבל, in SoM 21, where it appears in the phrase גוֹי נָבָל (foolish nation), synonymous with עַם נָבָל (foolish people) from SoM 6. YHWH's act, in SoM 21, of vexing the Israelites with a גוֹי נָבָל can be compared also with SoM 15cd, insofar as it represents a reversal of Israel's action scorning (וַיְנַבֵּל) YHWH. Thus, although the voices of YHWH, of the elders, and of the Song itself are distinct, they can also be seen working in concert.

60. I label four of the Song's attestations of the verb לֵאמֹר 'to say' with the symbol ø to indicate that according to my understanding they are not part of the poetic lines in which they appear (in SoM 20, 26, 37, 40). Contrast the way that the verb לֵאמֹר does form an integral part of its poetic contexts in SoM 7 and in SoM 27, where it is parallel to another verb which itself has a parallel subject. In SoM 7, the verb וְיֹאמְרוּ (that they may say) is parallel to וְיַגֵּד (that he may tell) preceding it; their subjects are זְקֵנֶיךָ (your elders) and אָבִיךָ (your father), respectively. The verbs also share a second person masculine singular indirect object, expressed without the preposition לְ 'to' in the case of וְיַגֵּדְךָ לְחַגִּיר (that he may tell you). In SoM 27, יֹאמְרוּ ([lest] they say) is parallel to יְנַכְּרוּ ([lest] they misconstrue) preceding it; צָרֵימוֹ (their adversaries) is the subject of both verbs (elided in the case of יֹאמְרוּ). These verbs are both marked by the negative volitive particle פֶּן 'lest'. However, the other four forms of לֵאמֹר in the Song are simple speech tags, each of which happens to introduce a speech of YHWH. In SoM 7 and 27, it is the fact that someone is speaking and the kind of speech being uttered that is at issue; in SoM 20, 26, 37, and 40 the speeches themselves are the focus. SoM 40 offers a possible exception to this characterization, since the act of uttering an oath formula would occur along with raising one's hand as part of making an oath. However, this parallel would stand even without the speech tag וְאָמַרְתִּי (when I say), which, additionally, seems to interrupt the rhythm of the line, hence I am labeling it too with the symbol ø. The other three speech tags appear before the poetic line begins, rather than dividing the poetic line, as in SoM 40.

18   θεὸν τὸν γεννήσαντά σε ἐνκατέλιπες, καὶ ἐπελάθου θεοῦ τοῦ τρέφοντός
      σε.
19   καὶ ἴδεν κύριος καὶ ἐζήλωσεν, καὶ παρωξύνθη δι᾽ ὀργὴν υἱῶν αὐτοῦ καὶ
      θυγατέρων·
20ø   καὶ εἶπεν

17d   whom their fathers did not know.
18   You left behind the god that begot you, and you forgot the god who
      nourished you.
19   And the Lord saw and was jealous he was stirred up with anger against
      his sons and daughters.[61]
20ø   And he said:

Speaker(s): With the reappearance of second-person address to Israel in SoM 17d, the performers reassume the voice of the Song's prophetic persona. In SoM 19, the prophetic persona ceases accusing the Israelites directly and prepares to introduce YHWH as the next speaker, referring both to YHWH and to the Israelites in the third person.

Addressee(s): The Israelites are directly addressed again in SoM 17d–18, with both singular and plural pronominal references. When they perform these lines, they are accusing themselves.

LXX: In the Greek, the ancestors of SoM 17d are not "yours" but "theirs"; with this reading, the shift in speaker from the Song's prophetic voice to the elders does not occur until the beginning of SoM 18, where the Greek agrees with the MT in having second-person pronouns. In SoM 18, where צור 'rock' is metaphorical in the MT, the Greek reads θεός, as expected (see discussion above at SoM 4).

Discussion: The word אֲבֹתֵיכֶם (your fathers) in SoM 17d refers to the ancestors of the performers, which is to say, to those who in SoM 7 are named as אָבִיךָ (your father) and זְקֵנֶיךָ (your elders) and whose voice the performers have been enacting since SoM 8. The voice of the Song, with the opening words of its speech in SoM 17d, finishes the poetic line begun in the elders' voice in SoM 17c, and further, by speaking of "[so-called gods] whom your fathers did not dread," the performers now, in the voice of the Song, reinforce what they had stated earlier as the elders: "YHWH alone led him, and there was with him no foreign god" (SoM 12). SoM 18 also picks up on the parental and specifically maternal imagery with which the elders' voice previously described YHWH's generosity: in SoM 13cd, YHWH suckled the people with honey from the cliff, with oil from the rocky flint; here YHWH himself is the

---

61. I follow Wever's translation closely here: "By understanding υἱῶν and θυγατέρων as objective genitives, the second line can be translated as 'and he was stirred up by anger against his sons and daughters'" (Wever 1995:520).

rock, having begotten and been in labor with the people. Moreover, in SoM 19 the Israelites are plainly called YHWH's sons and daughters. There is thus a movement in the poem regarding the identity of the present-day Israelites (that is, whichever generation happens to be performing the Song), from being spoken of as descendants of their human ancestors to being depicted as descendants of their divine forebear. Correspondingly, the speech of the Israelites' divine parent takes over from that of their human parents. Note the reappearance of parent/child imagery in SoM 18–19 in the introduction to YHWH's first speech, parallel to its use in SoM 7cd to introduce the elders' speech (where the existence of children is implied by the invocation of addressees who are to ask something of their parents).

SoM 20a–26ø

YHWH as composer: Moses's recitation: subsequent performers ... present performers ⇒ Song's prophetic voice: YHWH

20a–d	אַסְתִּירָה פָנַי מֵהֶם אֶרְאֶה מָה אַחֲרִיתָם
	כִּי דוֹר תַּהְפֻּכֹת הֵמָּה בָּנִים לֹא־אֵמֻן בָּם
21	הֵם קִנְאוּנִי בְלֹא־אֵל כִּעֲסוּנִי בְּהַבְלֵיהֶם
	וַאֲנִי אַקְנִיאֵם בְּלֹא־עָם בְּגוֹי נָבָל אַכְעִיסֵם
22	כִּי־אֵשׁ קָדְחָה בְאַפִּי וַתִּיקַד עַד־שְׁאוֹל תַּחְתִּית
	וַתֹּאכַל אֶרֶץ וִיבֻלָהּ וַתְּלַהֵט מוֹסְדֵי הָרִים
23	אַסְפֶּה[62] עָלֵימוֹ רָעוֹת חִצַּי אֲכַלֶּה־בָּם
24	מְזֵי רָעָב וּלְחֻמֵי רֶשֶׁף וְקֶטֶב מְרִירִי
	וְשֶׁן־בְּהֵמוֹת אֲשַׁלַּח־בָּם עִם־חֲמַת זֹחֲלֵי עָפָר
25	מִחוּץ תְּשַׁכֶּל־חֶרֶב וּמֵחֲדָרִים אֵימָה
	גַּם־בָּחוּר גַּם־בְּתוּלָה יוֹנֵק עִם־אִישׁ שֵׂיבָה
26ø	אָמַרְתִּי[63]

---

62. The consonants אספה as vocalized in Leningradensis (אַסְפֶּה) make no recoverable sense in this context, apparently indicating a first person singular, Hifil form of the prefix conjugation from the root ספה 'sweep away'. Starting from the consonants alone, repointings as אֹסְפָה (I will add; Hifil of the root יסף) and as אֶאֱסֹף '(I will gather; Qal of the root אסף) are possible. For the present analysis, the difference is not crucial; however, אֹסְפָה has the support of the versions (Sanders 1996:193) and allows for the parallel prepositions in this line to have an adversative meaning ("against").

63. On אָמַרְתִּי (I said) here in SoM 26ø and פֶּן־יֹאמְרוּ (lest they say) in SoM 27b: These two occurrences of the verb אמר do not belong in the same poetic lines as the quoted speech they introduce; rather, each line begins with the first quoted words (pace Sanders 1996:203). In SoM 26ab the first half of the quoted line is the single word אַפְאֵיהֶם (let me split them into pieces) and the second half is אַשְׁבִּיתָה מֵאֱנוֹשׁ זִכְרָם (let me put an end to their mention among humanity), while in SoM 27cd the first half of the quoted line is יָדֵינוּ רָמָה (our hand is exalted) and the second is וְלֹא יְהוָה פָּעַל כָּל־זֹאת (it is not YHWH who accomplished all this). Both first halves are short, but this resemblance only shows how these two short quotations go together, the one by YHWH and

20a–d "Let me hide my face from them, let me see what their end will be.
           For they are a generation of reversings, children with no reliability in
              them.
21   They made me jealous with what is no god, vexed me with their empty
              things,
           so I will make them jealous with what is no people, with a foolish
              nation I'll vex them.
22   For the fire of my anger is kindled; it burns to lowermost Sheol,
           consumes the land and its produce, and sets the foundations of the
              mountains in flame.
23   I will gather evils against them, my arrows will I spend against them.
24   Ones hungry from famine, ones fed with plague and bitter destruction,
           and the tooth of beasts will I send against them, along with the fury of
              dust-crawlers.
25   Outside, the sword will bereave, and indoors – terror! –
           for young man and young woman alike, for the nursing infant and the
              grey-headed man.
26ø   I said:

20a–d ἀποστρέψω τὸ πρόσωπόν μου ἀπ᾽ αὐτῶν, καὶ δείξω τί ἔσται αὐτοῖς ἐπ᾽
           ἐσχάτων ἡμερῶν.
           ὅτι γενεὰ ἐξεστραμμένη ἐστίν, υἱοὶ οἷς οὐκ ἔστιν πίστις ἐν αὐτοῖς.
21   αὐτοὶ παρεζήλωσάν με ἐπ᾽ οὐ θεῷ, παρώξυνάν⁶⁴ με ἐν τοῖς εἰδώλοις
           αὐτῶν·
           κἀγὼ παραζηλώσω αὐτοὺς ἐπ᾽ οὐκ ἔθνει, ἐπ᾽ ἔθνει ἀσυνέτῳ παροργιῶ
           αὐτούς.
22   ὅτι πῦρ ἐκκέκαυται ἐκ τοῦ θυμοῦ μου, καυθήσεται ἕως ᾅδου κάτω·
           καταφάγεται γῆν καὶ τὰ γενήματα αὐτῆς, φλέξει θεμέλια ὀρέων.
23   συνάξω εἰς αὐτοὺς κακά, καὶ τὰ βέλη μου συμπολεμήσω εἰς αὐτούς.
24   τηκόμενοι λιμῷ καὶ βρώσει ὀρνέων, καὶ ὀπισθότονος ἀνίατος·
           ὀδόντας θηρίων ἀποστελῶ εἰς αὐτούς, μετὰ θυμοῦ συρόντων ἐπὶ γῆν.
25   ἔξωθεν ἀτεκνώσει αὐτοὺς μάχαιρα, καὶ ἐκ τῶν ταμείων φόβος·
           νεανίσκος σὺν παρθένῳ, θηλάζων μετὰ καθεστηκότος πρεσβύτου.
26ø   εἶπα

20a–d "Let me turn my face away from them, and I will show what will
           happen to them in latter days.
           For it is a perverse generation, children in whom there is no
              trustworthiness.

---

the other by the enemies: if YHWH had completely carried out the intention expressed in SoM
26ab, then the enemies would have offered the interpretation given in SoM 27cd.
   64. From παροξύνω 'urge, prick'. The parallel verb in SoM 21d is from παροργίζω 'make
angry'.

21   They made me jealous with what is not god, stirred me up with their
       <u>images</u>,
       so I will make them jealous with what is not a people, with a people
       lacking understanding will I provoke them to anger.
22   For a fire flames up in my breast; it will burn unto Hades below,
       it will eat up the land and its produce and will burn the foundations of
       mountains.
23   I will gather evils against them, and my arrows will I make hostile
       against them.
24   Ones melted away from famine and dining of birds, with incurable
       convulsion.
       The teeth of wild animals will I send against them, with the fury of
       those crawling on the ground.
25   Outside, the sword will bereave them, and from the inner rooms, fear.
       Young man and girl, nursing infant and one who has become aged.
26ø   I said:

Speaker(s): SoM 19–20ø have made it clear that the words in SoM 20a–
26a belong to YHWH, and my definition of the characteristics of the divine
speaking voice is drawn from this speech: YHWH very often uses the first
person and refers to Israel in the third person. With the verb אָמַרְתִּי (I said) in
SoM 26ø, YHWH introduces another speech by himself, which he is about to
quote in SoM 26ab.

Addressee(s): YHWH does not use the second person nor is he speaking
here in response to a request, as the elders did in SoM 8–17. This speech is a
divine soliloquy.

Fokkelman characterizes this speech by the words "soliloquy" and
"monologue."[65] Similarly von Rad: "The Hebrew word (*ʾāmartî*) must be
understood in the sense of 'Then I thought'.... This section [SoM 26–35] is
therefore an interlude which takes us out of the turmoil of historical processes and allows us to overhear a soliloquy within the depths of the divine
heart."[66] It is possible to understand לֵאמֹר 'to say' in the sense of thought also
in SoM 26ø, 27b, and 37b, although the setting within a *rîb*, a genre of made
up of public speech, weighs against doing so. Or perhaps, to elaborate on von
Rad's suggestion, it is possible that SoM 20a–25 represents an audible speech
of YHWH that he then interrupts with his own mental reservations.

LXX: The Greek of SoM 20a–26a in Vaticanus contains nothing remarkable for the present analysis.

Discussion: In taking on YHWH's voice, the Israelites inhabit the per-

65. Fokkelman 1998:106.
66. Von Rad 1996:198.

formative center of the Song of Moses; here the poem comes full circle, revealing YHWH as the beginning and the end of the Song's performance tradition, the composer of the drama and the central actor within it. It is also at this point, not coincidentally, that the tension between the performers and YHWH reaches its highest pitch. At the beginning of the Song, the performers adopt a voice (that of the Song's prophetic persona) that says "I" and commands a "you," without speaking to or about the Israelites, although the "we" invoked in SoM 3 (אֱלֹהֵינוּ [our god]) does imply that it may be an Israelite voice (SoM 1–3). Then the performers take up the voice of heaven and earth, a voice that does not say "I" but speaks only in the third person, of YHWH, again without reference to the Israelites (SoM 4). After that they return to the voice of the Song's prophetic persona, not saying "I" this time (and not again in the Song) although still commanding a "you" – and now addressing the Israelites, which is to say, themselves (SoM 6–7). Next the performers take up the voice of their own ancestors – a more distant Israelite voice than that of the Song's prophetic persona, since the elders' discourse arises out of the past – speaking again solely in the third person, both of YHWH and of the Israelites themselves (SoM 8–14d). Then the performers alternate quickly between the Song's second-person address to themselves as Israelites and the elders' third-person description of themselves as Israelites (SoM 14e–20ø), after which point the performers finally come to find themselves speaking the words of YHWH (SoM 20a–26ø, etc.). Insofar as the performers here adopt a non-Israelite voice that says "I" and that uses "they" to refer to the Israelites, YHWH's speeches represent the high point of performative tension in the Song, in which the performers must identify with the voice that is the most distant from and antagonistic to their own while at the same time speaking of their people, of themselves, as distant referents.

The first two verses of this speech show that there is an affinity between the voice of YHWH, that of the prophetic persona, and that of the elders. I will focus on YHWH and the prophetic persona first, starting with SoM 20cd (divine speech) and SoM 5 (the prophetic persona). In these two verses, note the use of דּוֹר 'generation' and בָּנִים 'children, descendants', the motif of the Israelites' nature being distorted, and the similarity in sound between the semantically similar phrases דּוֹר תַּהְפֻּכֹת (a generation of reversals) and וּפְתַלְתֹּל (and perverse)[67] as well as the phrases בָּנִים לֹא־אֵמֻן בָּם (children with no reli-

---

67. Note the round vowel (i.e. ō or ū) followed by an *a* and then the final ō, as well as the consonant sounds *p* (one time) and *t* (two times).

ability in them) and לֹא בָּנָיו מוּמָם (not his children at all).[68] Further, the divine speech in SoM 21 (בְּלֹא־עָם בְּגוֹי נָבָל [with a no-people, with a foolish nation]) shares the prophetic persona's concern (in SoM 6: עַם נָבָל וְלֹא חָכָם [people that is foolish and not wise]) with the status of a nation as wise or foolish. Both voices also show an interest in recompense or reciprocity: as the prophetic persona inquired into the manner in which the nation requites their god (SoM 6: הֲ־לַיהוָה תִּגְמְלוּ־זֹאת [is it YHWH that you requite with this?]), now YHWH, even though the Israelites have not repaid his attentions in kind, continues to operate on a quid pro quo basis, at this point, evil for evil (SoM 21: הֵם ... וַאֲנִי [as for them ... as for me]). YHWH's voice in SoM 21 also resonates strongly with that of the elders, sharing[69] verbs of jealousy (קנא) and vexation (כעס) with SoM 16 and a denial of the divinity of the other worshipped entities with SoM 17 (לֹא אֱלֹהַּ [not-god]; SoM 21: לֹא־אֵל [not-god]). SoM 21 suggests that YHWH objects to the entities with which he has been replaced for two different reasons. One reason is the simple fact of the substitution itself. That is, Israel now looks elsewhere, vexing YHWH not simply with "empty things" but with "their empty things"; the Israelites are violating the relationship of belonging that exists between them and YHWH. The other objection YHWH states is that the replacements are not in fact divine, that they lack some necessary quality; they are לֹא־אֵל (not divine) and הֲבָלִים (empty things). YHWH thus responds to Israel's treatment in kind, by means of a לֹא־עָם (no-people). Though the phrase is clearly meant to be pejorative, it is not clear what not being a people would mean – especially since the term גוֹי 'nation, people' can still be applied to them (also in SoM 21). Perhaps, since עַם 'people' has connotations of kinship, the phrase לֹא־עָם (no-people) implies that YHWH too will violate the relationship of belonging that exists between him and Israel, that YHWH will make Israel jealous by means of a people with whom he has no special relationship. Albright argued that לֹא־עָם refers to Israel: "The foolish nation (*gôy nābāl*) [in SoM 21d] appears in verse 6 as an appellation of Israel itself (*ʿam nābāl we-lōʾ ḥākām*), so it seems clear that the expression *lōʾ-ʿam* [in SoM 21c] refers precisely to Israel, against whose follies God is warning its people. There is no need to turn to the Philistines or to any other non-Israelite nation in this particular context, though EISS-FELDT must be right in considering the former as the enemy par excellence

---

68. In addition to containing the words לֹא 'no, not' and בָּנִים 'children', both lines also end in a sequence of two nearly identically sounding syllables: a penultimate syllable beginning with *mū*- and a final syllable ending in -*ām* (SoM 5b: מוּמָם [*mūmām*]; SoM 20d: אֵמֻן בָּם [*ʾēmūn bām*]).

69. Fokkelman notes these connections (Fokkelman 1998:96).

in this poem."[70] Since לֹא־אֵל and הַבְלִים, however, refer to entities that are not-YHWH, in my view it is more likely that the parallel phrases לֹא־עָם and גּוֹי נָבָל refer to entities that are not-Israel. The value of Albright's insight comes in underlining the Song's emphasis on the gravity of the Israelites' lack of wisdom: by their folly they risk becoming – or have already become – YHWH's non-children (SoM 5a) and enemies (cf. SoM 27–29). This concern is reprised elsewhere in the book of Deuteronomy at 8.12–14, 17.

Finally, while the Song's prophetic voice and the elders have both spoken of YHWH's involvement in the nation's very beginnings (SoM 6c–7, 8–10), here YHWH speaks of the nation's end (SoM 20b), thus bringing all three of these voices together. The performers who unite these voices by virtue of performing each of them thus also find these voices converging by virtue of what they are saying, a fact that is not surprising given that, although they are now speaking explicitly in YHWH's voice for the first time in the Song, they have actually been performing YHWH's voice as composer all along. Moreover, having thus spoken against themselves in the voices of the elders and of the Song's prophetic persona and now speaking against themselves in the persona of YHWH, the Israelite performers here embody YHWH's emotional reactions of jealousy, vexation, and anger (SoM 21ab, 22) and learn that jealousy and vexation will be inflicted on them in turn by YHWH (SoM 21cd). The irony is that YHWH has already inflicted his jealousy and vexation on the Israelites by making them perform the Song and thus experience these emotions as their subjects (rather than as their objects).

In this speech, when YHWH says "let me hide my face from them, let me see what their end will be" (SoM 20ab), he is speaking from a position of knowledge, for YHWH in fact determines what their fate will be in the rest of the poem, at first proclaiming it, then modifying it. At this point the performers too are speaking knowledgeably, although not only because they are enacting YHWH. Because they are performing the Song under the influence of Deuteronomy, they know what YHWH has already said in Deuteronomy 31 about "their end." In addition, some of the performers will have personal experience of what happens when YHWH hides his face by virtue of living in the midst of the effects of the destruction of the land. This position of knowledge and YHWH's extending it to the Israelites add a particular poignancy to the history of the Song. It is not only that YHWH is composing in advance what he will say in the future while looking back on the Israelites' faithless deeds (which, from the point of view of YHWH's act of composition, have yet to take place), but the performers also, when

---

70. Albright 1959:344 (italics and capitalization in original).

looking back to the Israelites who would have learned the Song close to its moment of composition (Moses, Joshua, those assembled on the plains of Moab, etc., up to the point of the first turning to other gods in the land), would be able to imagine these early Israelites as participating in YHWH's future retrospective insight, aware of the failures for which the performers, their descendants, are guilty.

SoM 26ab

YHWH as composer: Moses's recitation: subsequent performers … present performers ⇒ Song's prophetic voice: YHWH: YHWH

26ab   אַפְאֵיהֶם[71] אַשְׁבִּיתָה מֵאֱנוֹשׁ זִכְרָם

26ab   Let me split them into pieces, let me put an end to their mention among humanity.'

26ab   διασπερῶ αὐτούς, παύσω δὴ[72] ἐξ ἀνθρώπων τὸ μνημόσυνον αὐτῶν·

26ab   'I will scatter them, let me put an end to their remembrance among humanity.'

    Speaker(s): The speaker is YHWH, having introduced himself by אָמַרְתִּי (I said) in SoM 26ø. The short speech in SoM 26ab also displays YHWH's characteristic use of the first person as well as the use of the third person with reference to Israel.

    Addressee(s): There is no addressee implicit in the speech, since the second person is not used, and any statements about possible addressees must

---

71. The root פאה occurs in biblical texts only this once as a verb. In light of the meaning of the biblical noun פֵּאָה 'corner, side', I render it "split into pieces." Sanders notes the Arabic root fw/y 'to cleave, to split', though he ultimately rejects it as a comparandum, remarking that אַפְאֵיהֶם seems to be formed from a root with consonantal ה, not from a ל"י root, and that the context requires it to denote "complete destruction" (Sanders 1996:202–3). I see the reason in both of these arguments, although I judge that splitting into pieces can in fact connote complete destruction in this context, regarding the topic of national fate evoked by the second half of the line: "let me put an end to their mention among humanity." Thus, אַפְאֵיהֶם would refer to YHWH splitting the nation (not merely its individuals, as could be happening in SoM 25) into pieces, construed as an undoing of YHWH's act of creating Israel alluded to earlier in the poem (SoM 6cd, 8–9) and reflected both elsewhere in Deuteronomy, for example, by the verb להפיץ 'to scatter' (4.27; 28.64; 30.3), as well as in Vaticanus's reading at this point: διασπερῶ αὐτούς (I will scatter them).

72. Vaticanus reads δεὲ; I follow Wevers's reasoning in translating δή: "The presence of δή is to ensure the reading of παύσω as a hortatory subjunctive, reflecting the long form אשביתה 'let me put to rest.' … B [Vaticanus] 848 + are secondary in their change of δή to δε. A δέ is quite inappropriate here, and is simply a copyist error" (Wevers 1995:524).

be based on the context – however, the speech within which SoM 26ab occurs also lacks a specified addressee.

LXX: There are no significant points to note.

Discussion: This speech is one of the most deeply embedded in quotation.
Recalling the cosmic setting of SoM 8 (the primordial division of gods and
nations), here YHWH threatens to undo the boundaries – both ethnographic
and geographic – that he had defined earlier. Elsewhere in Deuteronomy,
the report of YHWH's impulse to destroy the nation of Israel arrives in the
listening ears of the Israelites – whether in the narrative past of the book,
when the assembled Israelites heard Moses on the plains of Moab, or in the
performative, ritual present of the book, when the book of the law is read out
loud to the septennially assembled Israelites. In the Song, by contrast, the
listeners have been made into performers who express this destructive impulse in the first person, as their own. They are the ones speaking the words
that promise their own destruction, as have all Israelites who learned and
performed the Song during its history that stretches back to Moses – and,
ultimately, to YHWH. According to Deuteronomy's positioning of the Song,
YHWH has known all along that he would, in a paroxysm of rage, plan the
Israelites' destruction,[73] and SoM 26ab, insofar as it offers a summary of SoM
20a–25, seems to portray the moment when he consciously reflects on that
intention. Such a moment is quite fitting for a book such as Deuteronomy
that reflects on the possibilities and possible aftermath of the nation's vio-
lent destruction. Within the poem, YHWH reflects retrospectively; within
the performance tradition, YHWH reflects prospectively. By commanding
the Israelites to embody both aspects of YHWH's act of awareness, Deuteronomy in fact fosters a sense of continual reflection.

SoM 27ab

YHWH as composer: Moses's recitation: subsequent performers ... present performers ⇒
Song's prophetic voice: YHWH

27ab   לוּלֵי כַּעַס אוֹיֵב אָגוּר פֶּן־יְנַכְּרוּ צָרֵימוֹ פֶּן־יֹאמְרוּ

27ab   – except I feared the vexation of the enemy, lest their adversaries
            misconstrue, lest they say:

27ab   εἰ μὴ δι' ὀργὴν ἐχθρῶν, ἵνα μὴ μακροχρονίσωσιν, ἵνα μὴ συνεπιθῶνται
            οἱ ὑπεναντίοι· μὴ εἴπωσιν

---

73. Additionally, YHWH (as composer) has known all along that he would ultimately relent
from complete destruction, as subsequent verses make clear.

27ab   – if not for anger against[74] the enemies, lest they last long, lest the adversaries rally, lest they say:

Speaker(s): The speaker is still YHWH (though no longer quoting himself), using the first person and speaking of Israel and of their enemies in the third person.

Addressee(s): As with the speech of which this is a continuation, no addressee is specified.

LXX: There are no differences that would affect the present analysis of the Song.[75]

Discussion: It is customary in research on the Song to treat SoM 27ab as the counterfactual protasis to which SoM 26ab is the apodosis.[76] Such an understanding of this line, however, departs from the usual form of counterfactuals constructions in two respects. First, the particle לוּלֵי (or its by-form לוּלֵא [if not, unless]) is usually followed by a suffix-conjugation / "perfect tense" form (in eight out of fourteen occurrences in biblical Hebrew[77]). Although SoM 27ab is the only one of these passages in which לוּלֵי introduces a prefix-conjugation / "imperfect tense" form, this fact actually provides only a tenuous basis for argument, since in other cases לוּלֵי may also introduce a simple noun[78] or nominal predication.[79] The other difference, however, is more salient. In every case other than SoM 27ab, the protasis introduced by לוּלֵי precedes the apodosis, and there is no reason for supposing that SoM 27ab is an exception, especially given that there is a very good argument against reading SoM 26ab as the apodosis of SoM 27ab: the statement in SoM 26ab is not contrary to fact. YHWH has already said that he would wipe out his people completely, in SoM 20a–25. Witness the cosmic scope of YHWH's anger, consuming all the earth (SoM 22b–d), things inside and outside (SoM 25ab), and persons both male and female and young and old (SoM 25cd), as well as the total outpouring of that anger alluded to by the verb לכלות 'to finish, complete' (SoM 23b), and finally, the identical syntax of two first-person singular cohortative verbs in SoM 20ab (אַסְתִּירָה ... אֶרְאֶה [let me hide ... let me see]) and SoM 26ab (אַפְאֵיהֶם אַשְׁבִּיתָה [let me split them into pieces, let me

---

74. I follow Wevers in taking ἐχθρῶν as a specifically objective genitive construction: "what is referred to is divine anger against the enemies" (Wevers 1995:524).

75. There is an interesting variation in vocabulary in SoM 27a; for discussion and literature, see Sanders 1996:204–5.

76. E.g. Sanders 1996:202; Fokkelman 1998:107–8.

77. These eight are: Genesis 31.42; 43.10; Judges 14.18; 1 Samuel 25.34; 2 Samuel 2.27; Isaiah 1.9; Psalm 27.13; 106.23.

78. Psalm 124.1, 2. In these two cases, the noun – which is the Tetragrammaton – is further defined by a relative clause.

79. 2 Kings 3.14; Psalm 94.17; 119.92.

put an end]). That is, YHWH's words in SoM 26ab summarize the foregoing speech rather than proposing to go beyond it. Further, a counterfactual protasis, being part of a recognizable formula, can be intelligible even without a corresponding apodosis being stated explicitly. Rather, the incomplete syntax in SoM 27ab points to the self-interrupting nature of YHWH's thought process: YHWH, having pronounced his verdict, now begins to reconsider. Although he has been vexed by the Israelites and promised to vex them in return, YHWH does not wish to contemplate being vexed by the enemies.

As the root כעס 'vex' prompts a comparison between the Israelites and the enemies, so the verb יֹאמְרוּ ([lest] they say) prompts a comparison between the voices of the elders and of the enemies, appearing as it does both here and in SoM 7c. YHWH as composer makes successive generations of Israelites perform the commanded and prohibited speeches that follow יאמרו in both places. First, in the persona of the elders, the performers proclaim YHWH's generous deeds of provision for Israel in the land (SoM 8–14d). Second, in the persona of the enemies, the performers claim the credit for their military victory over the Israelites, specifically denying it to YHWH. Essentially, then, these two speeches are diametrically opposed.

In his discussion of all eight occurrences of the root אמר 'say' in the Song (the structure of which they serve to delineate, according to his schematization), Fokkelman remarks that the instances in SoM 7c and SoM 27b function as a pair, being morphologically identical, having collective subjects, and introducing "sensible" versus "deluded" speech.[80] There are three other ways in which they resemble each other or are perfectly opposed: 1) each is set in a volitive context, whether positive (following three imperatives in SoM 7) or negative (introduced by פֶּן [lest] in SoM 27ab); 2) the social role of the speaking subject is in each case denoted by both a singular noun and a plural noun (אָבִיךָ [your father] and זְקֵנֶיךָ [your elders] in SoM 7; אוֹיֵב [enemy] and צָרֵימוֹ [their adversaries] in SoM 27ab); and 3) the elders' speech is preceded by a chastisement for lack of wisdom and an exhortation to correct perception (SoM 6–7ab), while an observation of lack of perception and a wish for wisdom follows the enemies' speech (SoM 28–29).

SoM 27cd

YHWH as composer: Moses's recitation: subsequent performers … present performers ⇒ Song's prophetic voice: YHWH: enemies

27cd   יָדֵינוּ רָמָה וְלֹא יְהוָה פָּעַל כָּל־זֹאת

27cd   'our hand is exalted, it is not YHWH who accomplished all this.'

80. Fokkelman 1998:59–61, at 61; see also 140.

27cd   ἡ χεὶρ ἡμῶν ἡ ὑψηλὴ καὶ οὐχὶ κύριος ἐποίησεν ταῦτα πάντα.

27cd   'our hand is high, and it is not the Lord who did all these things.'

Speaker(s): The enemies were introduced by YHWH in SoM 27b as speaking the imagined words of this speech. They use the first person plural and speak of YHWH in the third person, inversely corresponding to the characteristic usages of YHWH's speech.

Addressee(s): The enemies do not address their statements to anyone, nor do they speak in response to any questioning or prompting.

LXX: There are no significant variations.

Discussion: YHWH and all who follow after him in the performance history of the Song here define what it means to be an enemy: to take credit for one's success or prosperity when it is really YHWH who has brought it about. As composer, YHWH has spoken the words of SoM 27cd before the enemies have, not simply foreseeing their arrogance but, in an ultimate display of the extent of his control, dictating the very terms in which they express their arrogance. Of course, YHWH has also dictated in advance the terms in which he is praised in the Song throughout the generations, from the elders' recitation of his founding acts of generosity (SoM 8–17) and the prophetic persona's announcement that "it's YHWH's name I proclaim" (SoM 3) to the Song's hymnic conclusion (SoM 43) and even his own verbal self-revelation (SoM 39–42).

SoM 28–30b

YHWH as composer: Moses's recitation: subsequent performers ... present performers ⇒ Song's prophetic voice: YHWH

28   כִּי־גוֹי אֹבַד עֵצוֹת הֵמָּה וְאֵין בָּהֶם תְּבוּנָה

29   לוּ חָכְמוּ יַשְׂכִּילוּ זֹאת יָבִינוּ לְאַחֲרִיתָם

30ab   אֵיכָה יִרְדֹּף אֶחָד אֶלֶף וּשְׁנַיִם יָנִיסוּ רְבָבָה

28   For they are a people devoid of counsel, and there is no understanding in them.

29   If only they were wise they might have figured this out, they might have understood about their end."

30ab   How could one pursue a thousand, or two make a multitude flee,

28   ἔθνος ἀπολωλεκὸς βουλήν ἐστιν, καὶ οὐκ ἔστιν ἐν αὐτοῖς ἐπιστήμη.

29   οὐκ ἐφρόνησαν συνιέναι ταῦτα· καταδεξάσθωσαν εἰς τὸν ἐπιόντα χρόνον.

30ab   πῶς διώξεται εἷς χιλίους, καὶ δύο μετακινήσουσιν μυριάδας,

28   It is a people lacking counsel, and there is no knowledge in them.
29   They were not wise enough to understand these things. Let them await
            the coming time."
30ab   How should one pursue thousands, and two displace multitudes,

Speaker(s): Although no voice is introduced (or reintroduced) as speaking here, these verses make no sense as a continuation of the enemies' speech.
The simplest hypothesis is that the quotation of the enemies' hypothetical
speech has ended and that YHWH, who was quoting them, continues speaking as before. In fact, here we find the third person plural used to describe the
characteristics of a people, which is typical of YHWH's speeches elsewhere
in the Song. Further, these verses pick up on YHWH's concern as expressed
in SoM 27, which is that the enemies should correctly understand his involvement in their success. Since they do not understand, they are a "people
devoid of counsel" – as well as the "foolish nation" foreseen in SoM 21.

Addressee(s): As with the preceding sections of this speech of YHWH,
there is no addressee.

LXX: There are no significant variations.

Discussion: Before laying out the relevant performative resonances of
this passage, I must discuss the question of who is the subject of YHWH's
speech, a question posed by the noun at the head of the passage: גּוֹי 'nation,
people' (SoM 28a). The גּוֹי most recently mentioned in the poem is the גּוֹי נָבָל
(foolish nation) of SoM 21d with whom YHWH will vex Israel (identical with
the לֹא־עָם [no-people] of SoM 21c with whom YHWH will make Israel jealous).
It seems clear, therefore, that the enemies, who have just been the subject
of YHWH's discourse and hypothetical quotation in SoM 27, are meant here,
especially since this גּוֹי is אֹבַד עֵצוֹת (devoid of counsel) and אֵין בָּהֶם תְּבוּנָה (without understanding in them), two descriptions that accord perfectly with
the adjective נָבָל 'foolish, stupid' in SoM 21d. As I have noted, however, with
respect to the parallel between גּוֹי נָבָל of SoM 21d, which does not refer to Israel, and עַם נָבָל וְלֹא חָכָם (foolish people, not wise) of SoM 6b, which does refer
to Israel, there is already some ambivalence in the poem concerning the respective characteristics of Israel and their enemies. Indeed the description
of the enemies in SoM 28–29 matches the description of Israel in yet other
ways: 1) The phrase כִּי־גוֹי אֹבַד עֵצוֹת הֵמָּה (kī gōy 'ōḇaḏ 'ēṣōṯ hēmā [for they are a
people devoid of counsel]) in SoM 28a contains a sequence of consonant and
vowel sounds, up to whole words, that recall SoM 20c's phrase כִּי דוֹר תַּהְפֻּכֹת הֵמָּה
(kī ḏōr tahpūḵōṯ hēmā [for they are a generation of reversings]): both begin
with kī 'for' immediately followed by a monosyllabic word with ō, contain an

ā vowel in the middle of the phrase, and end with a return to the *ō* vowel as part of the feminine plural ending -*ōt* followed immediately by the pronoun *hēmā* 'they'. 2) The phrases וְאֵין בָּהֶם תְּבוּנָה (*wəʾēn bāhem təḇūnā* [and there is no understanding in them]) in SoM 28b and בָּנִים לֹא־אֵמֻן בָּם (*bānīm lōʾ ʾēmun bām* [children with no reliability in them]) in SoM 20d both feature prominently the consonants *b* and *m* as well as the vowel sequence *ū-ā* at the end. 3) The counterfactual wish לוּ חָכְמוּ (*lū ḥāḵᵊmū* [if only they were wise]) in SoM 29a recalls the sound of the description of Israel in SoM 6b as לֹא חָכָם (*lōʾ ḥāḵam* [not wise]), while assuming what is stated there as a fact. 4) The demonstrative pronoun זֹאת 'this' is used here in SoM 29a and in SoM 27d to indicate what the enemies do not understand; its other occurrence in the poem is at SoM6a, referring to the manner in which the Israelites requite YHWH. 5) YHWH uses the phrase אַחֲרִיתָם (their end, their outcome) in SoM 29b with reference to the enemies' experience, having already used it in SoM 20b with reference to Israel. All these resemblances in the treatment of Israel and the enemies capitalize on the ambiguity inherent in the third person plural pronominal references in SoM 28–29;[81] the speech is ostensibly about the enemies, but the description matches Israel exactly.

If anything, this charged ambiguity heightens the performative tension within the poem. Already the performers, having begun speaking in YHWH's voice in SoM 20a, are stepping far outside themselves, referring to their Israelite selves as "they," a distant subject of speech, at the same time as identifying with an "I" that is angry with them. In SoM 27, then, the performers (as YHWH still) turn to disparaging their enemies instead, a move that promises to bring some relief from this tension – except that their ensuing tirade against their enemies echoes the very terms, concepts, and in some cases the very sounds with which they had to disparage themselves earlier. As they progress through SoM 28–30b, they must examine each part very closely to determine which people is meant and to whom the "they" of these verses refers: their enemies or themselves? At every turn it comes out unfavorably for the Israelites, thus this speech brings not relief from but rather a repetition and reinforcement of the divine anger that the performers are made to embody against themselves.

Notwithstanding the ambiguity of SoM 28–29, the topic of SoM 30ab is clearly the military defeat of the Israelites, for which they in the guise of their own enemies presume to take sole credit in SoM 27cd and which they

---

81. Note that YHWH speaks of the Israelites only in the plural, whereas the elders and the voice of the Song also use singular pronouns. YHWH's statements about the enemies are formally distinguished in no way from his statements about the Israelites.

allude to in SoM 25 (מִחוּץ תְּשַׁכֶּל־חֶרֶב [outside, the sword will bereave]) in the voice of YHWH. In the context of the Song's history of performance as constructed by Deuteronomy, every generation of the Israelites has meditated on this prediction of a humiliating defeat.

SoM 30cd

YHWH as composer: Moses's recitation: subsequent performers ... present performers ⇒ Song's prophetic voice: elders

אִם־לֹא כִּי־צוּרָם מְכָרָם וַיהוָה הִסְגִּירָם 30cd

30cd   unless their rock had sold them, YHWH had closed them in?

30cd   εἰ μὴ ὁ θεὸς ἀπέδοτο αὐτούς, καὶ κύριος παρέδωκεν αὐτούς ;

30cd   unless God had sold them, the Lord had given them over?

Speaker(s): Although the speaker is not explicitly identified, the use of the third person singular in SoM 30cd to refer to YHWH indicates a change in voice here. Since it is only in SoM 30d that YHWH is clearly referred to, it would be possible to group SoM 30c with YHWH's speech in SoM 28–30ab. Mid-line changes in speaker have already occurred in the poem at SoM 15a/b and SoM 17c/d. However, in my understanding the phrase צוּרָם (their rock) also refers to YHWH, given that SoM 30ab describes Israel's defeat as a result of YHWH having "sold them" (מְכָרָם), in the sense of handing them over, to their enemies; therefore, since he is referred to there, I exclude YHWH from being the speaker of SoM 30c (which I assign instead, for the reasons mentioned elsewhere in this paragraph, to the voice of the Song's prophetic persona). The voice speaking in SoM 30cd uses the third person plural for a group that suffers military defeat. Previously in the poem, the voices of both the Song's prophetic persona and of the elders have spoken of both YHWH and the Israelites in the third person. Of the two, it is the voice of the elders that the performers are most likely inhabiting here. The use of third-person plural pronouns for the Israelites is more characteristic of that voice, since second-person pronouns predominate in the speech of the Song's prophetic persona. Also, the content of SoM 30cd is a better match with the content of earlier speeches in the elders' voice, transformed by the compensatory reciprocity proclaimed (by YHWH) in SoM 21. As, in the re-performed words of the elders, the Israelites "forsook" YHWH (וַיִּטֹּשׁ; SoM 15c), YHWH has now "handed them over" to others (מְכָרָם; SoM 30c); YHWH once made the Israelites "ride on the heights of the land" (יַרְכִּבֵהוּ עַל־בָּמוֹתֵי אָרֶץ; SoM 13a) but has now "closed them in" (הִסְגִּירָם; SoM 30d).

It is worth devoting some time to Fokkelman's arguments about the identity of the speaking voice in SoM 30cd. He assigns the whole of SoM 30 to the enemies, asserting that nothing about the speech itself indicates who the speaker must be and therefore has recourse to looking for the preceding speaker.[82] However, the immediately preceding speaker is YHWH, while here in SoM 30 YHWH is spoken of in the third person. Therefore, Fokkelman assigns this verse to those who were speaking before that (SoM 27cd), namely, the enemies. In support of this designation, Fokkelman points out that the "diagnosis of stupidity" contained in SoM 28 can thereby be understood to be surrounded on either side by speeches of the enemies that exemplify their stupidity and that are introduced by counterfactual statements made by YHWH and marked by לוּלֵי and לוּ. That is, Fokkelman understands the structure of these verses to be: 1) a counterfactual statement marked by לוּלֵי, introducing: "our hand is exalted ..." (SoM 27); 2) YHWH's "diagnosis of stupidity": "for they are a people devoid of counsel ..." (SoM 28); 3) a counterfactual statement marked by לוּ, introducing: "how could one pursue a thousand ..." (SoM 29–30). As Fokkelman points out, the statement introduced at the third point is actually quite perceptive, not stupid, in the world of the Song and of Deuteronomy in general. Fokkelman interprets SoM 30, therefore, as exemplifying the enemies' stupidity not in a straightforward fashion (as does SoM 27cd) but rather by showing what they would say if they were actually as wise as YHWH laments that they are not: they would understand that their military success against Israel depends on YHWH's disposition toward his people. In my judgment, a hypothetical speech of hypothetically wise enemies would contrast too strongly with the "diagnosis of stupidity" in SoM 28, and it is more satisfactory to hear the performers enacting a different voice here: the voice of the Song's prophetic persona.

Fokkelman also raises the possibility that Moses could be the speaking voice in SoM 30, although he ultimately rejects it. His arguments against this "Moses" being the speaker should be considered, since he sometimes uses "Moses" as a stand-in for the default speaking voice in the poem – although limiting it to the first twenty verses: "Moses here means no more than the person who in first instance speaks until v.20 and no further, in the varying tones of hymn, reproach, exhortation, and especially (vv.8–19) of retrospection and narration."[83] His arguments amount to saying that SoM 30 is too deep within a set of embedded quotations to be Moses; if Moses were to interrupt, he would have to be re-introduced as a character, his speech explicitly marked. However, even in Fokkelman's understanding, SoM 30 is not

---

82. Fokkelman 1998:111.
83. Fokkelman 1998:68.

very far away, in terms of embedded quotation, from the level of the default speaker in the poem. As Fokkelman describes it, the narrator is the base speaking voice throughout all of Deuteronomy and therefore in the Song as well (Fokkelman's "first-level discourse"); the character of Moses is the default speaker in the Song itself, if only because in 31.30 it is related that he "said all the words of this song" ("second-level discourse"); YHWH is quoted as a speaker within the Song beginning at SoM 20 ("third-level discourse"); in SoM 27cd, YHWH quotes a hypothetical speech of the enemies ("fourth-level discourse"). However, in SoM 28–29 YHWH is speaking again in his own voice ("third-level discourse"). If Moses (or the default speaking voice in the Song) were to reappear in SoM 30, then, it would only be one step away from Fokkelman's "second-level discourse" – hardly the insurmountable gulf he portrays it as. Further, Fokkelman contradicts his own sensibilities as just outlined when he assigns speakers to some of the subsequent verses (SoM 31, 32, 36, 43). As for SoM 31, Fokkelman assigns it to someone he calls the author of the Song, distinct both from the narrator of Deuteronomy and from the Song's default speaking voice (= "Moses"), labeling it "zero-degree discourse." The resulting movement from "fourth-degree" to "zero-degree" discourse would be a better place to look before leaping. Further, Fokkelman waves off his earlier stated concern about introductory formulas when it comes to his discussion of SoM 32, 36, and 43: "in v.32, the return to God's discourse is not marked either, and neither is the momentary resumption by Moses in vv. 36 and 43."[84]

Addressee(s): There is no addressee specified for this or any preceding speech of YHWH.

LXX: There are no variations of note for the present analysis.

Discussion: Here the performers complete, in the voice of the Song's prophetic persona, the question that was begun by YHWH: "How could one pursue a thousand, or two make a multitude flee" – "unless their rock had sold them, YHWH had closed them off?" As earlier with the voices of the Song and of the elders, this kind of alternation or cooperation produces a front united against the performers' Israelite identity: no matter whose perspective they are embodying at any given point in the Song so far, the performers find no refuge from the accusations and misfortunes they are made to pronounce against themselves. For example (as just mentioned), earlier in the poem the performers described, through the personas of the Song itself and of the elders, the Israelites' lack of loyalty to YHWH.[85] When

---

84. Fokkelman 1998:111 n. 95.

85. In particular, see SoM 15d (the voice of the elders) and SoM 18a (the voice of the Song's prophetic persona), both of which feature the noun צוּר 'rock', as here, in a construction em-

they take on the Song's voice again here in SoM 30cd, it is now in order to describe YHWH's apparent turning away[86] from Israel, insofar as YHWH hands the Israelites over to their enemies.

SoM 31

YHWH as composer: Moses's recitation: subsequent performers ... present performers ⇒ Song's prophetic voice

31   כִּי לֹא כְצוּרֵנוּ צוּרָם וְאֹיְבֵינוּ פְּלִילִים[87]

31   For their rock is not like our rock, and our [own] enemies are judges [of it].

31   ὅτι οὐκ ἔστιν ὡς ὁ <u>θεὸς</u> ἡμῶν οἱ <u>θεοὶ</u> αὐτῶν· οἱ δὲ ἐχθροὶ ἡμῶν <u>ἀνόητοι</u>.

31   For their <u>gods</u> are not like our <u>god</u>, and our enemies are <u>unintelligent</u>.

Speaker(s): The voice of the Song's prophetic voice is foremost in SoM 31, which contains two of the poem's four attestations of first-person plural reference; a third is also spoken in the Song's voice, in SoM 3b: אֱלֹהֵינוּ (our god); and the fourth, in SoM 27c, belongs clearly to the enemies' persona.

Addressee(s): Without any second-person forms, this speech technically has no addressees, nor is it spoken in response to a direct request. However, a voice speaking to the other members of its group may address them not only by saying "you" but also by saying "we," and the Song's prophetic persona has in fact addressed the Israelites directly elsewhere in the poem so far (SoM 6–7, 14e, 15b, 17c–18). In this sense, then, the Israelites are addressed by SoM 31 (which provides, incidentally, another reason for assigning it to the prophetic persona, since it is that voice of which addressing the Israelites is typical).

LXX: Again, this speech in Vaticanus exhibits a few variations in vocabulary (including θεός 'god' where Leningradensis has צוּר 'rock'), but none have performative consequences. The Song is the speaker here as well as in the Hebrew Song.

Discussion: This interjection by the Song's prophetic persona provides a moment of referential clarity, firmly distinguishing between the Israelites

---

phasizing the relationship between YHWH and Israel: צוּר יְשֻׁעָתוֹ (the rock of his salvation); צוּר יְלָדְךָ (the rock that begot you); and here, more simply, צוּרָם (their rock).

86. Cf. also SoM 20a: אַסְתִּירָה פָנַי מֵהֶם (I will hide my face from them).

87. For a detailed discussion of the obscure word פְּלִילִים and of reasons for rendering it as something akin to "judges," see Sanders 1996:214–21. Its meaning, however, does not affect the delineation of speaking voices.

and their enemies, for both groups are referred to here by means of the mutually exclusive terms צוּרֵנוּ (our rock) and צוּרָם (their rock). Nevertheless, the performers must continue paying close attention to their words in order to sort out their own identity as Israelites from that of their enemies: in the preceding line, SoM 30cd, צוּרָם (their rock) referred to YHWH, their own god, whereas here it refers to the god of their enemies.

SoM 32–33

YHWH as composer: Moses's recitation: subsequent performers … present performers ⇒ Song's prophetic voice: elders

כִּי־מִגֶּפֶן סְדֹם גַּפְנָם וּמִשַּׁדְמֹת עֲמֹרָה   32
עֲנָבֵמוֹ עִנְּבֵי־רוֹשׁ אַשְׁכְּלֹת מְרֹרֹת לָמוֹ
חֲמַת תַּנִּינִם יֵינָם וְרֹאשׁ פְּתָנִים אַכְזָר   33

32   For their vine is of the vine of Sodom, from the fields of Gomorrah.
      Their grapes are grapes of poison, they have bitter clusters.
33   Their wine is the fury of serpents and the bitter poison of snakes.

32   ἐκ γὰρ ἀμπέλου σοδόμων ἡ ἄμπελος αὐτῶν, καὶ ἡ κληματὶς <u>αὐτῶν</u> ἐκ γομόρρας·
      σταφυλὴ αὐτῶν σταφυλὴ χολῆς, βότρυς πικρίας αὐτοῖς·
33   θυμὸς δρακόντων ὁ οἶνος αὐτῶν, καὶ θυμὸς ἀσπίδων ἀνίατος.

32   For from the vine of Sodom is their vine, and <u>their</u> branch from Gomorrah.
      Their cluster is a cluster of bile; a bitter bunch is theirs.
33   Serpents' fury is their wine, and incurable fury of asps.

Speaker(s): I assign SoM 32–33 to the persona of the elders, partly on the basis of the third-person plural pronouns (admittedly present in the preceding speech as well), as well as because the first-person references of the preceding speech have ceased. Further, the content of these lines shows an affinity with that of the elders' first speech, particularly the floral and faunal imagery in SoM 13–14d.

Fokkelman seems to assign SoM 32–33 to YHWH, although without particularly saying why.[88] The metaphors of snakes and venom in SoM 33 could provide a point of contact with the speech in YHWH's voice at SoM 24d (זֹחֲלֵי עָפָר [dust-crawlers]), as could מְרֹרֹת 'bitter' in SoM 32d and מְרִירִי 'bitter' in SoM 24b. These features of SoM 32–33, however, work better as a variation on use of food and drink in the speech of the elders (in which the Song's prophetic

88. Fokkelman 1998:59.

persona participates): YHWH fed them abundantly with the land's flora and fauna, but they themselves turned out to be a corrupt vine producing juice as poisonous as snake's venom.

Addressee(s): No addressees are specified here, nor is this speech pronounced in response to a direct request.

LXX: The identities of the speakers and addressees are the same as in the Hebrew.

Discussion: Having just performed a speech in which "they" refers to Israel's enemies, the performers are likely to feel that they are continuing to speak about their enemies in SoM 32–33, which contains four third person plural pronouns in its three lines of poetry. Indeed, nothing in these verses would be inappropriate if applied to the enemies. Nevertheless, as I mentioned above in the section on speakers, the imagery here resonates more strongly with what the performers have said about the Israelites elsewhere in the Song.[89] In performing this speech, as with YHWH's speech in SoM 28–30b, the performers start off thinking they are disparaging their enemies but must come to realize that their critique applies equally, if not more so, to themselves and that, if the critique of their enemies remains nonetheless true, the Israelite performers themselves have become indistinguishable from them.

SoM 34–35

YHWH as composer: Moses's recitation: subsequent performers ... present performers ⇒ Song's prophetic voice: YHWH

34 הֲלֹא־הוּא כָּמֻס עִמָּדִי חָתֻם בְּאוֹצְרֹתָי
35 לִי נָקָם וְשִׁלֵּם לְעֵת תָּמוּט רַגְלָם
כִּי קָרוֹב יוֹם אֵידָם וְחָשׁ עֲתִדֹת לָמוֹ

34 "Is it not stored up with me, sealed in my treasuries?
35 Vengeance and repayment belong to me, in time their foot will slip.
   For the day of their calamity is near, and the things prepared for them speed on."

34 οὐκ ἰδοὺ ταῦτα συνῆκται παρ' ἐμοί, καὶ ἐσφράγισται ἐν τοῖς θησαυροῖς μου ;

89. The connection of vegetal imagery with the theme of the Israelites' corruption is reflected in a passage such as Deuteronomy 29.17: פֶּן־יֵשׁ בָּכֶם אִישׁ אוֹ־אִשָּׁה אוֹ מִשְׁפָּחָה אוֹ־שֵׁבֶט אֲשֶׁר לְבָבוֹ פֹנֶה הַיּוֹם מֵעִם יְהוָה אֱלֹהֵינוּ לָלֶכֶת לַעֲבֹד אֶת־אֱלֹהֵי הַגּוֹיִם הָהֵם פֶּן־יֵשׁ בָּכֶם שֹׁרֶשׁ פֹּרֶה רֹאשׁ וְלַעֲנָה (lest there should be among you a man, woman, family, or tribe whose heart turns away today from YHWH our god, to go and serve the gods of those peoples – lest there should be among you a root bearing poison and wormwood).

35   ἐν ἡμέρᾳ ἐκδικήσεως ἀνταποδώσω, ὅταν σφαλῇ ὁ ποὺς αὐτῶν·
      ὅτι ἐγγὺς ἡμέρα ἀπωλίας αὐτοῖς, καὶ πάρεστιν ἕτοιμα <u>ὑμῖν</u>.

34   "Are not these things assembled by me and sealed up in my treasuries?
35   On the day of vengeance I will <u>recompense</u>, when their foot stumbles.
      For a day of destruction is close by them, and the things prepared for
          <u>you</u> arrive."

Speaker(s): The voice being performed here belongs to YHWH, recognizable despite not being marked by a speech tag. After the introduction to the poem (SoM 1–3), first-person singular forms have appeared only in speeches of YHWH, and the statements here would not be proper to any other figure.

Addressee(s): The performers do not speak to any "you" here through the voice of YHWH, nor does this speech answer any direct request. It is in that sense a continuation of the divine soliloquy begun in SoM 20a. In SoM 35b, at the verb תָּמוּט (she/it slipped, you slipped), it is initially ambiguous – until the third person (and grammatically feminine) subject is supplied (רַגְלָם [their foot]) – whether the performers are slipping into direct address (and thus into the prophetic persona); as elsewhere, the performers must continually assess who they are speaking of or addressing and in what way that overlaps with their own identities as the Song's Israelite performers in the present (according to Deuteronomy's narrative) generation.

LXX: In SoM 35d, a second person plural form appears in Vaticanus where the Leningradensis has the third person plural: "the things prepared for you are at hand." In the Greek, then, the speaking voice switches mid-line to the Song's prophetic persona, one half line sooner than in the Hebrew.

Discussion: Speaking as YHWH here, the performers allude to earlier parts of the poem spoken in the voices of YHWH, the Song's prophetic persona, and the elders. A number of items – נָקָם 'vengeance' and שִׁלֵּם 'recompense' in particular, but also כָּמֻס (stored up), עֲתִדֹת (prepared), and even לְעֵת (in time) – pick up on the interest in compensatory reciprocity shown earlier by the voice of YHWH in SoM 21 and by the Song's prophetic persona in SoM 6a (note there the verb לגמל 'to requite'). The idea of the slipping, unsteady foot in SoM 35b is easily seen as a reversal of the action, recounted in the elders' persona in SoM 13a, of YHWH setting the Israelites astride the high places of the land. The performers continue drawing on the elders' voice in the adjective קָרוֹב 'near': as YHWH's rivals are recently arrived (SoM 17c: חֲדָשִׁים מִקָּרֹב בָּאוּ[90] [new ones, recently arrived]), so the Israelites' moment of calamity

90. Note, too, the resemblance in sound between חֲדָשִׁים (ḥaḏāšîm / new [ones]) and חָשׁ (ḥāš / it hastens) in SoM 35d.

is not far behind (SoM 35c: קָרוֹב יוֹם אֵידָם [the day of their calamity is near]) – a logic that echoes the interest in compensation and consequence. Finally, this calamity (אֵידָם/ʾēdām) recalls the terror (אֵימָה/ʾēmā) that the performers promised earlier, also in YHWH's voice (SoM 25b). Through these allusions, the unified message of the poem is strengthened, even as the performers deliver it in different voices.

YHWH's place at the beginning of the Song's performance history adds another dimension to this passage with regard to timing of the Israelites' offense and YHWH's exacting of recompense. From the perspective of YHWH as composer, the vengeance and recompense prepared for the Israelites will lie stored up for quite a long time, and thus the day of calamity would not seem to be so "near" as YHWH says it is to be within the poem. On the other hand, however, although the Israelites' offense as described in the Song will only take place after they have entered the land, it is nevertheless as near to YHWH as "today," the day he delivers the Song to Moses on the plains of Moab, for he knows their "make," their nature, and thus knows in advance what they will do in the land (SoM 31.21). In the mind of YHWH, the Israelites' day of calamity is just as foreseeable, just as "near," as their eventual offense, and through the Song, then, YHWH hands over his burden of anger to be borne by the Israelites until such time as their corrupt nature bears its poisonous fruit.

SoM 36–37ø

YHWH as composer: Moses's recitation: subsequent performers ... present performers ⇒ Song's prophetic voice

36	כִּי־יָדִין יְהוָה עַמּוֹ וְעַל־עֲבָדָיו יִתְנֶחָם
	כִּי יִרְאֶה כִּי־אָזְלַת יָד וְאֶפֶס עָצוּר וְעָזוּב
37ø	וְאָמַר

36   For YHWH vindicates his people and feels for his servants.
       For he sees when the hand is weak, when leaders are no more,

37ø   and he says:

36   ὅτι κρινεῖ κύριος τὸν λαὸν αὐτοῦ, καὶ ἐπὶ τοῖς δούλοις αὐτοῦ
       παρακληθήσεται·
       ἴδεν γὰρ παραλελυμένους αὐτοὺς καὶ ἐκλελοιπότας ἐν ἐπαγωγῇ καὶ
       παρειμένους.

37ø   καὶ εἶπεν κύριος

36   For the Lord will give judgment for his people and towards his servants
       he will relent.

For he saw <u>them</u> undone and abandoned in captivity and neglected
37ø   and <u>the Lord</u> said:

Speaker(s): The performers pick up the voice of the Song's prophetic
persona here, naming YHWH and speaking of him and his people in the third
person before introducing the divine speech that follows in SoM 37–38.

It is worth considering a few arguments for assigning this speech to the
elders. As in this speech, the elders characteristically speak of YHWH and of
the Israelites in the third person (whereas earlier in the poem I used second-
person forms to distinguish the Song's prophetic persona from that of the
elders). As here, the elders speak of YHWH and his people, introduced by כִּי
'for', also in SoM 9a (כִּי חֵלֶק יְהֹוָה עַמּוֹ [for YHWH's people are his allotment]). Finally, if the elders are speaking here in SoM 36, they would be introducing a
speech in YHWH's voice (SoM 37–38) that has many points of similarity with
preceding speeches in the elders' voice: note the presence in SoM 15c–17c
of the verb לזבח 'to sacrifice', of אֱלֹהִים 'god, gods', and of צוּר 'rock', the last of
which occurs there in a phrase that matches SoM 37b in sound and rhythm.[91]
Note the presence also in SoM 13–14 of the verb לאכל 'to eat', of the noun
חֵלֶב 'fat', of the idea of drinking (cf. SoM 13c: וַיֵּנִקֵהוּ [he suckled him]), and of
wine (which is actually mentioned by the Song's prophetic persona at SoM
14e where it offers a brief interjection into the speech of the elders). The
foregoing notwithstanding, the Song's prophetic persona makes more sense
as the speaking voice here in the Hebrew for several reasons. First, except
for when the character of YHWH introduces his own speech (or, within his
speech, the enemies' speech), it is the prophetic persona that introduces or
prompts the other speakers in the poem (in SoM 1–3a introducing its own
speech, in SoM 3b prompting the earth and sky to speak, in SoM 7cd prompting the elders, in SoM 20ø introducing YHWH, and in SoM 43a prompting
the nations). Second, the particular form of introduction here matches the
one in SoM 19–20ø, where the prophetic persona is speaking: YHWH "sees"
(לראות) the Israelites, whether their idolatry or their weakened state; his
emotional reaction is described, whether contempt and vexation or compassion; and he makes a pronouncement introduced by לאמר 'to say'. Further
(though this reason is not operative at this point in a performance of the
poem, since it relies on a verse yet to be recited), עַמּוֹ (his people) and עֲבָדָיו
(his servants) reappear as parallel terms in SoM 43ab, which also belongs to
the voice of the prophetic persona.[92] Finally, in the Greek Song, this speech
more clearly (according to my guidelines for delineating speakers) belongs

91. See above at note 163.
92. Fokkelman 1998:121.

to the prophetic persona, insofar as it contains a second person pronoun where it begins (again, only in the Greek) at SoM 35d.

Addressee(s): There is no addressee specified.

LXX: In the Greek this speech begins with the shift in speaker at SoM 35d, marked by the appearance of a second person plural pronoun: ὑμῖν (to/for you), meaning that the Israelites are the direct addressees of this speech.

Discussion: Here the performers recite a narrative of compassion, although not directly addressing it to their Israelite selves in the way that has been associated with the prophetic persona elsewhere in the poem. Via the third person pronouns here, they speak of themselves as distant objects of compassion – as they do simultaneously in evoking the voice of YHWH as composer. Although these words are, by virtue of his authorship, necessarily YHWH's, they are nowhere echoed by the voice of YHWH within the poem.

SoM 37a–38b

YHWH as composer: Moses's recitation: subsequent performers ... present performers ⇒ Song's prophetic voice: YHWH

אֵי אֱלֹהֵימוֹ צוּר חָסָיוּ בוֹ   37ab

אֲשֶׁר חֵלֶב זְבָחֵימוֹ יֹאכֵלוּ יִשְׁתּוּ יֵין נְסִיכָם   38ab

37ab   "Where are their gods, the rock in whom they took refuge,

38ab   the fat of whose sacrifices they eat, the wine of whose libation they
        drink?"

37ab   ποῦ εἰσιν οἱ θεοὶ αὐτῶν, ἐφ' οἷς ἐπεποίθεισαν ἐπ' αὐτοῖς;

38ab   ὧν τὸ στέαρ τῶν θυσιῶν αὐτῶν ἠσθίετε, καὶ ἐπίνετε τὸν οἶνον τῶν
        σπονδῶν αὐτῶν·

37ab   "Where are their gods, the ones in whom they trusted,

38ab   the fat of whose sacrifices you ate, and you drank the wine of their
        libations?"

Speaker(s): The performers take on YHWH's voice again, as indicated by SoM 36–37ø. Although this passage lacks the use of the first person, it shows the other characteristic of YHWH's speeches, namely, treatment of the nation in the third person.

Addressee(s): There is no addressee specified.

LXX: In the Greek, SoM 37ab and SoM 38ab belong to two separate speeches, the first in the voice of YHWH, as in the Hebrew, and the second in the voice of the Song (continuing into SoM 38cd, where, in the Hebrew, the voice of the Song picks up again). Additionally, the second person forms prevent an ambiguity that is present in the Hebrew. Since both the Israelites and their gods (אֱלֹהֵימוֹ) in SoM 37a are grammatically plural and masculine, it is syntactically indeterminate in the Hebrew Song who is to be the subject of the third-person masculine plural verbs יֹאכֵלוּ (they eat) and יִשְׁתּוּ (they drink) in SoM 38ab. This ambiguity aligns with a tendency exhibited elsewhere in the poem of putting the Israelite performers in a position of figuring out whether they themselves are the target of the rhetoric they are pronouncing. However, corresponding to the fact that the Israelites' apostasy is linked with their eating and drinking at SoM 14–16, followed immediately thereafter by a reference to their sacrificing to other gods (SoM 17), it ultimately makes more sense for the Israelites to be the subjects of the verbs of eating and drinking in here SoM 38ab.

Discussion: In addition to the initial uncertainty of reference just mentioned in contrast with the Greek text of SoM 38ab, the two nouns in SoM 37ab also call for interpretation by the performers. Even though YHWH is clearly introduced as the leading voice through which they are speaking here, and even though the third-person forms presumably therefore refer to someone other than YHWH, it so happens that אֱלֹהֵימוֹ (their god/gods) and צוּר חָסָיוּ בוֹ (the rock in whom they took refuge) are nevertheless appropriate appellations for YHWH. He has been referred to as אלֹהֵינוּ (our god) at SoM 3b and as "rock" several times (SoM 4a, 18, 30, 31), including at SoM 15d in the phrase צוּר יִשְׁעָתוֹ (the rock of his salvation), which not only rhymes[93] with the phrase in SoM 37b and has the same rhythmic qualities but is also basically synonymous with it. Accordingly, YHWH's question in SoM 37ab holds two possible meanings that must be resolved into one. One possible meaning is, where is YHWH, Israel's god and rock? – his absence being suggested, perhaps, by the delay between offense and recompense (SoM 34–35), a gap that may also provide the enemies time to misconstrue the course of events (SoM 27). The other possible meaning is, where are the gods to whom Israel turned? – their absence presumably suggested by the pitiable state into which Israel has come (SoM 36), as evidence that they are unable to provide for Israel as YHWH has done in the past. The following line solidifies this question as referring to the other gods, by virtue of its plural pronouns (SoM 38ab). After the performers emphasize the other gods' absence in the words of the prophetic persona's challenge in SoM 38cd, however, they then answer the question's first sense by speaking again in YHWH's voice in SoM 39. If the question is, "where is YHWH?," the answer is רְאוּ עַתָּה (see now!)

---

93. SoM 15d contains two ū-vowels, an ā-vowel, and an ō-vowel (*ṣūr yašūʿātō*); in the same sequence, SoM 37b contains one ū-vowel, two ā-vowels, and an ō-vowel (*ṣūr ḥāśāyū ḇō*).

combined with YHWH's self-description that follows. The availability of this first sense of the question is reinforced by the Song's performance history, which is based in Deuteronomy 31.17, where YHWH predicts that a future generation of Israelites will ask, הֲלֹא עַל כִּי־אֵין אֱלֹהַי בְּקִרְבִּי מְצָאוּנִי הָרָעוֹת הָאֵלֶּה (is it not because my god is not with me that these evils have found me?). By giving them the Song, of course, YHWH ensures that they will ask this question, which it contains – except that by phrasing it in his own voice in the Song, he subverts it; YHWH, the deity supposed absent by the question posed in 31.17, himself poses a question that points out the absence of the (other) deities on which Israel has come to rely.

SoM 38cd

YHWH as composer: Moses's recitation: subsequent performers ... present performers ⇒ Song's prophetic voice

38cd	יָקוּמוּ וְיַעְזְרֻכֶם יְהִי עֲלֵיכֶם סִתְרָה

38cd   Let them rise up and come to your aid, let him be a hiding place for you.

38cd   ἀναστήτωσαν καὶ βοηθησάτωσαν ὑμῖν, καὶ γενηθήτωσαν ὑμῖν σκεπασταί.

38cd   Let them rise up and rescue you, and let them become your protectors.

Speaker(s): Given the presence of second person forms in SoM 38cd, the primary speaking voice is that of the Song's prophetic persona.

Addressee(s): The third person plural forms of SoM 37a–38b that refer to the Israelites in YHWH's voice become the second person plural forms in which the prophetic persona addresses them directly here in SoM 38cd.

LXX: SoM 38cd in Vaticanus also contains second person forms; however, in the Greek, the shift from YHWH's voice to that of the prophetic persona occurred in SoM 38ab, which also features direct address.

Discussion: This speech resonates most strongly with the exasperated tone of SoM 6ab, with which it shares second person plural forms and which is also spoken in the Song's prophetic voice. However, the performers also pick up, in oblique fashion, a few themes and motifs from elsewhere in the Song: elevation and power to save, provide, and protect. The verb יָקוּמוּ (let them rise up) invokes elevation as a metaphor for agency and ability. When, in SoM 27cd, the performers enacted the enemies' hypothetical boasting over YHWH, saying that their hand was רָמָה (high, exalted), they were claiming to have been the sole agents of their military success. The image of YHWH as צוּר 'rock, crag' also plays into this theme, insofar as an elevated feature of the landscape provides not only a place of superiority over an opposing force, a place in which one may be saved (cf. צוּר יִשְׁעָתוֹ [the rock of his salvation] in SoM 15d), but also a source of nourishment (SoM 13cd[94]), and it is in these two regards that the Song evaluates the suitability of the epithet צוּר – and the related ideas conveyed by לָקוּם 'to rise', סִתְרָה 'hiding place', לְעֹזֵר 'to help; to protect', and לַחְסוּת 'to take refuge' – for the other gods worshiped by the Israelites, from SoM 36cd up through the mocking challenge contained here.

In this speech, the performers are for the last time in the drama of the poem speaking as a character other than YHWH,[95] and insofar as that character is the Song's prophetic voice, the performers are thus addressing their Israelite selves directly for the last time – with the exception of the very first word of YHWH's subsequent speech (רְאוּ [see!]), by which YHWH as composer tips his hand. It is worth noting that the performers' final words before taking up YHWH's persona and his declaration of power (SoM 39–42) constitute self-mockery, which YHWH in his capacity as composer makes them perform.

Because YHWH is the Song's ultimate author, it is understandable that the voice of the prophetic persona – whose words YHWH composed – finally begins here to merge with YHWH's own voice within the poem. These are the poems' two primary speaking voices, and here at the end of it (starting at SoM 34) they are speaking together, switching back and forth from one to the other: first YHWH (SoM 34–35), then the Song (SoM 36–37ø), then YHWH again (SoM 37a–38b), then the Song again (SoM 38cd), with YHWH finally ending the speech (SoM 39–42). This alternation contributes to a merging effect, both voices delivering the same message from two perspectives, such as was also the case in the elders' long speech earlier in the poem (SoM 8–17c), into which the Song's prophetic voice inserted itself at SoM 14e and eventually took over, before introducing YHWH in SoM 20ø.[96] This overcoming of the distinctions between speaking voices is one of the high points of the rhetorical effect of the poem: to merge the identities of the characters in the Song (and of the persons participating in the performance tradition) with the identities of the current performer.

---

94. The synonymous noun סֶלַע 'cliff' is used in SoM 13c.

95. I am not hereby asserting that SoM 43 is only, as it were, an appendix, nor do I deny that its concerns are integral to those of the rest of the poem; however, SoM 43 very much has the feel of presenting the moral of the tale, after the plot has been resolved.

96. See discussions above on SoM 8–20ø.

Two other facts contribute to this merging in the present case. The plural verbs in SoM 38c – יָקוּמוּ (let them rise up) and יַעְזְרֻכֶם (let them come to your aid) – would seem to have their antecedents in the plural noun אֱלֹהֵימוֹ (their gods) in SoM 37a, while the singular predication יְהִי ... סִתְרָה (let him be ... a hiding place) in SoM 38d would seem to have its antecedent in the singular noun צוּר 'rock' in SoM 37b. The other is a point already mentioned: the second-person plural address of the first word of YHWH's subsequent speech: רְאוּ (see!). For more on רְאוּ and the effects of the voice of the prophetic persona merging with that of YHWH, see the discussion of SoM 39–40ø below.

The placement of this speech, along with the rest of the Song, within a performance tradition that stretches from YHWH and Moses all the way to the "present day" has one other effect worth noting here. SoM 38cd looks back on the Israelites' turning to other gods, encapsulating the futility of that turning into a moment of ridicule: as for those who have already been unable to help you (as established in SoM 36cd, for example), let them help you! By showing that the Israelites had this future retrospective insight from the beginning, the tradition emphasizes the foolishness (cf. the root נבל in SoM 6b, 15d) and perversity (cf. שִׁחֵת [it went corrupt], עִקֵּשׁ 'crooked', and פְּתַלְתֹּל 'perverse' in SoM 5 and תַּהְפֻּכֹת 'reversings' in SoM 20c) of the faithless generation, who were unable to help themselves even though they knew "their end" in advance.

SoM 39–40a, ø

YHWH as composer: Moses's recitation: subsequent performers ... present performers ⇒ Song's prophetic voice: YHWH

39   רְאוּ עַתָּה כִּי אֲנִי אֲנִי הוּא וְאֵין אֱלֹהִים עִמָּדִי
      אֲנִי אָמִית וַאֲחַיֶּה מָחַצְתִּי וַאֲנִי אֶרְפָּא
      וְאֵין מִיָּדִי מַצִּיל
40a, ø כִּי־אֶשָּׂא אֶל־שָׁמַיִם יָדִי וְאָמַרְתִּי

39   "See now that I – I am he, that there is no god with me.
      I am the one who kills and keeps alive; when I wound, it's also I who heals
      and no one can rescue from my hand.
40a, ø When I raise my hand to the skies, when I say:

39   ἴδετε ἴδετε ὅτι ἐγώ εἰμι, καὶ οὐκ ἔστιν θεὸς πλὴν ἐμοῦ·
      ἐγὼ ἀποκτέννω καὶ ζῆν ποιήσω, πατάξω κἀγὼ ἰάσομαι,
      καὶ οὐκ ἔστιν ὃς ἐξελεῖται ἐκ τῶν χειρῶν μου.

40a, ø   ὅτι ἀρῶ εἰς τὸν οὐρανὸν τὴν χεῖρά μου καὶ <u>ὀμοῦμαι τὴν δεξιάν μου</u>, καὶ
         ἐρῶ

39   "See, <u>see</u>, that I am, and there is no god besides me.
         I am the one who kills and brings to life; I strike, and I heal,
         and no one can snatch from my <u>hands</u>.
40a, ø   When I raise to the sky my hand and <u>I swear by my right hand</u> and say:

Speaker(s): Given what the "I" in these verses says about itself, it is clear
that YHWH is the speaker, even though he is not named or formally introduced by another speaker. See also the discussion below.

Addressee(s): The statements made here are so general that one might
be tempted to say that רְאוּ (see!) has as general an address as הַרְנִינוּ (shout
out!) in SoM 43 (which is another second-person plural imperative introducing a speech, with גּוֹיִם understood as nations in general and not specifically
as the enemy nations, that is, in a sense that would accord more with the
broad scope of the LXX's version of SoM 43: οὐρανοί [skies], υἱοὶ θεοῦ [sons
of god], ἔθνη [nations], and πάντες ἄγγελοι θεοῦ [all the messengers of
god]). However, רְאוּ occurs immediately after the use of the second person
in SoM 38, and the statements here in SoM 39 have particular relevance for
an Israelite audience as defined in the Song: if they have been partaking of
the sacrifices of other gods (SoM 17a, 37a–38b), it would seem that they have
been looking to them for help; this speech, particularly SoM 39, contradicts
the idea that any but YHWH offers help.

LXX: None of the minor variations are of note for a performative analysis of the Song.[97]

Discussion: While for the rest of the poem I have been taking second-
person forms as a feature solely of the prophetic voice and defining YHWH's
voice, in part, by its use of third- and first-person forms (such as in SoM
20a–26ø), in SoM 39 this distinction must break down, for none other than
YHWH can be the speaker of the speech that begins here.

One possibility for preserving the distinction intact would be to observe
that רְאוּ (see!), while undeniably a second-person form, is nonetheless an
ordinary way of beginning a speech, on the order of the verb לָקוּם 'to rise up'
when used merely as the introduction to a primary statement, such as in Exodus 32.1: קוּם עֲשֵׂה־לָנוּ אֱלֹהִים (come, make gods for us). Even such an innocuous
usage, however, being an imperative, implies an addressee of some kind, the
very kind of feature that is important to the present performative analysis

---

97. At the beginning of SoM 40, the Greek offers two parallel phrases regarding the raising of hands and oath-taking (as opposed to just one in the MT). For more on this point, see
McGarry 2005.

of the Song. Further, רְאוּ appears immediately following three volitive forms that occur in a second-person context.[98] For the performers, the seam between the speeches of the prophetic persona and of YHWH at SoM 38d/39a is barely detectable until it has passed, when it finally becomes obvious that YHWH must be speaking now instead.[99] In the context of this performative analysis, then, רְאוּ represents the moment when YHWH reveals, within the poem, his authorship thereof (already presumed in the history created by Deuteronomy, at 31.19) by speaking directly to those for whom he intends the Song.

SoM 39 encapsulates an essential teaching of the Song and of Deuteronomy in general: YHWH, as a deity, is incomparable and controls the fates, or "ends," of humans. By this point the rhetoric of the poem has reached such a pitch that the precipitation to which the teaching was compared in SoM 2 has become more of a torrential downpour, lashing at the herbage rather than falling gently upon it. The performance of this verse, then, which insists so strenuously that its speaker is the deity, brings home a central message of the Song, forcing the performers to confront the contrast between themselves and YHWH by effacing themselves completely, replacing their own point of view with YHWH's: "I – I am he."[100]

YHWH introduces a short speech of his own in SoM 40ø, following a metonymic reference to standard oath-taking practice in SoM 40a: "when I raise my hand to the skies."

As Sanders reports, there has been some discussion whether raising one's hand, at least in the present context, has anything to do with oath-taking.[101] For a review and refutation of arguments marshaled against the association, see not only Sanders but also the thorough treatment by McGarry.[102] It is worth noting that the alternative reading links YHWH's raising his

---

98. Note the second-person pronominal suffix in the form יַעְזְרֻכֶם (let them come to your aid). The addressee of the clause containing יְהִי (let him be), a third-person form, appears in a prepositional phrase: עֲלֵיכֶם (for you).

99. The reasons just named could also be given as partial justifications for assigning this speech to YHWH, along with the fact that the second person – which I have been taking as a marker of the prophetic persona's voice – appears in the immediately following verse in what can only be YHWH's voice, given the statements that ensue. The word רְאוּ (see!) at the beginning of SoM 39, is one indisputable instance of YHWH using the second person in the Song.

100. As Fokkelman says: "the self-revelation of God ... is finally granted to the audience" (Fokkelman 1998:124). However, this self-revelation is not simply granted, it is actually handed over for the "audience" to act out, so that they may not just be confronted with but may embody YHWH's indignation at not being recognized for what he is.

101. Sanders 1996:241, 241 nn. 805–7, 242 n. 809.

102. McGarry 2005:218–27.

hand with "displaying [his] power"[103] – or, as expressed by Levy: "JHVH raises up His hand to the heavens not to take an oaths [sic] but to strike the enemy heavily"[104] – which is in fact a major preoccupation of the Song. (Further, following from this understanding, Levy emends וְאָמַרְתִּי in SoM 40 to the third-person form וְאָמְרוּ, thus introducing a change in speakers: "When to heaven my hand I'll raise they'll say that I live forever," thus allowing the performers to voice this orthodox statement either in their own persona, if "they" refers to the Israelites, or perhaps as the enemies, harking back to their unorthodox pronouncement in SoM 27cd that their hand is ascendant.)[105]

SoM 40b

YHWH as composer: Moses's recitation: subsequent performers ... present performers ⇒
Song's prophetic voice: YHWH: YHWH

                                                         חַי אָנֹכִי לְעֹלָם   40b

40b   'as I live forever,'

40b   ζῶ ἐγὼ εἰς τὸν αἰῶνα·

40b   'I live forever,'

Speaker(s): The speaker is YHWH; he has introduced himself in SoM 40ø with the verb וְאָמַרְתִּי (when I say), where he was also the speaker.

Addressee(s): There is no addressee specified. However, it functions as an illustration for the preceding speech and is therefore spoken to the addressees of רְאוּ (see!), for which see above.

LXX: There are no variations of note.

Discussion: The content of SoM 40b, although it is a quotation within a quotation and would thus seem to provide suitable material for the present performance analysis, is almost as mutely iconic as the symbolic gesture of hand-raising in SoM 40a, both of which serve merely to evoke YHWH's oath-taking. Oath-taking does at least align with the concepts of consequence and delay evident elsewhere in the poem, particularly in SoM 34–35, for which see the discussion above, as well as in SoM 21. As the performers' proclamation here and in the following two verses will reiterate to them, when YHWH makes a solemn pronouncement and prepares to settle accounts, results are certain to follow.

103. Sanders 1996:241 n. 805.
104. Levy 1930:58.
105. Levy 1930:58.

Although חַי אָנֹכִי לְעֹלָם (I live forever) does function primarily as a metonym for oath-taking, its allusion to YHWH's ageless vitality can take on a particular meaning within the context of the Song's performance tradition. As YHWH is the main actor both in the events of "days of old" and "generation upon generation" ago (SoM 7ab) that brought Israel into being (as narrated in the elders' voice), as well as in the present facts of recompense after unfaithfulness, so also is YHWH, as narrated by Deuteronomy, active both at the origin of the Song's performance tradition as well as in each of its successive present moments down through the ages.

SoM 41–42

YHWH as composer: Moses's recitation: subsequent performers ... present performers ⇒
Song's prophetic voice: YHWH

41   אִם־שַׁנּוֹתִי בְּרַק חַרְבִּי וְתֹאחֵז בְּמִשְׁפָּט יָדִי

אָשִׁיב נָקָם לְצָרָי וְלִמְשַׂנְאַי אֲשַׁלֵּם

42   אַשְׁכִּיר חִצַּי מִדָּם וְחַרְבִּי תֹּאכַל בָּשָׂר

מִדַּם חָלָל וְשִׁבְיָה מֵרֹאשׁ פַּרְעוֹת אוֹיֵב

41   when I sharpen the lightning of my sword and my hand takes hold in
          judgment,
      then I take vengeance against my adversaries and settle up with those
          who hate me.

42   I make my arrows drunk with blood – and my sword eats flesh –
      with the blood of the slain and of the captive, from the long-haired
          head of the enemy."

41   ὅτι παροξυνῶ ὡς ἀστραπὴν τὴν μάχαιράν μου, καὶ ἀνθέξεται κρίματος
      ἡ χείρ μου,
      καὶ ἀποδώσω δίκην τοῖς ἐχθροῖς, καὶ τοῖς μισοῦσίν ἀνταποδώσω·

42   μεθύσω τὰ βέλη μου ἀφ' αἵματος, καὶ ἡ μάχαιρά μου καταφάγεται κρέα
      ἀφ' αἵματος τραυματιῶν καὶ αἰχμαλωσίας, ἀπὸ κεφαλῆς ἀρχόντων
      ἐχθρῶν.

41   for I will provoke as lightning my sword and my hand will cling to
          judgment,
      and I will give back justice to my adversaries and repay those who hate
          me.

42   I will make my arrows drunk with blood, and my sword will eat flesh
      with the blood of the wounded and the captives, from the head of the
          rulers of the enemies."

Speaker(s): YHWH is no longer quoting himself but goes back to his speech that began in SoM 39.

Addressee(s): Although at this point there are only first- and third-person forms, as is typical of YHWH's other speeches, the Israelites remain the addressees of this speech; see above at SoM 39–40a, ø.

LXX: There are no significant variations.

Discussion: Here the performers continue enacting YHWH's speech that they began in SoM 39 and of which a summary might be: it is I, YHWH, who holds all power, and when I promise, I then fulfill. Although this speech is addressed to their Israelite selves, the enemies are also in view, a fact that perpetuates the overlap that the Song creates between the identities of the Israelites and their enemies. The address to the Israelites is constituted 1) by the second-person form רְאוּ (see!) in SoM 39a; 2) by the evocation of compensatory reciprocity through the verbs אָשִׁיב (I will send back) and אֲשַׁלֵּם (I will settle [accounts]) and through the noun נָקָם 'vengeance' in SoM 42cd; 3) relatedly, by the reversal of the motifs of eating and drink in SoM 42ab, whereby the actions through which Israel offended YHWH (SoM 13–15) reappear in the characterization of their punishment; 4) by the reappearance here also of two instruments of YHWH's judgment, his sword (SoM 41a, 42b) and his arrows (SoM 42a), that played a role in his first pronouncement of judgment against the Israelites (SoM 23b, 25a); and 5) by the fact that, in the context of the performance history envisioned by Deuteronomy 31, the Israelite performers of this speech answer the equally Israelite question of 31.17 – "Is it not because my god is not with me that these evils have found me?" While the performers are thus addressing their Israelite selves, with respect to this speech's direct references and allusions, they are also, on the same kinds of grounds, speaking of the enemies. First, performing YHWH's proclamation of his own power in SoM 39 recalls the hypothetical misperception and rhetorical question regarding his power that they enacted earlier, also in YHWH's voice, with reference to the enemies, in SoM 27cd and SoM 30ab. Not only so, but the nouns צָרָי (my adversaries) and אוֹיֵב 'enemy' and the nominal participle מְשַׂנְאַי (those who hate me), which is parallel to צָרָי, are direct references making it abundantly clear that "the enemies" are the objects of YHWH's vengeance in this speech. As composer, YHWH thus makes the Israelite performers draw out for as long as possible – especially in his own speeches within the poem – the question of whether he considers them to be his enemies or his own people, that is, based on whether they are acting like his enemies or his own people, for it is only in SoM 43, the last speech of the poem, where צָרָיו (his enemies) and עַמּוֹ (his people) (with its parallel עֲבָדָיו [his servants]) appear together and are thus able to be distinguished. To take a step back, the composers of Deuteronomy, reflecting on the imminent possibility and/or immediate aftermath of destruction and exile, evidently found the Song's meditation on ambivalence to be a key to understanding their history and not only situated it prominently in their own composition but also, through the performance history envisioned in Deuteronomy 31, made it a central object of previous generations' ruminations, even though destined to be comprehended fully only by a later – that is, their own – generation.

SoM 43

YHWH as composer: Moses's recitation: subsequent performers ... present performers ⇒ Song's prophetic voice

43   הַרְנִינוּ גוֹיִם עַמּוֹ כִּי דַם־עֲבָדָיו יִקּוֹם
וְנָקָם יָשִׁיב לְצָרָיו וְכִפֶּר אַדְמָתוֹ עַמּוֹ

43   O nations, shout out on account of his people, for he avenges the blood of his servants;

he takes vengeance against his adversaries and brings atonement for the land of his people.

43   εὐφράνθητε, οὐρανοί, ἅμα αὐτῷ, καὶ προσκυνησάτωσαν αὐτῷ υἱοὶ θεοῦ·

εὐφράνθητε, ἔθνη, μετὰ τοῦ λαοῦ αὐτοῦ, καὶ ἐνισχυσάτωσαν αὐτῷ πάντες ἄγγελοι θεοῦ·

ὅτι τὸ αἷμα τῶν υἱῶν αὐτοῦ ἐκδικᾶται, καὶ ἐκδικήσει καὶ ἀνταποδώσει δίκην τοῖς ἐχθροῖς,

καὶ τοῖς μισοῦσιν ἀνταποδώσει· καὶ ἐκκαθαριεῖ κύριος τὴν γῆν τοῦ λαοῦ αὐτοῦ.

43   Be glad, o skies, with him, and let the sons of God bow down to him.

Be glad, o nations, with his people, and confirm for him, o all God's messengers,

that the blood of his sons will be avenged, and he will punish and repay justice to the enemies.

And he will repay the haters and the Lord will cleanse the land of his people.

Speaker(s): Given that YHWH and Israel are spoken of in the third person, the Song is the speaker of this verse.

Addressee(s): The beginning of this verse is addressed, in an imperative, to the גּוֹיִם 'nations', presumably not including Israel, since Israel, as עַמּוֹ (his people), is the object of the verb. Although the three subsequent parts of the verse (SoM 43b–d) are relevant to the concerns of the enemy – YHWH avenges the blood the enemy has spilled (SoM 43b), YHWH settles accounts with his adversaries (SoM 43c), and he atones for Israel's land (SoM 43d), presumably on account of impurity incurred by the blood the enemy has spilled – it is preferable to understand גּוֹיִם as referring to nations in general rather than specifically to the enemies from earlier in the Song. First, when גּוֹי 'nation' is used in connection with the enemies, it is singular (SoM 21d, 28a), not plural as it is here. Further, the plural גּוֹיִם does occur elsewhere in the poem, at SoM 8, referring to all nations taken together in a cosmic setting, when YHWH assigns them their territorial inheritances and borders in primordial time. Finally, the variations found in the Greek text elaborate on this larger meaning rather than on a sense of גּוֹיִם as specifically hostile nations.

LXX: Although the Greek of this verse is famously divergent from the Hebrew of the Masoretic Text, none of these divergences have substantial ramifications for a performance analysis of the Song, since no new speakers are introduced. The Greek does broaden the addressees of the verse from the nations alone to include the heavens, "the sons of God," and "all the messengers of God." If there could be a question in the MT of whether the "nations" are synonymous with the enemies spoken of elsewhere in the poem (including, most recently, at the end of SoM 42d, the immediately preceding line), in the Greek the "nations" definitely have a broader referent.

Discussion: With the opening words of the Song's last speech, the performers do several things at once. The imperative הַרְנִינוּ (harnīnū / shout out!) recalls the first word of the entire Song: הַאֲזִינוּ (ha'azīnū / give ear!); the two words show resemblances in form, in sound, in being addressed to entities of cosmic scale, and in dealing with speech – the first, with attentiveness to it, and the second, with producing it. As mentioned above, גּוֹיִם 'nations' evokes the cosmic setting of SoM 8–9, where YHWH parcels out gods, nations, and territories, with "his people" Israel (עַמּוֹ) belonging to him; this is recalled in SoM 43 by the double occurrence of עַמּוֹ.[106] This coming full circle signals the end of YHWH's rîḇ, which began in SoM 1, with a return to the state of the relationship between YHWH and Israel as it existed at first.

By contrast with the rest of the poem, in this final speech the performers are allowed by YHWH the composer to un-blur the distinction between their Israelite identity and that of YHWH's enemies, both of which are referred to here. The reconciliation between YHWH and Israel just mentioned contributes to making this distinction, in concert with the directing of YHWH's vengeance solely and clearly against the enemies, in SoM 43c. Not only so,

---

106. Note that עַמּוֹ evokes a moment of sympathy between YHWH and Israel in SoM 36ab, where it also occurs alongside עֲבָדָיו (his servants).

but in this speech that he composed for the prophetic persona, YHWH proclaims his ultimate loyalty to his people Israel, resolving what has up to this point in the Song been the open question of whether he will treat Israel as his enemy or as his people.

Also against the backdrop of the performance tradition constituted by Deuteronomy, the גּוֹיִם 'nations' as addressees take on another connotation. Here in SoM 43, and also to some extent in SoM 8–9, the nations of the world are the audience or foil for YHWH's relationship with and treatment of Israel. In SoM 8–9, it is Israel that is assigned to YHWH out of all the nations. In SoM 43, the nations are to shout out (with joy, as this verb is often translated) over YHWH's vindication of and reconciliation with his people. Within the narrative of Deuteronomy, these moments are anticipated, in 4.6, by the words of הָעַמִּים[107] אֲשֶׁר יִשְׁמְעוּן (the nations who will hear) – in this case, who will hear of YHWH's gift of wisdom and understanding to the Israelites in the form of the commandments.

---

107. Although the plural of עַם is used here, note that גּוֹי appears in the following two verses, 4.7–8, which also deal with Israel's uniqueness among the nations because of YHWH.

Song of Moses, Speaker by Speaker (Vaticanus)

Song:
1   πρόσεχε οὐρανέ, καὶ λαλήσω· καὶ ἀκουέτω ἡ γῆ ῥήματα ἐκ στόματός
         μου.
2   προσδοκάσθω ὡς ὑετὸς τὸ ἀπόφθεγμά μου, καὶ καταβήτω ὡς δρόσος τὰ
         ῥήματά μου·
     ὡσεὶ ὄμβρος ἐπ' ἄγρωστιν, καὶ ὡσεὶ νιφετὸς ἐπὶ χόρτον.
3   ὅτι ὄνομα κυρίου ἐκάλεσα· δότε μεγαλωσύνην τῷ θεῷ ἡμῶν.

Skies and Earth:
4   θεός ἀληθινὰ τὰ ἔργα αὐτοῦ, καὶ πᾶσαι αἱ ὁδοὶ αὐτοῦ κρίσεις·
     θεὸς πιστός, καὶ οὐκ ἔστιν ἀδικία· δίκαιος καὶ ὅσιος κύριος.

Song:
5   ἡμάρτοσαν, οὐκ αὐτῷ τέκνα, μωμητά, γενεὰ σκολιὰ καὶ διεστραμμένη.
6   ταῦτα κυρίῳ ἀνταποδίδοτε οὕτω, λαὸς μωρὸς καὶ οὐχὶ σοφός ;
     οὐκ αὐτὸς οὗτός σου πατὴρ ἐκτήσατό σε, καὶ ἐποίησέν σε.
7   μνήσθητε ἡμέρας αἰῶνος, σύνετε ἔτη γενεῶν γενεαῖς.
     ἐπερώτησον τὸν πατέρα σου καὶ ἀναγγελεῖ σοι· τοὺς πρεσβυτέρους σου
         καὶ ἐροῦσίν σοι.

Elders:
8   ὅτε διεμέριζεν ὁ ὕψιστος ἔθνη, ὡς διέσπειρεν υἱοὺς Αδαμ,
     ἔστησεν ὅρια ἐθνῶν κατὰ ἀριθμὸν ἀγγέλων θεοῦ.
9   καὶ ἐγενήθη μερὶς κυρίου λαὸς αὐτοῦ Ἰακώβ, σχοίνισμα κληρονομίας
         αὐτοῦ Ἰσραήλ.
10   αὐτάρκησεν αὐτὸν ἐν τῇ ἐρήμῳ, ἐν δίψει καύματος, ἐν γῇ ἀνύδρῳ·
     ἐκύκλωσεν αὐτὸν καὶ ἐπαίδευσεν αὐτόν, καὶ διεφύλαξεν αὐτὸν ὡς
         κόραν ὀφθαλμοῦ.
11   ὡς ἀετὸς σκεπάσαι νοσσιὰν αὐτοῦ, καὶ ἐπὶ τοῖς νοσσοῖς αὐτοῦ
         ἐπεπόθησεν,
     διεὶς τὰς πτέρυγας αὐτοῦ ἐδέξατο αὐτούς, καὶ ἀνέλαβεν αὐτοὺς ἐπὶ τῶν
         μεταφρένων αὐτοῦ.
12   κύριος μόνος ἦγεν αὐτούς, οὐκ ἦν μετ' αὐτῶν θεὸς ἀλλότριος.
13   ἀνεβίβασεν αὐτοὺς ἐπὶ τὴν ἰσχὺν τῆς γῆς, ἐψώμισεν αὐτοὺς γενήματα
         ἀγρῶν·
     ἐθήλασαν μέλι ἐκ πέτρας, καὶ ἔλαιον ἐκ στερεᾶς πέτρας·
14   βούτυρον βοῶν καὶ γάλα προβάτων μετὰ στέατος ἀρνῶν καὶ κριῶν,
     υἱῶν ταύρων καὶ τράγων μετὰ στέατος νεφρῶν πυροῦ,
     καὶ αἷμα σταφυλῆς ἔπιεν οἶνον.
15   καὶ ἔφαγεν Ἰακὼβ καὶ ἐνεπλήσθη, καὶ ἀπελάκτισεν ὁ ἠγαπημένος,
     ἐλιπάνθη, ἐπαχύνθη, ἐπλατύνθη·
     καὶ ἐνκατέλιπεν τὸν θεὸν τὸν ποιήσαντα αὐτόν, καὶ ἀπέστη ἀπὸ θεοῦ
         σωτῆρος αὐτοῦ.

The Lord:

16 παρώξυνάν με ἐπ' ἀλλοτρίοις, ἐν βδελύγμασιν αὐτῶν παρεπίκρανάν με·

Elders:

17 ἔθυσαν δαιμονίοις καὶ οὐ θεῷ, θεοῖς οἷς οὐκ ᾔδεισαν·
καινοὶ πρόσφατοι ἥκασιν, οὓς οὐκ εἴδησαν οἱ πατέρες αὐτῶν.

Song:

18 θεὸν τὸν γεννήσαντά σε ἐνκατέλιπες, καὶ ἐπελάθου θεοῦ τοῦ τρέφοντός
σε.

19 καὶ ἴδεν κύριος καὶ ἐζήλωσεν, καὶ παρωξύνθη δι' ὀργὴν υἱῶν αὐτοῦ καὶ
θυγατέρων·

20ø καὶ εἶπεν

The Lord:

20abcd ἀποστρέψω τὸ πρόσωπόν μου ἀπ' αὐτῶν, καὶ δείξω τί ἔσται αὐτοῖς ἐπ'
ἐσχάτων ἡμερῶν.
ὅτι γενεὰ ἐξεστραμμένη ἐστίν, υἱοὶ οἷς οὐκ ἔστιν πίστις ἐν αὐτοῖς.

21 αὐτοὶ παρεζήλωσάν με ἐπ' οὐ θεῷ, παρώξυνάν με ἐν τοῖς εἰδώλοις
αὐτῶν·
κἀγὼ παραζηλώσω αὐτοὺς ἐπ' οὐκ ἔθνει, ἐπ' ἔθνει ἀσυνέτῳ παροργιῶ
αὐτούς.

22 ὅτι πῦρ ἐκκέκαυται ἐκ τοῦ θυμοῦ μου, καυθήσεται ἕως ᾅδου κάτω·
καταφάγεται γῆν καὶ τὰ γενήματα αὐτῆς, φλέξει θεμέλια ὀρέων.

23 συνάξω εἰς αὐτοὺς κακά, καὶ τὰ βέλη μου συνπολεμήσω εἰς αὐτούς.

24 τηκόμενοι λιμῷ καὶ βρώσει ὀρνέων, καὶ ὀπισθότονος ἀνίατος·
ὀδόντας θηρίων ἀποστελῶ εἰς αὐτούς, μετὰ θυμοῦ συρόντων ἐπὶ γῆν.

25 ἔξωθεν ἀτεκνώσει αὐτοὺς μάχαιρα, καὶ ἐκ τῶν ταμιείων φόβος·
νεανίσκος σὺν παρθένῳ, θηλάζων μετὰ καθεστηκότος πρεσβύτου.

26ø εἶπα

The Lord (quoting himself):

26ab διασπερῶ αὐτούς, παύσω δὴ ἐξ ἀνθρώπων τὸ μνημόσυνον αὐτῶν·

The Lord:

27ab εἰ μὴ δι' ὀργὴν ἐχθρῶν, ἵνα μὴ μακροχρονίσωσιν, ἵνα μὴ συνεπιθῶνται
οἱ ὑπεναντίοι· μὴ εἴπωσιν

Enemies:

27cd ἡ χεὶρ ἡμῶν ἡ ὑψηλὴ καὶ οὐχὶ κύριος ἐποίησεν ταῦτα πάντα.

The Lord:

28 ἔθνος ἀπολωλεκὸς βουλήν ἐστιν, καὶ οὐκ ἔστιν ἐν αὐτοῖς ἐπιστήμη.

29 οὐκ ἐφρόνησαν συνιέναι ταῦτα· καταδεξάσθωσαν εἰς τὸν ἐπιόντα
χρόνον.

30ab πῶς διώξεται εἷς χιλίους, καὶ δύο μετακινήσουσιν μυριάδας,

Elders:

30cd εἰ μὴ ὁ θεὸς ἀπέδοτο αὐτούς, καὶ κύριος παρέδωκεν αὐτούς;

Song:

31 ὅτι οὐκ ἔστιν ὡς ὁ θεὸς ἡμῶν οἱ θεοὶ αὐτῶν· οἱ δὲ ἐχθροὶ ἡμῶν ἀνόητοι.

Elders:

32 ἐκ γὰρ ἀμπέλου σοδομων ἡ ἄμπελος αὐτῶν, καὶ ἡ κληματὶς αὐτῶν ἐκ
   γομορρας·
  σταφυλὴ αὐτῶν σταφυλὴ χολῆς, βότρυς πικρίας αὐτοῖς·

33 θυμὸς δρακόντων ὁ οἶνος αὐτῶν, καὶ θυμὸς ἀσπίδων ἀνίατος.

The Lord:

34 οὐκ ἰδοὺ ταῦτα συνῆκται παρ' ἐμοί, καὶ ἐσφράγισται ἐν τοῖς θησαυροῖς
  μου ;

35 ἐν ἡμέρᾳ ἐκδικήσεως ἀνταποδώσω, ὅταν σφαλῇ ὁ πούς αὐτῶν·
  ὅτι ἐγγὺς ἡμέρα ἀπωλίας αὐτοῖς, καὶ πάρεστιν ἕτοιμα ὑμῖν.

Song:

36 ὅτι κρινεῖ κύριος τὸν λαὸν αὐτοῦ, καὶ ἐπὶ τοῖς δούλοις αὐτοῦ
   παρακληθήσεται·
  ἴδεν γὰρ παραλελυμένους αὐτοὺς καὶ ἐκλελοιπότας ἐν ἐπαγωγῇ καὶ
   παρειμένους.

37ø καὶ εἶπεν κύριος

The Lord:

37ab ποῦ εἰσιν οἱ θεοὶ αὐτῶν, ἐφ' οἷς ἐπεποίθεισαν ἐπ' αὐτοῖς;

Song:

38 ὧν τὸ στέαρ τῶν θυσιῶν αὐτῶν ἠσθίετε, καὶ ἐπίνετε τὸν οἶνον τῶν
   σπονδῶν αὐτῶν·
  ἀναστήτωσαν καὶ βοηθησάτωσαν ὑμῖν, καὶ γενηθήτωσαν ὑμῖν
   σκεπασταί.

The Lord:

39 ἴδετε ἴδετε ὅτι ἐγώ εἰμι, καὶ οὐκ ἔστιν θεὸς πλὴν ἐμοῦ·
  ἐγὼ ἀποκτέννω καὶ ζῆν ποιήσω, πατάξω κἀγὼ ἰάσομαι,
  καὶ οὐκ ἔστιν ὃς ἐξελεῖται ἐκ τῶν χειρῶν μου.

40a, ø ὅτι ἀρῶ εἰς τὸν οὐρανὸν τὴν χεῖρά μου καὶ ὀμοῦμαι τὴν δεξιάν μου, καὶ
   ἐρῶ

The Lord (quoting himself):

40b ζῶ ἐγὼ εἰς τὸν αἰῶνα·

The Lord:

41 ὅτι παροξυνῶ ὡς ἀστραπὴν τὴν μάχαιράν μου, καὶ ἀνθέξεται κρίματος
   ἡ χείρ μου,

καὶ ἀποδώσω δίκην τοῖς ἐχθροῖς, καὶ τοῖς μισοῦσιν ἀνταποδώσω·

42 μεθύσω τὰ βέλη μου ἀφ' αἵματος, καὶ ἡ μάχαιρά μου καταφάγεται κρέα
   ἀφ' αἵματος τραυματιῶν καὶ αἰχμαλωσίας, ἀπὸ κεφαλῆς ἀρχόντων
   ἐχθρῶν.

Song:

43 εὐφράνθητε, οὐρανοί, ἅμα αὐτῷ, καὶ προσκυνησάτωσαν αὐτῷ υἱοὶ
   θεοῦ·

   εὐφράνθητε, ἔθνη, μετὰ τοῦ λαοῦ αὐτοῦ, καὶ ἐνισχυσάτωσαν αὐτῷ
   πάντες ἄγγελοι θεοῦ·

   ὅτι τὸ αἷμα τῶν υἱῶν αὐτοῦ ἐκδικᾶται, καὶ ἐκδικήσει καὶ ἀνταποδώσει
   δίκην τοῖς ἐχθροῖς,

   καὶ τοῖς μισοῦσιν ἀνταποδώσει· καὶ ἐκκαθαριεῖ κύριος τὴν γῆν τοῦ λαοῦ
   αὐτοῦ.

Chapter 4

Song of Deuteronomy

Introduction

AVING EXAMINED IN THE PRECEDING CHAPTER the dynamic act of performing the Song of Moses as Deuteronomy creates it, I now turn to another aspect of the relationship between Deuteronomy and the Song: although Deuteronomy speaks explicitly of the Song's meaning for future generations, which includes the accumulation of its meaning(s) in all antecedent generations, there are also indications of the Song's meaning for Deuteronomy itself. That is to say, their composition reveals that the Deuteronomists are already interpreting their own history, just as they intend the Israelites of the future to do, with the Song in their collective, notional mouth (31.19) – or with the Song in their Deuteronomic pen, so to speak.[1] The thesis of this chapter is that the Song's influence is found throughout Deuteronomy, not only at the places in the exilic frame that Levenson pointed out in his 1975 article.[2] This influence is a matter not simply of Deuteronomy adopting the Song's language and themes but also – and intrinsically related to its preoccupation with performance – of Deuteronomy acting out, or acting as, the Song in more substantial ways.

In the main part of this chapter I will proceed by identifying a theme or motif in the Song of Moses, then the passages in the frame identified by Levenson that pick up on or extend the theme, then passages elsewhere in Deuteronomy that do the same, while at the same time arguing for these passages' dependence on the Song. As a control, I will also show that Deuteronomy's use of each theme or motif has little, if anything, in common with its treatment by the other Pentateuchal sources, when it appears in them at all. By way of preparation, however, I will first highlight the striking parallels to the Song exhibited by a few passages in Deuteronomy that lie outside the exilic frame, after which I will offer a brief survey of scholarly identifications of Pentateuchal themes and argue that the Song has very little in common with them, with the goal of rendering the hypothesis of the Song's unique influence on Deuteronomy more credible.

---

1. Of course, the Israelites of the "future," with respect to Deuteronomy's narrative present, are contemporary with the book's composers.

2. Levenson 1975.

As I have described elsewhere, Levenson has shown that the Song inspired the composers of Deuteronomy's exilic frame.[3] The frame tends to borrow themes and one or two associated lexemes, rather than whole phrases, from the Song. In accordance with his thesis that the frame is a unified composition, Levenson also demonstrates that the phrases thus composed under the Song's influence take identical or virtually identical forms when they happen to appear more than once in the frame.[4] Since I am not proposing that Deuteronomy as a whole is a unified composition but only that borrowing from the Song is evident at many more points than in the exilic frame, my argument does not need to go so far as adducing instances of identical phrasing. Take, for example, the following five passages, the first three of which belong to Dtr₁, the other two of which belong to the exhortatory material introducing the legal core of the book, and each of which shows striking parallels to the Song of Moses.[5]

1.31: This verse seems to draw its inspiration from SoM 10–12. The passages exhibit five points of commonality, comprising both theme and vocabulary. The events concerned in both texts occur in an unnamed wilderness (denoted by the noun מִדְבָּר), with the Israelites moving on toward their destination in the land. YHWH's manner of leading them is compared (כְּ 'like, as') to that of a parent carrying (לשׂאת) offspring, whether an eagle with its nestlings[6] or a human with its child. Finally, the larger concern in both is the proclamation of YHWH's past beneficent actions that are known to the Israelites; in SoM 10–12, the elders of the community are responding to an inquiry about the past by reciting YHWH's creation of Israel as a nation, while in 1.31 the addressees themselves are the ones who have witnessed YHWH's deeds and who would thus be prepared to respond in the manner called for in the Song.[7]

3. Levenson 1975:215–17. Note particularly the following summary characterization: "The Song of Moses exerted not only an influence of a literary nature on the exilic hand, evident in his recomposition of the covenant at Moab, but also a profound theological influence over the entirety of his bracket. The exilic frame to Dtn is the sermon for which the Song of Moses is the text" (Levenson 1975:217).

4. These passages are 4.19 and 29.25, from SoM 8–9; 4.26, 30.19, and 31.28, from SoM 1; 31.17–18, from SoM 20; 4.25 and 31.29, from SoM 16, 21.

5. These observations coincide in part with the thesis advanced by Leuchter that the Song was incorporated into Deuteronomy during Josiah's reign (Leuchter 2007:passim).

6. The image of YHWH as an eagle carrying the Israelites appears in Exodus 19.4 as well as in the Song (and nowhere else). For arguments that the direction of influence runs from Deuteronomy to Exodus, see Blenkinsopp 1999, esp. 87–91.

7. The root אמן 'firm, trustworthy' in 1.32 is also a point of comparison between Deuteronomy 1 and the Song, although it does not appear in the near context of SoM 10–12 but only in SoM 20d (cf. also SoM 4c). On the other hand, as the next paragraph will show, SoM 19–20 seems to have inspired 1.34–35.

1.34–35: For these verses it will be instructive to set them side-by-side
with SoM 19–20.
SoM 19–20:

וַיַּרְא יְהוָה וַיִּנְאָץ מִכַּעַס בָּנָיו וּבְנֹתָיו: וַיֹּאמֶר אַסְתִּירָה פָנַי מֵהֶם אֶרְאֶה מָה אַחֲרִיתָם כִּי דוֹר
תַּהְפֻּכֹת הֵמָּה בָּנִים לֹא־אֵמֻן בָּם:

YHWH saw and felt contempt because of the vexation of his sons
and his daughters, and he said: "Let me hide my face from them, let
me see what their end will be, for they are a generation of reversals,
children with no reliability in them."

1.34–35:

וַיִּשְׁמַע יְהוָה אֶת־קוֹל דִּבְרֵיכֶם וַיִּקְצֹף וַיִּשָּׁבַע לֵאמֹר: אִם־יִרְאֶה אִישׁ בָּאֲנָשִׁים הָאֵלֶּה הַדּוֹר הָרָע
הַזֶּה אֵת הָאָרֶץ הַטּוֹבָה אֲשֶׁר נִשְׁבַּעְתִּי לָתֵת לַאֲבֹתֵיכֶם:

YHWH heard the sound of your words and was angry and took an
oath: "If even one of these men, this evil generation, sees the good
land that I took an oath to give to your fathers … "

The similarities between these two passages begin at a basic level, with the
plot development of YHWH's anger: once YHWH perceives the Israelites'
offense,[8] he experiences an emotion of anger,[9] and then he solemnly announces the action he will take.[10] Further, the faculty of sight (לראות 'to see')
plays a role in the action YHWH announces in each case: in the Song, YHWH
says he will seek to see the outcome of the Israelites' actions, while in 1.34
YHWH will keep the current generation of Israelites from seeing the land.
Alternatively we may focus on YHWH's action of hiding something from
the Israelites: in SoM 20 he hides his face, and in 1.35 he effectively hides
the land from them (though without using the word "hide"). The parallels
here also include the idea of a corrupt generation, which appears not only in
the noun דוֹר 'generation' and its negative descriptors (1.34: הַדּוֹר הָרָע הַזֶּה [this
evil generation]; SoM 20: דוֹר תַּהְפֻּכֹת הֵמָּה [they are a generation of reversings])
but also in the associated language of ancestors (1.35: אֲבֹתֵיכֶם [your fathers])

8. By hearing in 1.34; by sight in SoM 19. A change from seeing to hearing could be explained on the basis of the fact that in Deuteronomy 1 YHWH is responding to the Israelites'
speech, whereas in the Song YHWH is responding to actions more generally construed.

9. 1.34: לקצף 'to be angry'; SoM 19: לנאץ 'to condemn, spurn'.

10. In 1.34 he takes an oath (להשבע 'to swear'), while in SoM 20 he is speaking in verse. The
addition of the concept and vocabulary of oath-taking could be explained not only as a way of
lending solemnity to YHWH's prose speech but also as a way of anticipating – and producing
tension with – the oath that YHWH will mention in 1.35.

and descendants (SoM 19–20: בָּנָיו וּבְנֹתָיו [his sons and his daughters]; בָּנִים [his children]). Finally, these two passages share the theme of compensatory reciprocity, insofar as once the Israelites fail to act properly towards YHWH, he also reverses the way that he treats them.

1.42–45: These verses draw on multiple points in the Song, although most of their verbal parallels are with SoM 1. A handful of lexemes from the opening verse of the Song appear throughout the passage: the pairing of the verbs of hearing לשמע 'to hear' and להאזין 'to give ear' (1.45); the 1cs form of the prefix conjugation form of the verb לדבר (to speak; 1.43: וָאֲדַבֵּר [I spoke]; SoM 1: וַאֲדַבֵּרָה [that I may speak]); and the noun פֶּה 'mouth' (1.43).[11] Additionally, the theme of compensatory reciprocity appears again, with YHWH adopting the Israelites' manner of treating him in his continued dealings with them: as they have not listened to him, so will he not listen to them (1.43, 45). Compare the Song's elaborate expression of this reciprocity in SoM 21: הֵם קִנְאוּנִי בְלֹא־אֵל כִּעֲסוּנִי בְּהַבְלֵיהֶם וַאֲנִי אַקְנִיאֵם בְּלֹא־עָם בְּגוֹי נָבָל אַכְעִיסֵם (they made me jealous with a no-god, vexed me with vanities, so I will make them jealous with a no-people, with a foolish nation I'll vex them.) A further shared theme is that of the Israelites' enemies defeating them (or not) according to YHWH's direction, appearing along with the verb לרדף 'to pursue' in both 1.42, 44 and SoM 30. Finally, Israel's misfortune is described with animal imagery both in 1.44 (bees) as well as in SoM 24, 33 (snakes, specifically, as well as other animals).

Chapter 8: As a whole this chapter reflects several of the Song's important themes and topoi, such as: 1) the depiction of the relationship between YHWH and Israel as a parent-child relationship involving discipline or punishment (8.5; SoM 5–6, 18b–20); 2) a list-like elaboration on the land's abundance (8.7–9; SoM 13–14); 3) the pivotal nature of the moment when the Israelites have enough to eat (8.10, 12–14; SoM 15); 4) the phrasing [אשר] [אבותיכם] לא ידעו (which your ancestors did not know; 8.16; SoM 17b, d); 5) the pretension of one's success being due to one's own efforts rather than to YHWH's actions, coupled with the use of יָד 'hand' as a metaphor for agency (8.17–18; SoM 27cd[12]); and 6) forgetting (לשכח) YHWH as a description of the primary offense that the Israelites have committed or may yet commit (8.11, 14, 19; SoM 18).

9.26:[13] This verse exhibits the phrase עַמְּךָ וְנַחֲלָתְךָ (your people, your in-

---

11. Note that in both places the "I" of the verb represents someone who is speaking YHWH's words and the noun "mouth" is a metonym for those words.

12. Cf. the related use of the adjective רָם 'high' in 8.14, where it modifies the noun לֵב 'heart', and in SoM 27c, where it modifies the noun יָד 'hand'.

13. See below in this chapter for a more detailed discussion of this verse.

heritance), two terms that appear in parallel in SoM 9: כִּי חֵלֶק יְהֹוָה עַמּוֹ יַעֲקֹב
חֶבֶל נַחֲלָתוֹ (for his people are YHWH's allotment, Jacob the border-rope of his
inheritance). The use of the verbal root שחת 'destroy, become corrupt' in 9.26
in the phrase אַל־תַּשְׁחֵת עַמְּךָ (do not destroy your people) is a play on its use in
9.12 (שִׁחֵת עַמְּךָ [your people have become corrupt]), which in turn mimics its
use in SoM 5 (שִׁחֵת לוֹ לֹא בָּנָיו [(his people) became corrupt toward him – (they
are) not his children]). Note too the occurrence of יָד 'hand' and גֹּדֶל 'greatness' with reference to agency and action that can properly be ascribed only
to YHWH (cf. SoM 3b, 27c, 39d).

Based on such examples as these, it seems clear that the composers of
the Dtr₂ frame were not the only contributors to Deuteronomy to draw on
the Song of Moses. As I have stated above, in the rest of this chapter I will
explore such parallels organized according to the theme or topos in question. In order to bring these examples into higher relief, my argument will
incorporate a demonstration that the (other) sources used by Deuteronomy's various composers do not treat the same themes and topoi in a way
similar to their treatment in the Song. As a preliminary to this second part
of my argument, in the next few pages I will show that the Song is relatively
unconcerned with the themes of the Pentateuch and its sources as defined
in the past half century by Martin Noth, by Hans Walter Wolff and Walter
Brueggemann, and by David Clines.

Noth's 1948 examination of Pentateuchal themes, *Überlieferungsgeschichte des Pentateuch*, is the classic work in this area.[14] Noth categorized
Pentateuchal themes as either major (the rescue from Egypt; the guidance
into arable land; promises to the patriarchs; and revelation and covenant
at Sinai) or minor (the guidance in the wilderness; Baal Peor and Balaam;
thirst, hunger, and enemies in the wilderness; murmuring of the people; and
episodes connected with the occupation). As I will show, the Song exhibits
only vague affinities with some – not all – of them.

According to Noth, YHWH's rescuing of Israel from Egypt by means of
the events at the Reed Sea constitutes perhaps the most basic theme of the
Pentateuch.[15] The Song of Moses, however, includes not a single reference to
Egypt, any pharaoh or pharaoh-like figure, enslavement to another people
or in another land, or the Reed Sea or any body of water. Further, if the Song
is at all concerned with the Israelites' movement from one locale to another,
it emphasizes the land that YHWH brought them into rather than a place he
brought them out of.[16] Noth's theme of guidance into arable land concerns

14. Noth 1948. I will be citing page numbers from the 1981 translation.

15. Noth 1981:47–51.

16. This movement thus presents a better potential match with Noth's theme of guidance
into arable land.

tracing the route by which the people entered the land,[17] but all the Song offers in this regard is an an image of YHWH as a bird carrying his nestlings through the air into the land (SoM 11) – a distinctly untraceable route. The theme of YHWH's guidance of and provision for Israel in the wilderness[18] is present in the Song, if at all, in a purely allusive summary – "He found him in a wilderness land, in a howling, desert emptiness; he enclosed him, he took thought for him; he guarded him as the pupil of his eye" (SoM 10) – a summary that lacks, notably, this theme's most distinct feature, the encounter with drinkable water where none was expected. Noth hypothesized that guidance in the wilderness is a secondary theme that developed only in dependence on the primary themes of guidance out of Egypt and guidance into arable land.[19] Suffice it to say that the Song in and of itself does not lend support to this hypothesis, since the Song's (minimal) attestation to guidance in the wilderness (SoM 10) exists in the complete absence of the Egypt theme and in association with only the barest hint of guidance into arable land (SoM 11–12). With respect to Noth's theme of the promises made to the patriarchs,[20] the Song mentions no patriarchs by name, nor are the anonymous ancestors who do appear in the Song spoken of as recipients of any promise. Nor does the Song contain any material related to revelation and covenant at Sinai:[21] YHWH does not appear to anyone in the Song, and the mountains in SoM 22d are nothing like a site of meeting, law-giving, or covenant-making. In fact, the Song contains no explicit mention of a covenant, merely presuming a somewhat reciprocal relationship between YHWH and Israel as god and people (e.g. SoM 6, 9, 21) without elaborating on the origin or terms of that relationship.

A number of Noth's themes would resonate more with the Song if they pertained to Israel's experience after entering the land. Take, for example, the secondary theme of "Baal Peor and Balaam."[22] Although in the Song the Israelites are said to give their worship to other gods (e.g. SoM 15c–17c), this change of allegiance apparently takes place after they have entered the land, rather than before. The same is the case with Noth's theme "Thirst, Hunger, and Enemies in the Wilderness."[23] YHWH does provide food and drink for his people (SoM 13–14),[24] and, by the end of the Song, he announces his in-

17. Noth 1981:51–54.
18. Noth 1981:58–59.
19. Noth 1981:47.
20. Noth 1981:54–58.
21. Noth 1981:59–62.
22. Noth 1981:74–79.
23. Noth 1981:115–22.
24. Note, as well, that this alimentation is not provided as a remedy for thirst and hunger

tention to (vindicate his people and) turn his wrath against his and their enemies (SoM 36ab, 41–43) – but, again, all this occurs in the land, not in a wilderness. As for something like Noth's "Murmuring of the People,"[25] the Song depicts the Israelites not as complaining about YHWH's provision but rather, it would seem, as attributing that provision to the wrong parties (as evidenced by the fact that they offer sacrifice to gods other than YHWH; SoM 17–18).

By contrast to Noth's approach of tracing themes throughout the Pentateuch as a whole, Hans Walter Wolff and Walter Brueggemann published a series of essays proposing the "kerygma" of each of the Pentateuchal sources.[26] While the word "kerygma" carries theological overtones, it is nevertheless broadly similar to theme and as such provides a useful metric by which to estimate the Song's degree of overlap with the other Pentateuchal sources.[27] This overlap appears to be quite meager when judged against the analyses of Wolff and Brueggemann.

According to Wolff's essay on the Yahwist, that source is primarily concerned with divine blessing coming to all nations through Abraham and his descendants, especially as a result of their intercession with YHWH.[28] Such a theme is wholly unrelated to the Song. If anything, other nations ultimately suffer violence at YHWH's hands in connection with Israel (SoM 41–42), not blessing, and although YHWH does change his mind in the Song, it is not as the result of intercession.[29] At most all that the Song may be said to have in common with this theme is the presupposition of a unique relationship

---

but as evidence of YHWH's generosity in giving the Israelites access to a land of such abundance. Although the rock (צוּר; also סֶלַע 'cliff') that is the source of honey and oil in SoM 13cd may call to mind scenes from Israel's wilderness wanderings, the motif has been substantially modified, not least by making the rock a feature of the land into which Israel was brought rather than of the wilderness.

25. Noth 1981:122–30.

26. Brueggemann and Wolff 1982. Wolff's essay on the Yahwist was originally published as Wolff 1964 and its translation as Wolff 1966. Wolff's essay on the Elohist was originally published as Wolff 1969 and its translation as Wolff 1972. Brueggemann's essay on the Priestly Writers was originally published as Brueggemann 1972.

27. I am leaving out of consideration the essays of Wolff and of Brueggemann that address the D source, both because they treat D and the Deuteronomistic History together as a single work and also because the very thesis of this chapter is that Deuteronomy and the Song share certain themes, regardless of whether Wolff and Brueggemann would identify such items as themes of D as a whole. The relevant essays are Wolff 1961, which was not published in translation before its appearance in Brueggggemann and Wolff 1982, and Brueggemann 1968, which was not included in Brueggemann and Wolff 1982.

28. Brueggemann and Wolff 1982:49, 56.

29. See below in this chapter, however, where I argue that Moses's intercession with YHWH in Deuteronomy 9 shows the Song's influence in a different manner.

between Israel, out of all the nations, and YHWH (SoM 8–9). The conclusion is similar in the case of the Elohistic source, of which the primary theme (again according to Wolff) is the fear of God, particularly as measured by obedience during moments of testing.[30] The Song, however, portrays the Israelite's offense as comprised of corruption, stupidity, forgetfulness, and a failure to reciprocate (SoM 5–6, 15cd, 18) rather than specifically as a lack of the fear of God, and it makes no reference to testing or to commands that may or may not be followed. As for the Priestly source, Brueggemann defines its theme as the divine blessing of Israel (as well as of humanity more generally) with large numbers of descendants, with dominance, and with possession of land,[31] with the caveat that the Israelites may lose YHWH's gift of land by being unfaithful.[32] The element of land possession offers a minor point of comparison with the Song, which shows YHWH bringing the Israelites to live in a land of abundance (SoM 8–14) – and yet, in the Song, Israel's unfaithfulness threatens to result not in their losing the land but more simply in their total destruction at the hands of YHWH (SoM 20–26). In summary, then, although these three sources may have certain background elements in common with the Song, in no way can the Song be said to contribute actively or specifically to any of their major themes as analyzed by Wolff and Brueggemann.

In his book *The Theme of the Pentateuch*, David Clines returns to an approach based on the Pentateuch as a finished product, which in a way Noth also had taken.[33] By contrast, however, and as his title indicates, Clines does not examine the Pentateuch's individual constituent themes but rather seeks a single theme for the whole,[34] which he summarizes in the following statement:

> The theme of the Pentateuch is the partial fulfillment – which implies also the partial non-fulfillment – of the promise to or blessing of the patriarchs. … The promise has three elements: posterity, divine-human relationship, and land. The posterity-element of the promise is dominant in Genesis 12–50, the relationship-element in Exodus and Leviticus, and the land-element in Numbers and Deuteronomy.[35]

The Song refers to no words of promise spoken by YHWH, as I have noted

30. Brueggemann and Wolff 1982:71–72, 77.

31. Brueggemann and Wolff 1982:103, 106.

32. Brueggemann and Wolff 1982:109–10.

33. Clines 1997.

34. The "kerygmata" of the individual sources discussed by Wolff and Brueggemann would seem to be analogous to the kind of theme Clines proposes.

35. Clines 1997:30 [italics omitted].

above, nor does it refer to words of blessing. Furthermore, the Song takes the elements of posterity, divine-human relationship, and land as givens, not susceptible to any further fulfillment.[36] The points of anxiety in the Song can at most be said to revolve around whether the blessings that have already been achieved will be reversed: Will the images of flora and fauna in the land of abundance (SoM 13–14) be turned into sources of curse (SoM 24, 32–33)? Will the old and the young (SoM 7), symbols of the passing of generations, be destroyed together (SoM 26)? And, most importantly for the Song, what will YHWH do now that the relationship of reciprocity between YHWH and Israel has become a source of vexation and jealousy (SoM 16, 21)? If the Song could thereby be construed as furthering the theme of the Pentateuch, then so could nearly any other biblical passage.

The foregoing introductory pages have established that a certain number of passages outside the Dtr₂ frame exhibit the Song's characteristic influence, as well as that it should be possible to disentangle the Song's influence on Deuteronomy from what Deuteronomy has taken from its other sources. I now proceed to the main part of this chapter, an analysis of several of the Song's distinctive themes and motifs that appear to have been taken over in various ways by various parts of Deuteronomy.

Corruption and Integrity throughout the Generations

I have taken the title of this section from the roots שחת 'destroy, become corrupt', appearing in SoM 5a, and תמם 'be perfect, complete', appearing in SoM 4a. The theme of transgenerational corruption and integrity can be seen as a very broad one, with which several sub-themes and motifs interact, both in the Song and elsewhere in Deuteronomy. The Song's language of "twistedness" (SoM 5: דּוֹר עִקֵּשׁ וּפְתַלְתֹּל [a crooked and perverse generation]; SoM 20c: דּוֹר תַּהְפֻּכֹת [a generation of reversals]) and of "straightness" (SoM 4d: יָשָׁר הוּא [(YHWH) is upright]) plays into this theme in an obvious way, as do evocations of animals and plants that are either rich sources of nourishment (SoM 13–14) or deadly (SoM 24cd) and poisonous (SoM 32–33). As indicated by the association between the root שחת and idolatry elsewhere in the book (and highlighted by Levenson specifically within the exilic, Dtr₂ frame[37]), Deuteronomy sees idolatrous practices as one manifestation of the Israelites' corruption in any given generation. Below I will discuss the linking of the root שחת with idolatry in a passage from outside of the exilic

---

36. In this way, it is quite appropriate that Deuteronomy gives the Song a mission for the future, a mission of speaking to, as it were, a post-Pentateuchal Israel.

37. Levenson 1975:214.

frame (Deuteronomy 9) before moving on to discuss transgenerational continuity and discontinuity in Deuteronomy more broadly, where it becomes primarily a question of whether successive generations of Israelites will adhere to YHWH (with some instances of comparison to YHWH's consistent treatment of the Israelites from generation to generation). As I will show, Deuteronomy's use of this theme – indeed, the theme itself – shows the distinct influence of the Song.

Let me begin by reviewing the relevant elements of Levenson's discussion regarding שחת and idolatry in the exilic frame. Levenson has noted the association of the Hiphil verb form לְהַשְׁחִית 'to destroy, to become corrupt' with "material idolatry in the future" at 4.16 and at 31.29.[38] Of the two verses, 4.16 includes a direct reference to idols: וַעֲשִׂיתֶם לָכֶם פֶּסֶל ([lest] you make an idol for yourselves), while in 31.29 the reference is metonymic, by means of the phrase מַעֲשֵׂה יְדֵיכֶם (the work of your hands). Levenson does not include 4.25: וְהִשְׁחַתֶּם וַעֲשִׂיתֶם פֶּסֶל (when you become corrupt and make an idol), even though it too refers to "material idolatry in the future." This omission seems relatively unimportant, however, since the verse's evidence supports and does not contradict Levenson's thesis.

Levenson does not include 4.16 (25); 31.29 in his list of verbal parallels between the Song and the exilic frame, presumably because the vocabulary with which they refer to idolatry[39] does not appear in the Song in connection with its sole attestation of the root שחת (SoM 5a). As I will argue, however, Deuteronomy's Song-influenced treatment of the theme of Israel's "corruption" incorporates features not only from SoM 5–6, which is the near context of שחת in the Song, but also from other parts of the Song. As a necessary prelude, I must discuss the specifically future aspect of the idolatry as identified by Levenson in the frame and as it appears in the Song.

The mentions of idolatry pointed out by Levenson (plus the one in 4.25) clearly do take place in the future with reference to the narrative present of the book of Deuteronomy. The occurrences in Deuteronomy 4 appear in the context of commands and warnings, indicating that idolatry must be prevented from happening: "guard yourselves well … lest you become corrupt and make an idol for yourselves" (4.15–16); "guard yourselves lest you forget the covenant and make an idol for yourselves in the image of anything concerning which YHWH your god has commanded you … when you

---

38. Levenson 1975:214.

39. The vocabulary in question would seem to be the verb לַעֲשׂוֹת 'to do, to make' in association with words for idol – particularly the noun פֶּסֶל 'idol, image' but including the metonym מַעֲשֵׂה יְדֵיכֶם (the work of your hands) mentioned above – and/or the motifs of doing what YHWH considers evil (לַעֲשׂוֹת אֶת הָרַע בְּעֵינֵי יְהוָה [to do what is evil in the eyes of YHWH]) and/or of vexing (להכעיס [to vex]) YHWH.

produce children and grandchildren and grow old in the land and become corrupt" (4.23, 25).[40] While those verses treat idolatry as an indefinite prospect for the future, the occurrence in 31.29 is a simple prediction: "for I know that, after I die, you will in fact become corrupt ... vexing him with the work of your hands."[41] Now, the timing of the idolatry mentioned in the Song is more complicated, not limited to the future. In the Song's narrative context within Deuteronomy, particularly as dictated by chapter 31, the idolatry that the Song recounts (SoM 16–17, 37–38) occurs in the future. In fact, the introductory material in Deuteronomy 31 iterates four distinct times that the events with which the Song is concerned take place in the future (31.16–17, 18, 20–21, 29[42]). Nevertheless, within the Song considered as an isolated text, the idolatry in question occurs in the past; it forms part of the elders' historical résumé (SoM 16–17c) and serves as the point of departure for the announcement of YHWH's anger and anticipated acts of retribution (SoM 19–21). Therefore, we should not refuse to consider that an account of idolatrous actions in Deuteronomy might exhibit the Song's influence based specifically on the timing, whether future or past, of those actions as recited by the account in question.

The most relevant example of a passage outside the exilic frame that shows the influence of the Song's treatment of idolatry is Deuteronomy 9.12–29, generally understood to be a Dtr$_1$ text. As a preliminary observation, note that the overall plot of the relationship crisis between YHWH and Israel as told by 9.12–29 matches that of the Song:[43] first Israel's material idolatry (SoM 15c–18; 9.12, 16), then YHWH's announcement of a decision to destroy his people (SoM 20–26; 9.14, 25), followed by a discourse that considers the outcome of such a course of action and takes the opinions of other nations into account[44] (SoM 26–27, where it is spoken by YHWH; 9.26–29, where it is

---

40. 4.15–16: הִשָּׁמְרוּ לָכֶם פֶּן־תִּשְׁכְּחוּ אֶת־בְּרִית 25, 4.23; וְנִשְׁמַרְתֶּם מְאֹד לְנַפְשֹׁתֵיכֶם ... פֶּן־תַּשְׁחִתוּן וַעֲשִׂיתֶם לָכֶם פֶּסֶל; כִּי־תוֹלִיד בָּנִים וּבְנֵי בָנִים וְנוֹשַׁנְתֶּם בָּאָרֶץ וְהִשְׁחַתֶּם וַעֲשִׂיתֶם פֶּסֶל ....

41. כִּי יָדַעְתִּי אַחֲרֵי מוֹתִי כִּי־הַשְׁחֵת תַּשְׁחִתוּן ... לְהַכְעִיסוֹ בְּמַעֲשֵׂה יְדֵיכֶם.

42. Only the last of these refers to idolatry explicitly; all four place the Israelites' unfaithful actions in the future.

43. The crisis is introduced differently in each text, however. The Song offers a recitation of YHWH's generosity as a prelude (SoM 8–14), highlighting the emotional shock that is the basis for his subsequent anger, following on Israel's failure to reciprocate. By contrast, the preceding part of Deuteronomy 9 (see vv. 4–7) dwells on Israel's history of stubbornness and provocation with YHWH, creating instead a wholly different expectation for Israel's behavior.

44. In commenting on a similar moment of hypothesizing discourse in Exodus 32.12, William Propp notes parallels to it in Numbers 14.13–16; Joshua 7.9; Ezekiel 20.14; 36.22–23; and Joel 2.17 (Propp 2006:555). In commenting on Exodus 32.14 (which recounts the changing of YHWH's mind as a result of Moses's persuasive hypothesizing), J. Philip Hyatt mentions Amos 7.1–6, although this human attempt to persuade does not carry on through the remainder of

spoken by Moses), and finally YHWH's revised decision (SoM 36, 41–42; 9.19 [see also 10.10]).[45] Within the context of this broad narrative resemblance, there are a number of shared motifs and means of expression related to the idolatry theme. Because of the complexity of the passage as a whole and its numerous parallels or allusions to the Song, I will proceed verse-by-verse as through Deuteronomy 9.12–29 and then re-focus the discussion on idolatry and its relation to transgenerational integrity and corruption.

9.12: The verb שִׁחֵת (he/it became corrupt) is this verses's most striking parallel with the Song of Moses. Precisely the same form occurs in SoM 5, where the noun עַם 'people' is likewise notionally (although not syntactically) the subject of the verb. These two instances are the only Piel forms of the root שׁחת out of its ten (or eleven, depending on how one counts the infinitive absolute construction in 31.29[46]) occurrences in the book of Deuteronomy.

The noun דֶּרֶךְ 'way' is also a parallel, occurring in שֶׁחֵת's near context in the Song. It appears in the plural two lines before, in SoM 4b, where it refers to YHWH's consistent, integrity-filled ways of acting. Here in 9.12, it refers to a way of acting that Israel has not kept to but has, rather, departed from. Each of these instances serves the larger idea that YHWH can be trusted while Israel cannot.

Amos's vision, in vv. 7–9 (Hyatt 1971:307). Given that the passages in Exodus 32 and Numbers 14 exhibit numerous other Song-reminiscent parallels with Deuteronomy 9 (as well as with Deuteronomy 1, in the case of Numbers 14), how can we be sure that such features of Deuteronomy 9 derive from the Song and not from Exodus and/or Numbers? Although I will not pursue it in detail here, scholars have long noted that the Exodus and Numbers passages are characterized by Deuteronomic language (in general, without further distinguishing Song-related language) and have accordingly proposed that the writers of Deuteronomy or at least Deuteronomy-influenced redactors composed them and/or inserted them into their current contexts. On Exodus 32, see Hyatt 1971:306: "This section [vv. 7–14] is recognized by many critics as coming from a Deuteronomic Redactor (RD). Much of the material, in similar terminology, is found in Dt. 9:12–19, 25–29. The vocabulary and ideas are more closely related to Deuteronomy than to E." See also Propp 2006:148: "Many have noticed, however, that Yahweh's speech in 32:7–13 strongly manifests D-like language." On Numbers 14, see Davies 1995:142: "It is generally agreed that the passage is permeated by Deuteronomistic ideas and phrases ..., and, in particular, there are clear points of contact with Dt. 1:34–40. It is uncertain, however, whether Num. 14:11–25 provided the prototype for the Deuteronomic version ..., or whether it represents a later amplification of the Deuteronomic passage." Even though consensus is lacking in this second case, the possibility that Numbers 14 depends on Deuteronomy is enough for my argument to proceed.

45. Although YHWH's actions may be interpreted as those of a rash character, YHWH is at least possessed of wisdom and insight as the Song defines it in SoM 29: he considers the effect of his actions on himself.

46. In Deuteronomy the root שׁחת appears in the Song (SoM 5), in the exilic frame (4.16, 25, 31; 31.29), in the law code's introductory material (9.12, 26, along with a resumptive use in 10.10), and in the unrelated law of the trees in Deuteronomy 20.19, 20.

While מַסֵּכָה 'casting, cast image' is not a strict verbal parallel, it never-theless functions allusively with respect to the idolatry mentioned in SoM 16–17.

9.13: The verb לראות 'to see' is used both here and in SoM 39 by YHWH in conjunction with a generalization about a person's (or nation's) true character. In SoM 39, before making a few salient generalizations about his nature and his role, YHWH commands others to see him (רְאוּ [see!]), while in 9.13 YHWH offers his assessment of Israel's nature as a stiff-necked people,[47] based on his having seen (רָאִיתִי [I have seen]) them. Although such a use of לראות is not unusual insofar as seeing is a metaphor for knowing,[48] its presence in both these texts nevertheless constitutes a link between them, a link that is strengthened by the fact that the motif is used in exactly op-posite ways in each. In SoM 39, YHWH is to be the object of sight, and his character is to be observed, while in 9.13, YHWH is the subject, observing the character of the Israelites. This reversal corresponds to several others shared by these texts.

9.14: The clause אֶמְחֶה אֶת־שְׁמָם מִתַּחַת הַשָּׁמָיִם (I will wipe their name from un-der the skies) expresses an idea parallel to that expressed in SoM 26b by אַשְׁבִּיתָה מֵאֱנוֹשׁ זִכְרָם (I will put an end to their mention among humanity), where YHWH is also the speaker. Even though the only vocabulary items that they technically share are the preposition מִן 'from' and the 3mp possessive pro-nominal suffix, the other words are basically synonymous in context, while the syntax of the two clauses is highly similar. YHWH is the subject of each 1cs verb; the Israelites are the antecedent of the 3mp suffixes, which are attached to the direct objects; and the prepositional phrases introduced by מִן each indicate the all-encompassing extent to which YHWH will nullify Israel's mark of identity.

9.15: This verse shares with the Song of Moses an association between mountain, fire, and YHWH's anger at Israel's idolatry. SoM 22 speaks of the fire of YHWH's anger enveloping the earth, particularly the "mountain foundations." While the clause וְהָהָר בֹּעֵר בָּאֵשׁ (the mountain burning with fire) – or even the word אֵשׁ 'fire' on its own – does not evoke anger in and of itself,[49]

---

47. To be clear, the epithet "stiff-necked" does not appear in the Song.

48. E.g. Genesis 6.2, 12; 7.1; Exodus 2.2. The usage can also be applied to non-animate enti-ties, as in Genesis 1.4, where the nature of light is described. Cf. also the appearance of לדעת 'to know' alongside generalizations in Deuteronomy 31.21 (YHWH speaking), 27 (Moses speak-ing).

49. The exact same phrase occurs in 4.11 and 5.23 without any connotation of divine emo-tion, whether anger or any other emotion. Anger is also absent from the other instances of אֵשׁ 'fire' in chs. 4 and 5, which likewise refer to the events at Horeb (4.12, 15, 33, 36; 5.4, 5, 22, 24, 25). The sole exception to this rule is 4.24, where YHWH is described in the temporal and

in Deuteronomy 9 it clearly occurs in a context of divine anger over idolatry (see 9.7–14, especially vv. 7–8 for the verbs לְהַקְצִיף 'to make angry' [twice] and לְהִתְאַנַּף 'to be angry'), a provocation to anger that is particularly expressed in YHWH's speech as it comes to an end in v. 14).

9.16: As in 9.12, while מַסֵּכָה 'casting, cast image' does not precisely parallel any vocabulary in the Song, it nevertheless functions allusively with respect to the idolatry mentioned in SoM 16–17.

9.18: The phrase לַעֲשׂוֹת הָרַע בְּעֵינֵי יְהוָה לְהַכְעִיסוֹ (to do what is evil in the eyes of YHWH, vexing him) is of note here. Levenson includes the virtually identical phrasing in 4.25 and 31.29 among the pieces of evidence that a unified, exilic composition frames Deuteronomy;[50] not only so, but he characterizes these two passages as drawing on the use of the verb לכעס / להכעיס 'to vex' in the Song of Moses in association with the theme of idolatry (SoM 16, 21),[51] the definition of which as taking place in the future excludes 9.18 from his consideration. And yet, if 4.25 and 31.29 draw on the Song, then surely the wording in Deuteronomy 9 must have been formed under the influence of the Song as well – unless it was formed under the influence of texts that were themselves formed under the influence of the Song (such as 4.25 and 31.29, in which case the phrasing in 9.18 would represent a late insertion, contemporaneous with or later than Dtr₂). Or, perhaps, 4.25 and 31.29 were composed under the influence of 9.18. In a way, this last possibility coincides most easily with Levenson's thesis: If 9.18 and its context were written under the influence of the Song at a time when the Song was an independent text (or at least not introduced by 31.29 in its current form and thus not part of the exilic frame nor, therefore, of the Dtr₂ edition of Deuteronomy), then 9.18's setting of Israel's idolatry in the past would make sense insofar as the Song itself also speaks of idolatrous practices that have already taken place. Then, whatever innovation occurred by which the Song of Moses came to be read as a message for the future – whether it was an innovation original to Dtr₂ or an intervening one that Dtr₂ adopted – once such an interpretation

---

geographical abstract as a consuming fire and, significantly, as "jealous" – קַנָּא, from the same root that is used as a verb in SoM 21, directly adjacent to the angry fire of SoM 22. Cf. also 9.3, 10; 10.4.

50. 4.25: וַעֲשִׂיתֶם הָרַע בְּעֵינֵי יְהוָה־אֱלֹהֶיךָ לְהַכְעִיסוֹ ([when] you do what is evil in the eyes of YHWH your god, vexing him); 31.29: כִּי־תַעֲשׂוּ אֶת־הָרַע בְּעֵינֵי יְהוָה לְהַכְעִיסוֹ. Levenson 1975:214.

51. Levenson 1975:216. Levenson does not include the phrase [אֱלֹהֶיךָ] בְּעֵינֵי יְהוָה (in the eyes of YHWH [your god]) at this point, perhaps because, even though it only strengthens the links between 4.25 and 31.29, it does not have a clear parallel in the Song. The phrasing לַעֲשׂוֹת [אֶת] הָרַע בְּעֵינֵי יְהוָה (to do what is evil in the eyes of YHWH) seems to appear for the first time in Numbers 32.13 (along with the motif of a generation gone bad), a verse that itself has strong affinities with the Song (SoM 5, 20) and that appears in a section said, for example, by Davies to be "couched in the Deuteronomistic-Priestly style" (Davies 1995:331–32). Cf. also Genesis 38.7.

of the Song became operative, it would be natural for 4.25 and 31.29 both to draw on the Song-influenced phrasing in 9.18 as well as to be concerned with the possibility of Israelite idolatry in the future, in accordance with the new understanding of the Song's temporal reference. In any case, for the moment it suffices to observe that both the Song and Deuteronomy 9 exhibit the use of the root כעס 'vex' to indicate something that Israel does to YHWH by means of idolatrous behavior.

9.23: The same root (אמן 'firm, trustworthy') is used both here (לֹא הֶאֱמַנְתֶּם לֹו [you did not believe him]) and in the Song (SoM 20: בָּנִים לֹא־אֵמֻן בָּם [children with no faithfulness in them]) to address Israel's failure to keep faith with YHWH.

9.26–29: As noted above, these verses relate Moses's thought experiment on the outcome of YHWH's decision to destroy his people, taking into account what YHWH's (and Israel's) enemies will surely think. Something similar occurs in SoM 26–27, where it is YHWH who performs the thought experiment.

9.26: I observed above that שִׁחֵת (he/it became corrupt) in 9.12 is exactly parallel to SoM 5, with עַם 'people' as subject. Here in 9.26, Israel – represented again by עַם – is now the object of אַל־תַּשְׁחֵת (do not destroy; the Hiphil and Piel forms convey the same meaning), whereas YHWH is the subject. The two occurrences in Deuteronomy 9 can be seen as a play on its use in the Song of Moses. In the Song, after the people have become corrupt (SoM 5: שִׁחֵת), YHWH initially decides to destroy them but changes his mind about it after musing on the consequences. The same sequence takes place in Deuteronomy 9 (with שִׁחֵת appearing in 9.12), except that it is Moses who does the thinking for YHWH and then specifically entreats him with a negated instance of the root שחת in 9.26.

The noun עַם 'people' is an integral part of the play on שִׁחֵת (he/it became corrupt), as can be seen from the preceding paragraph, but עַם participates in yet another parallel with the Song by being paired with the noun נַחֲלָה 'inheritance' where each of them has a possessive pronominal suffix. In his direct address to YHWH here in Deuteronomy 9, Moses describes Israel to YHWH as עַמְּךָ וְנַחֲלָתְךָ (your nation, your inheritance); in SoM 9, the narrators of that verse's third-person speech (the ancestors and elders mentioned in SoM 7cd) describe Israel's relationship to YHWH with the same terms in parallel lines of poetry: עַמּוֹ ... נַחֲלָתוֹ (his nation ... his inheritance). The narrative context in both places is YHWH's taking a people as his own and bringing them into possession of a land of their own.

Finally, although this is a minor point, 9.26 does happen to use the same noun that SoM 3 does in describing YHWH's "greatness": גֹּדֶל.

9.27: Just as in the Song, the imperative זְכֹר (remember!) is used here to introduce an appeal to former generations. In SoM 7, the Israelites are commanded to remember the past by asking the mass of their ancestors to recount it to them. Here in Deuteronomy 9, YHWH is the addressee and was himself present in the past, so Moses implores him to remember Israel's ancestors directly (and by name).

9.28: This verse and SoM 27 share the phrase פֶּן־יֹאמְרוּ (lest they say), which further has as its subject in each place a singular noun denoting a group with whom Israel and YHWH are in conflict. Moreover, the content of the hypothetical speech of these adversaries is to minimize the extent and effectiveness of YHWH's actions. In the Song, the unnamed enemies specifically deny YHWH's involvement in Israel's military defeat, taking the credit for themselves. In Deuteronomy 9, the Egyptians interpret YHWH's punishment of Israel (announced but not yet carried out) as evidence of weakness on YHWH's part, particularly as evidence of an inability to secure a land for his people. In both texts, the hypothetical speech functions to persuade YHWH to refrain from destroying his people completely.

9.29: The terms עַם 'people' and נַחֲלָה 'inheritance' appear again as the phrase עַמְּךָ וְנַחֲלָתֶךָ (your people, your inheritance), a striking resemblance to their use as parallel terms in SoM 9 in a similar narrative context. On this point, see the discussion above at 9.26.

Let me summarize the strongest of these arguments that roughly the final two-thirds of Deuteronomy 9 was shaped with the Song of Moses in mind, perhaps by someone who was obeying the call to recount the former days. First, and most broadly speaking, both the poem and this section of chapter 9 portray a scene in which YHWH relents from his decision to destroy his people (at whose idolatrous practices he has taken offense) following a discourse that considers the effect on his reputation if he were to carry out the planned destruction. Beyond this general resemblance, which is not entirely unique to these two texts, they also share several words and phrases associated with identical concepts and narrative references: 1) the phrase פֶּן־יֹאמְרוּ (lest they say), introducing a hypothetical quotation of YHWH's adversaries expressing a highly undesirable interpretation of YHWH's actions; 2) the imperative זְכֹר (remember!), marking an appeal to earlier generations of Israelites; 3) the semantically and syntactically parallel clauses וְאֶמְחֶה אֶת־שְׁמָם מִתַּחַת הַשָּׁמָיִם (let me wipe out their name from under the skies) and אַשְׁבִּיתָה מֵאֱנוֹשׁ זִכְרָם (I will put an end to their mention among humanity), which are both uttered as YHWH's initial reaction to Israel's idolatry; 4) the pairing of עַם 'people' and נַחֲלָה 'inheritance' along with possessive suffixes, describing Israel's relationship to YHWH and referring to the narrative theme of

YHWH bringing Israel into possession of their own land; and 5) the use of the roots שחת 'destroy, become corrupt' and כעס 'vex' in association with Israelite idolatry. Finally, it's not just that these striking parallels appear in both texts but that the meaning of several of them is explicitly reversed with respect to the context of the relationship between YHWH and Israel. In the Song, the Israelites are to remember days gone by and to inquire of their ancestors in order to do so (SoM 7); in Deuteronomy 9, it is YHWH who is to recall the Is-raelite ancestors (9.27). In the Song, the parallel terms עַמּוֹ ... נַחֲלָתוֹ (his people ... his inheritance) occur in a context that shows YHWH creating a relation-ship of belonging between him and Israel (SoM 9); when the phrase עַמְּךָ וְנַחֲלָתְךָ appears in 9.26, it is in the mouth of Moses, imploring YHWH not to abandon that relationship.[52] The Song's use of the roots כעס 'vex' and קנא 'be jealous'[53] may have provided the inspiration for Deuteronomy 9's reversal of the fore-going motifs. In SoM 21, these two roots are used in such a way as to indicate the reciprocity that exists between YHWH and Israel: as Israel vexed YHWH, so will he vex them; as Israel made YHWH jealous, so will he make them jeal-ous. In Deuteronomy 9, although the root כעס does appear there, it is instead the root שחת that is subject to a question of reciprocity: Israel has become corrupt (9.12: שִׁחֵת), and now Moses must plead with YHWH to refrain from destroying (9.26: אַל־תַּשְׁחֵת [do not destroy]) Israel in reciprocation.

I believe it is clear, then, that Deuteronomy 9 has borrowed in a number of ways from the Song, including the use of שחת 'destroy, become corrupt' in association with material idolatry, which is a parade example of the Song's influence on Deuteronomy outside of the exilic frame identified by Levenson. In fact, in seven of the nine places that it appears elsewhere in Deuteronomy, שחת denotes either Israelite idolatry or YHWH's (possible) reaction to that idolatry.[54] I now wish to turn from idolatry specifically to the broader generational aspect of the theme of corruption and integrity. This element of generational continuity is signaled especially by the noun דּוֹר 'generation' as well as by the language of descent in general. Thus the other main keywords are אָב 'father; ancestor' and בֵּן 'son, child; descendant', although vegetal imagery is also pertinent.

To begin with, the qualities of successive generations are a major preoc-cupation for the Song, where the noun דּוֹר 'generation' appears four times. In its two occurrences in SoM 7, it simply invokes the succession of genera-

---

52. Cf. further 9.12, where YHWH tells Moses that Israel is עַמְּךָ, that is, "your [Moses's] people."

53. Unlike כעס, the root קנא is not picked up by Deuteronomy 9.

54. 4.16, 25, 31; 9.12, 26; 10.10; 31.29. The other two appear in the law concerning the treat-ment of trees during a siege (20.19, 20).

tions, parallel to the passage of time: יְמוֹת עוֹלָם ... שְׁנוֹת דּוֹר־וָדוֹר (the days of old ... the years of generation after generation). The word also appears twice in conjunction with nouns denoting perversion or unnaturalness of some sort: SoM 5b: דּוֹר עִקֵּשׁ וּפְתַלְתֹּל (a crooked and perverse generation); SoM 20c: דּוֹר תַּהְפֻּכֹת הֵמָּה (they are a generation of reversals). Notably, the other halves of each of these poetic lines casts the Israelites as children who are deficient in some way: SoM 5a: לֹא בָּנָיו מוּמָם (not his children at all); SoM 20d: בָּנִים לֹא־אֵמֻן בָּם (children with no reliability in them).[55]

As a whole, Deuteronomy reflects this generational preoccupation through its focus on the extent to which each successive generation of Israelites acts in accordance with the nation's "original identity," that is, whether any given generation of Israelites recompenses YHWH for his initial solicitude for the nation. Whenever there is an Israelite failure to reciprocate, Deuteronomy points out the contrast with YHWH's steadfastness in action. Further, and in coordination with its overall interest in varied points of view, Deuteronomy also imagines situations of dialogue between successive Israelite generations where the topic is each generation's performance in recompensing YHWH and the consequences thereof.

In laying out the evidence for Deuteronomy's unique emphasis on this theme, I will begin by summarizing the seven occurrences of דּוֹר 'generation' in Deuteronomy outside of the Song. The three most closely related to the theme are 1.35 and 2.14 (which belong to a single narrative context in Dtr$_1$) and 29.21 (Dtr$_2$). In 1.35 (following a verse that alludes syntactically and semantically to SoM 19–20ø[56]), YHWH characterizes an entire generation as רַע 'evil' and pronounces judgment on them (much as happens in SoM 20a–d). Deuteronomy 2.14 relates the fulfillment of YHWH's pronouncement, char-

---

55. The contexts of דּוֹר 'generation' in SoM 5 and SoM 20cd are linked in several other ways. Consider, for example, the extensive assonance between the phrasing in both poetic lines. Further, while אֵמֻן 'faithfulness' appears in SoM 20d as a quality lacking in the Israelites, the nearly identical noun formation אֱמוּנָה 'faithfulness' appears in SoM 4 (in the near context of SoM 5) as a quality that characterizes YHWH. Likewise, in the near contexts of each occurrence of דּוֹר, Israel and YHWH show opposite tendencies with regard to reciprocity or recompense: in SoM 6, the Israelites are accused of failing to reciprocate YHWH's behavior toward them (הֲ־לַיהוָה תִּגְמְלוּ־זֹאת [is this how you requite YHWH?]), while in SoM 21, YHWH shows a strict adherence to the principle of recompense, treating the Israelites exactly as they treated him: הֵם קִנְאוּנִי בְלֹא־אֵל כִּעֲסוּנִי בְּהַבְלֵיהֶם וַאֲנִי אַקְנִיאֵם בְּלֹא־עָם בְּגוֹי נָבָל אַכְעִיסֵם (they made me jealous with a no-god, vexed me with their vanities, so I will make them jealous with a no-people, with a foolish nation I'll vex them). Lastly – although this is evidence not from the Song itself but rather from its reception in Deuteronomy – the roots שחת 'destroy, become corrupt' (juxtaposed with דּוֹר in SoM 5) and כעס 'vex' (appearing in SoM 21b, d immediately following דּוֹר in SoM 20) are both reused in distinctive ways by Deuteronomy in association with the topic of idolatry, as discussed at length above.

56. See my discussion of these parallels above in the introduction to this chapter.

acterizing the generation in question not as evil but simply as אַנְשֵׁי הַמִּלְחָמָה (warriors). An entire generation is also the subject in 29.21, distinguished in this case not by their lack of loyalty to YHWH but by their location in time as הַדּוֹר הָאַחֲרוֹן (the latter generation). Implicitly, then, this generation's questions and the answer they receive concern a generation that came earlier and that could presumably – based on its fate, at least – be described as "evil" (29.21–27). Although 29.21–27 is not an intergenerational dialogue in the sense of two Israelite generations speaking directly with each other, one generation is nevertheless being talked about by another.

The keyword דּוֹר 'generation' also appears in 7.9, where it highlights YHWH's consistent reciprocity towards those who keep faith with him: לְאֶלֶף דּוֹר (to a thousand generations). The subsequent verse proclaims YHWH's direct reciprocity towards those who "hate" him, which, although it is worded without דּוֹר, conforms with the idea that the punishment for an evil generation's actions is limited to that generation and that a later generation can look back unaffected by it, as in, for example, 29.21–27.[57]

There are, finally, three occurrences of דּוֹר 'generation' in Deuteronomy 23 (vv. 3, 4, 9), which seem to have no connection to the theme of generational continuity/discontinuity, dealing as they do with whether and the point at which certain categories of people may (Edomites, Egyptians) or may not (the מַמְזֵר, Ammonites, Moabites) become part of the Israelite people. Indeed, the reasoning behind the prohibitions does not consider the effect on Israel's continuity of behavior with YHWH, as is the case, for example, in 7.3–4, where intermarriage is seen as having the potential to turn the next generation away from worshiping YHWH.

As 7.3–4 indicates, the theme of generational continuity or integrity is also of interest for Deuteronomic passages that do not contain the noun דּוֹר 'generation'. Here I will survey the major ways this overarching concern is worked out in Deuteronomy, which are: 1) distinctions between the moral qualities (and fates) of Israelite generations; 2) statements of YHWH's transgenerational loyalty to Israel; 3) statements of Israel's (potential, required) loyalty to YHWH in every generation, including instructions for Israelites to pass on their experiences with YHWH and YHWH's commands to following generations; and 4) instances of conversation between Israelite generations.

First, the Song itself evidences a concern for distinguishing between various Israelite generations in the abstract, particularly according to their moral qualities and places in Israelite history, characterizing some

---

57. This is by contrast to Deuteronomy 5.9–10 (= Exodus 20.5–6) and Exodus 34.6–7, where punishment is passed on.

as "crooked and perverse" (SoM 5) and as "backwards" (SoM 20) while also introducing earlier generations who are able to testify to YHWH's acts on behalf of the nation (SoM 7). This same distinguishing tendency is apparent elsewhere in Deuteronomy, although with a greater emphasis on the consequences of a particular generation's actions, at 1.39; 4.25; 7.3–4; 11.2–7; 24.16; 29.21–27; and 31.20. Outside of Deuteronomy, the rhetoric of schematically distinguishing one generation from another in moral terms appears only in passages that are quite possibly influenced by Deuteronomy anyway (i.e. Exodus 32.7–14; Numbers 14.11–25).[58]

Second, although direct statements of YHWH's transgenerational loyalty to the Israelites do not appear in the Song,[59] such statements nevertheless form a second important outworking of the corruption/integrity theme in Deuteronomy, where they serve as a foil to the Israelites' lack of loyalty to YHWH. Most of these statements have to do with YHWH fulfilling his promise of land to earlier generations by in fact giving the land to later generations: 1.8, 21; 6.3, 10, 23; 7.9, 12–13; 9.5; 10.11; 11.9, 21; 19.8; 26.3, 15; 27.3; 28.11; 30.5, 20; 31.7, 20. Some contain no mention of land at all, speaking only of YHWH treating subsequent generations according to the covenant, love, promise, or pleasure that dictated his earlier treatment of Israel: 4.31, 37; 7.8; 8.18; 13.18; 29.12; 30.9. Such statements do appear outside of Deuteronomy, but much less frequently, especially when the ones that may in fact depend on Deuteronomy are removed from consideration.[60]

Third, although the Song serves as an indictment of a later generation

---

58. Although the P story of the flood, where nearly all of humankind becomes corrupt despite starting off well, shows a superficial similarity to this theme, it is ultimately quite different. For example, while the root שחת 'destroy, become corrupt' appears in Genesis 6.11, 12, it is used there in a Niphal form and refers not to idolatry but to violence. Further, although Noah is said to be exemplary among the people of his generation (the usage in Genesis 6.9 is actually plural: דרתיו (his generations); cf. the J version in Genesis 7.1: בַּדּוֹר הַזֶּה [in this generation]), the idea is of a progressive and cumulative corruption (corresponding to the Priestly conception of contamination) rather than of a single generation exhibiting corruption without a particular relationship to preceding or subsequent generations. Some other passages offer a negative characterization comparable to the way the Song uses עִקֵּשׁ 'crooked', פְּתַלְתֹּל 'perverse', and תַהְפֻּכֹת 'reversings' in SoM 5 and 20, but they are speaking not of a specific generation but of the people as a whole; see the epithet קְשֵׁה-עֹרֶף (stiff-necked) in Exodus 32.9; 33.3, 5; 34.9, which Deuteronomy also uses (9.6, 13; 10.16; cf. 31.27). Exodus 1.8 shows a different kind of similarity to this idea, except that it concerns a succession not of generations but of individual pharaohs; note that the verse contains two items that also appear together in SoM 17 (although in the plural): חָדָשׁ 'new' and the phrase לֹא יָדַע (he did not know) in a relative clause.

59. Notwithstanding general praise of YHWH as trustworthy, as in SoM 4: אֵל אֱמוּנָה (a god of trustworthiness).

60. See Genesis 24.7; 26.3; 50.24; and Exodus 13.5, 11. Those appearing in D-influenced passages make up almost half the total: Exodus 32.13; 33.1; and Numbers 14.16, 23.

(or of later generations) of the Israelite people for failing to live up to the experiences of their own ancestors regarding YHWH's generous treatment of them, it contains little that specifically exhorts them to transgenerational loyalty to YHWH. It is, rather, implied: if certain generations can be noticeably deviant (SoM 5b, 20c) and lacking in faithfulness (SoM 20d), then the imperative must be to adhere steadfastly to YHWH in every generation. The rest of Deuteronomy, however, takes this kind of exhortation much further, where virtually all such exhortations are couched in terms of maintaining obedience to YHWH's commands. Of these, about half are combined with (the possibility of) the fulfillment of YHWH's promise of land to earlier generations (as is the case with statements of YHWH's loyalty, discussed above): 4.1, 40; 6.3, 18, 7.12–13; 8.1; 11.8–9; 12.1; 31.20.[61] The others mention not possession of the land but rather more general outcomes of prosperity for the Israelites: 5.29; 6.2; 7.9; 12.25, 28; 29.25;[62] 30.2. There are numerous examples outside of Deuteronomy of exhortations to the Israelites to transgenerational loyalty to YHWH, but they use specific language that differs from the expressions in Deuteronomy. For example, while the sabbath law in Exodus 31.12–17 contains references to דֹרֹתֵיכֶם (your generations; 31.13) and דֹרֹתָם (their generations; 31.16), Deuteronomy does not actually use the word דּוֹר in hortatory contexts. Further, Exodus calls the sabbath an אוֹת 'sign' (31.13, 17) and a בְּרִית 'covenant' (31.16), words that Deuteronomy uses in very different senses. To take another example, the phrase חֻקַּת עוֹלָם (an eternal statute) is very common in Leviticus, where it is almost always accompanied by לְדֹרֹתֵיכֶם (throughout your generations).[63] Neither phrase, however, appears in Deuteronomy, which also engages in second-person address but tends, in exhortations, to indicate other generations by referring to אֲבֹתֶיךָ (your fathers) and to בִּנְךָ (your son) or בָּנֶיךָ (your sons). To summarize, although Deuteronomy does not exhibit entirely unique ways of speaking of the Israelites' obedience to YHWH's commands, it does sound fairly distinct when it puts them in a transgenerational context.

Additionally, a corollary to Deuteronomy's emphasis on maintaining obedience to YHWH's commands is the requirement to pass the commands on to subsequent generations, from generation to generation: 4.10, 6.7, 11.19, 31.12–13. Note that 4.9 also calls for the Horeb generation to pass along their

---

61. Of this subset of passages, 31.20 is unique insofar as it is phrased negatively. It does not mention commands but speaks of Israel violating the covenant.

62. Of this subset of passages, 29.25 is unique insofar as it is phrased negatively. It does not mention commands but speaks of Israel worshiping gods other than YHWH.

63. Leviticus 3.17; 7.36; 10.9; 16.29, 31, 34; 17.7; 23.14, 21, 31, 41; 24.3; cf. Leviticus 6.11: חָק־ עוֹלָם לְדֹרֹתֵיכֶם.

experiences with YHWH, in addition to the commands they received.[64] Also, 11.21, which is a continuation of 11.19, connects the act of passing on the commands (distinct from the act of obeying them) with the concept of possession of the land. This specific combination does not appear in the other Pentateuchal sources.

Fourth and finally, there are two instances of Israelite intergenerational conversation in Deuteronomy outside of the Song: 6.20–25 and 29.21–27. In both cases, the later generation (indicated by "your son" or "your sons") initiates the conversation with an inquiry, as is the case in the Song, where the Israelite performers of the Song are to ask their ancestors about earlier times (SoM 7). In 6.20–25, the question has to do with YHWH's commands, and the answer gives the previous generation's experiences with YHWH (specifically, the rescue from Egypt) as the ground for those commands. In 29.21–27, partially discussed above, the question (which is posed also by "the foreigner who will come from a far land" as well as by "all the nations") has to do with a previous generation's experiences with YHWH, and the answer portrays these experiences as the outcome of their forsaking YHWH's covenant. The only two other cases of intergenerational conversation occur in Exodus 12.26–27 and 13.8, for both of which Deuteronomic redaction or composition has been proposed.[65]

YHWH's Sovereignty Over Boundaries

SoM 8–9 are the main locus of this theme in the Song: YHWH[66] separates humankind into nations, one nation for each בן אלם (son of the gods), and gives each nation an inheritable/ancestral territory with fixed borders; under this distribution, YHWH and the nation of Israel belong together.[67] Levenson has pointed out parallels between SoM 8–9 on the one hand and 4.19 and 29.25 on the other, focusing on YHWH's action of "parceling out gods to the nations."[68] The parallels between 4.19 and 29.25 themselves are striking, extending to vocabulary and phraseology.

---

64. See Exodus 10.2, which may have been redacted by a Deuteronomy-influenced hand (Hyatt 1971:123, 137).

65. Hyatt 1971:137, 143.

66. I.e. with עֶלְיוֹן 'most high' taken as an epithet of YHWH.

67. Other verses in the Song gain in intelligibility in connection with the narrative alluded to in SoM 8–9, particularly YHWH's acquiring, creating, and establishing of the people in SoM 6, but also YHWH's care and solicitous generosity in installing the people in their land in SoM 10–14 and even his providing atonement for both land and people in SoM 43.

68. Levenson 1975:213, 215.

4.19 (excerpted):

וְנִדַּחְתָּ וְהִשְׁתַּחֲוִיתָ לָהֶם וַעֲבַדְתָּם אֲשֶׁר חָלַק יְהוָה אֱלֹהֶיךָ אֹתָם לְכֹל הָעַמִּים תַּחַת כָּל־הַשָּׁמָיִם:

[Lest ...] you be drawn away and bow down to them and serve them,
whom YHWH your god has allotted to all the peoples under all the
skies.

29.25:

וַיֵּלְכוּ וַיַּעַבְדוּ אֱלֹהִים אֲחֵרִים וַיִּשְׁתַּחֲווּ לָהֶם אֱלֹהִים אֲשֶׁר לֹא־יְדָעוּם וְלֹא חָלַק לָהֶם:

They went and served other gods and bowed down to them, gods
whom they had not known and whom he had not allotted to them.

The parallels between 4.19 and 29.25 are comprised of the following elements: Israel as the subject of a verb of motion (whether להנדח 'to be drawn
away' or ללכת 'to go'), of לעבד 'to serve', and of להשתחוות 'to bow down'; a plural
number of divinities as the object of לעבד; the relative pronoun אֲשֶׁר 'which,
whom'; YHWH as the subject of the verb לחלק 'to allot' within the relative
clause; the plural divinities as the object of לחלק; and the preposition ל 'to,
for' introducing the parties to whom said divinities were (or were not) par-
celed out. Narratively speaking, in 4.19 and 29.25, YHWH assigns certain
deities to other nations, and Israel is (in danger of) serving those deities as
well. One difference is that 4.19 refers to the future and 29.25 to the past.

The parallels between these two prose verses and SoM 8–9 have to do
not so much with precise lexical matches, to which I have already alluded,
but do involve the theme of YHWH overseeing a process of allotment by
which peoples, territories, and gods are put into fixed relationships with
each other – one people to one territory to one god. The root חלק 'allot' appears in SoM 9, not as the verb לחלק 'to allot' but as the noun חֵלֶק 'allotment';
Israel is the nation that is YHWH's חֵלֶק. In 4.19 and 29.25, the process of allotment is treated summarily: YHWH assigns gods to nations. In SoM 8–9, the
nations, not the gods, are the object of YHWH's actions, and the process is
more complicated. Taking the number of divine beings into account (לְמִסְפַּר
בְּנֵי אֵלִם [according to the number of the sons of the gods]), YHWH separates
humankind (בְּהַפְרִידוֹ בְּנֵי אָדָם [when he distributed the sons of Adam]) into "peoples" (עַמִּים), assigning to these peoples their rightful territorial possessions
(בְּהַנְחֵל עֶלְיוֹן גּוֹיִם [when the high one made the nations (into) inheritances]; יַצֵּב
גְּבֻלֹת עַמִּים [he set up the boundaries of the peoples]). Then the description
broadens, such that YHWH is not only the agent of allotment but also a recipient, with the nation of Israel being YHWH's allotted portion and rightful

possession (כִּי חֵלֶק יְהוָֹה עַמּוֹ יַעֲקֹב חֶבֶל נַחֲלָתוֹ) [for his people is YHWH's allotment, Jacob the boundary-rope of his inheritance]).[69]

Now, while it is clear that 4.19 and 29.25 draw on the Song in the way they use the verb לַחֲלֹק 'to allot', theirs is not the only Song-dependent manifestation of the theme of YHWH as boundary-maker and apportioner of gods and nations. I will continue my analysis by examining the ways in which other passages in the exilic frame elaborate on this theme, and then I will discuss how other passages in Deuteronomy show the same – and still further – elaborations. The passages within the exilic frame that I will discuss first are 4.19–21, 27; 29.25–27; and 30.1–5.

As already discussed, in 4.19–21 YHWH allots gods to all nations (4.19), which is a verbal and thematic elaboration of SoM 8–9. Further, by removing the Israelites geographically from the land of Egypt (4.20), YHWH exerts mastery over human national boundaries (though the word "boundary" does not appear here), as he does in SoM 8c. Since the events of 4.20 do not take place in primordial time – insofar as they transgress existing boundaries rather than establishing them for the first time – they must also be seen as an elaboration, rather than as a simple parallel, of SoM 8–9.[70] YHWH again appears in the role of giver of rightfully possessed lands to peoples, by giving land to the Israelites as their נַחֲלָה 'inheritance' (4.21), which is parallel to (or a specifically elaborated instance of) בְּהַנְחֵל עֶלְיוֹן גּוֹיִם (when the high one made the nations [into] inheritances) in SoM 8a. Further, the Israelites themselves are said to be YHWH's עַם נַחֲלָה (inheritance-people) (4.20), a phrase comprised of two terms that are parallel to each other in SoM 9.

In 4.27, YHWH again shows mastery over human boundaries when he reverses the assignments of lands and peoples that he is said to have made in SoM 8–9, at least in the case of Israel, by scattering the Israelites and driv-

---

69. This shift may be a play on the possible semantic relationships between the verb לְהַנְחִיל 'to cause to inherit' and its syntactic direct objects. An object of לְהַנְחִיל may either be the entity that rightfully possesses or the entity that is rightfully possessed, as illustrated in Deuteronomy 21.16: בְּיוֹם הַנְחִילוֹ אֶת־בָּנָיו אֵת אֲשֶׁר־יִהְיֶה לוֹ (on the day he causes his sons to inherit his belongings). At the beginning of SoM 8–9, it seems that the גּוֹיִם 'nations' are being given their rightful possessions. Indeed, when לְהַנְחִיל has only one object, that object is the entity that rightfully possesses. (See Deuteronomy 12.10; 19.3; 1 Samuel 2.8; Jeremiah 3.18; 12.14; Ezekiel 46.18; Proverbs 13.22; cf. 1 Chronicles 28.8.) In SoM 9, however, the nation of Israel has become the entity that is rightfully possessed, described in an explicitly geographic manner: חֶבֶל נַחֲלָתוֹ (the boundary-rope of his inheritance). It would seem that as territories are rightfully possessed by nations, so are nations rightfully possessed by gods, according to SoM 8–9.

70. Another dimension of YHWH's authority over human boundaries is shown by his control of who exactly may cross into the land, i.e. Moses may not (4.21).

ing them to the territories of other nations: וְהֵפִיץ ... אֶתְכֶם בָּעַמִּים ... גּוֹיִם אֲשֶׁר יְנַהֵג יְהֹוָה אֶתְכֶם שָׁמָּה (he will scatter you ... among the peoples, ... the nations where YHWH drives you). The nouns עַמִּים 'peoples' and גּוֹיִם 'nations' appear to be metonyms for the territories they possess, given the spatial connotations of the verbs לְהָפִיץ 'to scatter' and לְנַהֵג 'to drive' and of the preposition בּ 'in'. Significantly, YHWH does not simply send the Israelites back to Egypt, which would be a specific reversal of his actions in 4.20, but he scatters them to many nations, which recalls the more cosmic setting mentioned in both 4.19 and SoM 8.

In 29.25–27, in addition to the already discussed motif of YHWH allotting gods to nations and here, specifically, with respect to Israel (29.25: אֱלֹהִים אֲשֶׁר ... לֹא חָלַק לָהֶם [gods whom ... he had not allotted to them]), there also reappears the motif of YHWH reversing or undoing a previously made assignment of land and people, again in the case of Israel (29.27: וַיִּתְּשֵׁם ... מֵעַל אַדְמָתָם ... וַיַּשְׁלִכֵם אֶל־אֶרֶץ אַחֶרֶת [he rooted them up ... from their land ... and cast them into another land]). Also like 4.27, 29.26 exhibits an instance of metonymy between land and people, except that here it is the land that stands for the human inhabitants, rather than vice versa: וַיִּחַר־אַף יְהֹוָה בָּאָרֶץ הַהִוא (YHWH grew angry against that land).[71] In 30.1–5, we see the same features again, including an additional elaboration.[72] The words גּוֹיִם 'nations' (30.1) and עַמִּים 'peoples' (30.3) are again used as metonyms for the lands inhabited by those peoples, given that they represent places to which the Israelites can be driven (30.1) and scattered (30.3) and from which they can be gathered (30.3). Further, by this driving and scattering of the Israelites into other lands, YHWH again shows his mastery over human boundaries, not by creating boundaries but rather by moving the Israelites across them. YHWH's mastery in this

71. This passage also shows an instance of compensatory reciprocity of the kind found in SoM 21, which similarly deals with god-nation relationships (but where the word play employs the roots קנא 'jealous' and כעס 'vex'; the concept of otherness represented by the play on the adjective אַחֵר 'other' in 29.25, 27 is only implicit in SoM 21): once the Israelites violate the god-nation relationship that YHWH has allotted for them by serving אֱלֹהִים אֲחֵרִים (other gods; 29.25), YHWH then also violates the nation-land relationship that he has created for them by removing them to אֶרֶץ אַחֶרֶת (another land; 29.27). By comparison to the Song, this passage from the exilic frame adds a focus on land.

72. Like 29.25–27 (see the previous footnote), this passage also shows an instance of compensatory reciprocity of the kind found in SoM 21. Here the word play centers on the verb לשוב 'to return.' Once the Israelites "return" (וְשַׁבְתָּ; 30.2) to their designated god-nation relationship with YHWH by means of obeying him, YHWH will also return to the relationship by "turning [their] captivity" (וְשָׁב ... אֶת־שְׁבוּתְךָ; 30.3) and "returning and gathering them" or "again gathering [them]" (וְשָׁב וְקִבֶּצְךָ; 30.3). Insofar as 30.2–3 exhibits not a simple parallel or rewording of the reciprocal antagonism of SoM 21 but instead reverses it, envisioning a reciprocal return, it should be characterized as an elaboration of the Song's contents; note that it is intertwined with the novel elaboration of the theme of YHWH's mastery over human boundaries also contained in 30.1–5.

regard is further represented by the Nifal participle of נדח 'to drive' and by another phrase metonymically indicating the locations to which the Israelites have been driven, קְצֵה הַשָּׁמָיִם (the ends of the heavens), both of which occur in 30.4. This passage further elaborates the theme under discussion by envisioning YHWH remaking the assignment of the Israelites to a specific land that he had earlier undone; note particularly לָשׁוּב 'to return' in 30.3, לְקַבֵּץ 'to gather' in 30.3, 4, לָקַחַת 'to take' in 30.4 (cf. the use of the same verb in 4.20, denoting the first iteration of the land-people assignment that is being remade here), and וֶהֱבִיאֲךָ יְהוָה אֱלֹהֶיךָ אֶל־הָאָרֶץ אֲשֶׁר־יָרְשׁוּ אֲבֹתֶיךָ וִירִשְׁתָּהּ (YHWH your god will bring you into the land that your ancestors took possession of and you will take possession of it) in 30.5. While both the people and land of Israel are described as נַחֲלָה 'inheritance' in 4.20, 21, no forms of the root נחל 'inherit' appear in 30.1–5. Instead, the root ירשׁ 'possess' is used, as a verb, and the land alone is the object of possession (in 30.5, twice).

The elaboration that consists of YHWH remaking existing assignments of lands and peoples appears in Deuteronomy outside of the exilic frame. In 2.12b, 24, 31; 3.2; 19.1–3, 8, 10, and 14 (like 4.21, 27; 29.27; and 30.1, 3–5 in the exilic frame), it concerns the land that YHWH assigns to Israel, dealing exclusively with the moment of Israel coming into possession of that land for the first time (while passages in the exilic frame also depict the moments when YHWH removes them from that land and brings them back to it). In 2.5, 9, 12a, 21, 22, YHWH shows his mastery over the territorial boundaries of other nations, without particular reference to Israel except insofar as Israel is specifically forbidden from attempting to take their land.

Some of these same parallels to the Song and elaborations thereof appear in Deuteronomy outside of the exilic frame. The most basic, the concept of YHWH assigning lands and nations,[73] appears in Deuteronomy 2.5, 9, 12, 19; 19.1, 2, 8, 10. The idea of YHWH further showing his mastery over human boundaries by remaking some of the earlier assignments appears in 2.12, 21, 22, 24, 31; 3.2; and 19.1 (and, implicitly, 19.8), where YHWH gives one nation's land to another nation. In the passages drawn from the exilic frame, just discussed, this remaking of earlier land-nation assignments centers on YHWH's dealings with Israel, whether removing them from the land to which he had assigned them or, subsequently, returning them to that land. The passages under discussion here, especially those from chapter 2, highlight YHWH's mastery over the territorial boundaries of other nations.

---

73. The motif of YHWH giving land to Israel – which is ubiquitous in Deuteronomy and quite common throughout the Pentateuch – could be considered one particular manifestation of this concept; however, I am focusing on passages that show YHWH allotting land to Israel as one nation among many or allotting land to other nations entirely. Such passages are much closer to the concept contained in the Song (SoM 8–9).

None of the passages discussed above are taken over by Deuteronomy from earlier Pentateuchal sources; they are seen as relatively free compositions of the Deuteronomistic authors. This is especially clear in Deuteronomy 2 and the early part of 3, in which texts that are adapted from the Elohistic source (2.6–8, 13–16, 26–29, 32–37) alternate with new compositions (2.2–5, 9–12, 17–25, 30–31; 3.1–11).[74] Only in the new texts do this theme and its elaborations appear.

Now, this theme is admittedly not completely unknown in the other Pentateuchal sources, albeit with different phrasing or with different actors in view. Specific parts of the Abraham cycle present the most notable instances of vaguely similar material, which, if they are parallel to anything in Deuteronomy, are parallel to what I have been calling elaborations of the theme as contained in the Song. But of YHWH dividing humankind into nations in primordial time according to the number of divine beings and assigning them inheritable territories – the theme itself as expressed in SoM 8–9 – we see nothing. However, we do encounter what could be called the results of such primordial actions, insofar as certain lands and certain individuals or peoples are understood already to belong together: Genesis 12.1 (אַרְצְךָ [your land]), 5 (אַרְצָה כְּנַעַן [to the land of Canaan] *bis*), 6 (וְהַכְּנַעֲנִי אָז בָּאָרֶץ[75] [the Canaanite was then in the land]); 15.7 (אוּר כַּשְׂדִּים [Ur of the Chaldeans]), 13 (אֶרֶץ לֹא[76] אֶת־הָאָרֶץ הַזֹּאת ... לָהֶם [a land not theirs]), 18–21 (אֶת־הַקֵּינִי וְאֶת־הַקְּנִזִּי וְאֶת הַקַּדְמֹנִי וְאֶת־ הַחִתִּי וְאֶת־הַפְּרִזִּי וְאֶת־הָרְפָאִים וְאֶת־הָאֱמֹרִי וְאֶת־הַכְּנַעֲנִי וְאֶת־הַגִּרְגָּשִׁי וְאֶת־הַיְבוּסִי [this land ... the Kenite, the Kenizzite, the Kadmonite, the Hittite, the Perizzite, the Rephaim, the Amorite, the Canaanite, the Girgashite, and the Jebusite])[77]. Further, YHWH shows mastery over these boundaries by moving people across them: Genesis 12.1 (לֶךְ־לְךָ מֵאַרְצְךָ ... אֶל־הָאָרֶץ אֲשֶׁר אַרְאֶךָּ[78] [go from your land ... to the land that I will show you]); 15.7 (הוֹצֵאתִיךָ מֵאוּר כַּשְׂדִּים [I brought you out of Ur of the Chaldeans]). Finally, YHWH shows mastery by giving (or at least by promising to give) currently possessed territories to others: Genesis 12.7 (לְזַרְעֲךָ אֶתֵּן אֶת־הָאָרֶץ הַזֹּאת [to your descendants will I give this land]); 15.7 (לָתֶת לְךָ אֶת־הָאָרֶץ הַזֹּאת לְרִשְׁתָּהּ [to give you this land to take possession of]).

74. For the division of these verses, see Joel S. Baden 2009:137–41. For arguments for assigning Deuteronomy 3.1–3 to D rather than to E (pace Baden), see Mayes 1979:142–43.

75. Although this particular phrasing in Genesis 12.6 suggests a non-identification of people and land (insofar as it implies that "the Canaanite" was not or will not be always in the land), in combination with אֶרֶץ כְּנַעַן in Genesis 12.5 it shows that "Canaan" is not just the name of the land itself but also of a people, such that the two can belong together.

76. That is, the land in question belongs to some other nation.

77. Here people and land are treated as identical, both objects of YHWH's giving and as such clearly related to each other.

78. See also Genesis 12.4–6, where Abram obeys the command given here.

Situations of Speaking

With speaking, or quotation, it is not particularly the case that Deuteronomy has adopted distinctive vocabulary from the Song. Although the occurrences of the verb לאמר 'to say' in the Song are important to its functioning, and although the verb appears numerous times throughout Deuteronomy, the argument can hardly be made that the Deuteronomic uses depend on the Song; the action of speaking and this verb denoting it are so common throughout biblical texts as to lack distinctiveness. Nevertheless, Deuteronomy does mirror some of the speeches that are indicated in the Song by לאמר and by other verbs. In this section I will argue that Deuteronomy both adopts the form of quoted, layered speech that plays such an important role in the Song and in the performance history created for it by Deuteronomy 31.19–22, 30 as well as reproduces some of the settings of the speeches that occur in the Song. An example of the second phenomenon would be the question-and-answer between ancestor and descendant that takes place in SoM 7–17 (interrupted though this passage is towards its end by the voice of the Song) and is mirrored in Deuteronomy 6.20–25.

Since the layered speech of the Song is analyzed extensively in the previous chapter of this book, here I will give only a few memory-inducing examples. The most notable examples of layered speech in the Song include SoM 26ab and 40b, where the voice of the Song quotes YHWH in the act of quoting himself, whether something he has said in the past (SoM 26ab) or something he will say in order to indicate the solemnity of his intent to take vengeance (SoM 40b). Another example is SoM 27cd, where the voice of the Song is quoting YHWH in the act, this time, of quoting the hypothetical speech of enemies. Furthermore, once the Song is read within the performance history created for it by its introduction in Deuteronomy 31.19–22, 30, several more layers of quotation are added to every instance that already occurs within the Song. For example, while the intended performers of the Song are singing it and thereby quoting YHWH quoting himself (SoM 26ab, 40b), they are also thereby quoting their ancestors who taught them the Song, who themselves were quoting all the Israelites assembled on the plains of Moab, who in turn were quoting Moses delivering it on the plains of Moab, who – finally – was quoting YHWH's act of composition that was delivered to him (and Joshua) in the tent of meeting on the plains of Moab. Moreover, because YHWH (in the narrative of Deuteronomy 31) creates this performance history with a public intention, the layers of quotation work in a forward-looking direction as well, such that YHWH's act of composing the Song (or at least of presenting it to Moses) constitutes an advance quotation of what Moses (and Joshua) will say to the assembled Israelites, which quotes in advance what they will say to their descendants, which quotes in advance what generation after generation of Israelites will pass on, which quotes in advance what the current generation at any given time will be saying whenever they too perform the Song, which is to quote, for example, the speech of the earth and skies in SoM 4, the speech of the ancestors in SoM 8–17, the speech of YHWH in SoM 20–30, in which YHWH, as already discussed, quotes both himself in SoM 26ab and his enemies in SoM 27cd. The entirety of the performance tradition as imagined by Deuteronomy is present in any and every moment of performance.

Deuteronomy exhibits layered quotation, or re-performance, as much as or even more than the Song does. First of all, virtually the whole book of Deuteronomy is on some level a quotation, in which the narrator is quoting Moses. Further, to return to SoM 27cd for a moment, note that this passage may be described as a three-layer quotation (within the Song itself), since there are three overlapping voices: the voice of the Song (beginning at SoM 1), the voice of YHWH (beginning at SoM 20), and the hypothetical voice of enemies (speaking only in SoM 27cd). When read in the context of Deuteronomy, SoM 27cd becomes a four- or five-layer quotation, with the narrator quoting Moses – who is quoting the Song quoting YHWH hypothetically quoting enemies. Four passages elsewhere in Deuteronomy may also be described as three- or four-layer quotations – three if the counting starts with Moses and four if the counting starts with the Deuteronomic narrator.

1.42: Here the narrator is quoting Moses (whose speech began in 1.6), who is quoting YHWH (who begins speaking here with אֱמֹר לָהֶם [say to them]), who is quoting Moses in advance, passing on verbatim to the Israelites a command expressed in YHWH's point of view (the first person singular of אֵינֶנִּי בְּקִרְבְּכֶם [I am not among you] refers to YHWH). If one counts YHWH's point of view separately, then this is a five-layer quotation, as are the following two instances.

2.4b–6: The narrator is quoting Moses (continuing the speech he began in 1.6), who is quoting YHWH (who began speaking in 2.3), who is quoting Moses in advance, again passing on verbatim to the Israelites a command expressed in YHWH's point of view.

5.27b: The narrator is quoting Moses (whose present speech began in 5.1), who is quoting YHWH (who began speaking this time in 5.26), who is quoting Moses in advance, once again passing on a command to the Israelites (which is expressed either in YHWH's or Moses's point of view).

22.17b: The narrator is quoting Moses (continuing the speech he began in 5.1), who is quoting a hypothetical offended father (who began speaking in 22.16), who is quoting his hypothetical son-in-law (whose hypothetical speech Moses too has quoted in 22.14 in a two- or three-layer quotation).

Now, this same degree of layering of quotations is not unheard of in Genesis through Numbers. There are several three- or four-layer quotations in Genesis 20.13 (the narrator quoting Abraham quoting himself quoting Sarah); 24.32 (the narrator quoting Abraham's servant quoting himself himself yet again); 24.44 (the narrator quoting Abraham's servant quoting himself quoting Rebecca); and Exodus 3.16–17 (the narrator quoting God quoting Moses quoting God). There is also a four- or five-layer quotation in Exodus 4.23 (the narrator quoting YHWH quoting Moses quoting YHWH quoting himself). Extensive but less-layered quotation too is common outside of Deuteronomy; for example, almost all of the book of Leviticus (with the exception of chapters 8–10) quotes either what YHWH says to Moses or what YHWH tells Moses to say to the Israelites. Where Deuteronomy betrays the Song's distinctive influence is in its actualization of the model of intergenerational question-and-answer concerning YHWH's past deeds found in SoM 7–17, in its prominent use of advance quotations (including in laws), and particularly (which is a subset of the previous item) in its use of advance quotations to be avoided.

As noted, in SoM 7–17 there occurs an implied question-and-answer between a future generation of Israelites on the one hand (understood as those who are performing the Song at any point in its future history as charted in Deuteronomy 31), who are commanded to interrogate their ancestors about YHWH's past deeds in constituting the people of Israel, and their ancestors on the other. The Song's performers, having commanded this inquiry into the past in the voice of the Song (SoM 7), are then also cast in the role of the ancestors (SoM 8–17), answering their own question by reciting YHWH's actions in bringing the nation into the land. In Deuteronomy 6.20–25, the enactment of just such a situation is portrayed, with the narrator quoting Moses quoting future Israelites and their children. Although in Deuteronomy 6 the question (6.20) and the last part of the answer (6.24–25) have to do with הָעֵדֹת וְהַחֻקִּים וְהַמִּשְׁפָּטִים (the testimonies, statutes, and ordinances), which go unmentioned in the Song, and although the first part of the answer (6.21–22) has to do with YHWH's deeds in taking Israel out of Egypt (also unmentioned in the Song), other parallels to the Song remain. The central part of the answer (6.23) concerns YHWH's bringing of Israel into the land, which is the subject of SoM 13, and, in the narrative of Deuteronomy at least, the rescue from Egypt and the giving of the laws take place in days past, when the people of Israel was constituted by YHWH (cf. SoM 6c–7). Elsewhere in the Pentateuch, this same form of future question-and-answer between descendant and ancestor occurs only in Exodus 12.26–27 and 13.14–15,[79] which is to say, in contexts that sound so much like Deuteronomy (both at 6.20–25 and elsewhere) that they are considered by some to have been written under the influence of Deuteronomy.[80] Beyond this schematic example in 6.20–25, Deuteronomy goes so far as to enact, through the figure of Moses, the paradigm of the ancestor speaking about YHWH's past deeds. Moses's recitation of YHWH's deeds is not prompted within the book of Deuteronomy by a question posed by Israelites who come after Moses, much less by Moses's own children. Nevertheless, the content of Moses's speeches does concern the times when YHWH constituted Israel as a people (cf. לקנות 'to acquire', לעשות 'to make', and לכון 'to establish' in SoM 6cd), not so much by leading them into the land (as in SoM 12–13, although that too is explicitly anticipated throughout Deuteronomy) but by taking them out of Egypt and by leading them through the intervening territories. The other major focus of Moses's Deuteronomic speeches is the law. According to Deuteronomy,[81] the law is closely linked to the unique relationship between YHWH and Israel vis-à-vis other nations and gods, and while the Song does not mention the law, the unique relationship between YHWH and Israel is one of the Song's primary concerns (SoM 6cd, 8–9, 15c–18, 21).

Deuteronomy also adopts the Song's use of advance quotations, the primary example of which is SoM 27cd, where YHWH quotes enemies speaking in the future. (As an advance quotation that is to be prevented from being uttered, SoM 27cd also provides the paradigm for the specifically hypothetical advance quotations detailed in the following section.) Moreover, whatever the inspiration that led Deuteronomy to incorporate the Song and to give it a destined moment of performance in the far future – thus creating or imagining a performance history for it (based, of course, on the Song's real performance history up to that point, which had given the Song the prestige and currency that Deuteronomy then attached to itself) – this move turned the entire Song into an advance quotation, a phenomenon that became characteristic of the rest of Deuteronomy. While advance quotations occur elsewhere in narration[82] and in instructions on specific situations,[83] Deuteronomy formulates an appreciable number of laws using this technique: 12.20; 15.16; 17.14; 18.21; 20.3–4, 5–8; 21.7–8, 20; 22.14–17; 25.7–10; 26.3, 5–10, 13–15. Although occurring outside the legal core of the book, 6.20–25 may

---

79. Cf. Exodus 13.8, where the "answer" appears without a question.

80. See e.g. Hyatt 1971:137, 141–43.

81. Deuteronomy 4.6–8; 5.26; 6.20–21; 7.12–14; 10.12–15; 11.22–23; 12.1–4, 28–32; 20.18; 28.1; 30.2–3.

82. E.g. Genesis 24.14; Exodus 7.9; 11.8; cf. Deuteronomy 4.6.

83. E.g. Exodus 7.9, 19; Leviticus 1.2–3.17; cf. Deuteronomy 27.15–26.

also be considered a law, insofar as it offers generalized instructions. Outside of Deuteronomy, laws are formulated with advance quotations in only three places: Exodus 21.5 (which is the same law as found in Deuteronomy 15.16); 22.9; and Numbers 5.19–22.

A particular form of advance, layered quotation that is shared between the Song and the rest of Deuteronomy represents an opinion or course of action that must be avoided. In the Song this occurs at SoM 27cd, where the Song quotes YHWH (in the middle of a speech beginning at SoM 20), who hypothetically quotes enemies claiming credit for a victory over the Israelites that YHWH is actually responsible for. A very close parallel to this occurs at Deuteronomy 8.17, where the narrator quotes Moses (in the speech beginning at 5.1), who hypothetically quotes future Israelites claiming credit for the prosperity that YHWH has provided them with.[84] Several other passages in Deuteronomy exhibit a similar form, with their themes clustering around agency (whether YHWH's or others') and the distinctiveness of – and the distinct relationship between – YHWH and Israel vis-à-vis other nations and their gods.[85]

7.17: The narrator quotes Moses (continuing the speech he began at 5.1) who hypothetically quotes future Israelites expressing a lack of confidence in their ability to defeat the nations already living in the land – the remedy for which, as 7.18 makes clear, is to recall the effectiveness of YHWH's actions against Egypt.

9.2: The narrator quotes Moses (continuing the speech he began at 5.1), who quotes hearsay that implies that the Anakim living in the land cannot be defeated – in answer to which Moses asserts that YHWH will indeed defeat the Anakim (9.3).

9.4: The narrator quotes Moses (continuing the speech he began at 5.1), who hypothetically quotes future Israelites expressing, after the completion of the conquest, their worthiness to have been made owners of the land – in response to which Moses offers evidence of the Israelites' unworthiness (9.4–27).

9.28: The narrator quotes Moses (continuing the speech he began at 5.1), who quotes himself (in the prayer to YHWH beginning at 9.26) hypothetically quoting the Egyptians interpreting YHWH's proposed destruction of the Israelites at Horeb as inability and hatred for the Israelites on YHWH's part – which will be prevented, as the rest of Moses's prayer makes clear,

84. Additionally, both passages use the word יָד 'hand' as a metaphor for agency and ability.

85. Again, the only instances of such a phenomenon outside of Deuteronomy occur in D-influenced passages: Exodus 32.12 and Numbers 14.18.

by YHWH remembering that he is capable of acts of power, by his ignoring Israel's unworthiness, and by his recalling the (transgenerational) relationship of belonging between him and Israel (9.26–29).

12.30: The narrator quotes Moses (continuing the speech he began at 5.1), who hypothetically quotes future Israelites inquiring, after the completion of the conquest, into adopting the cultic practices of the nations who previously lived in the land and worshipped their own gods – in order to prevent which Moses notes that those cultic practices are hateful to YHWH (12.31).

13.3: The narrator quotes Moses (continuing the speech he began at 5.1), who hypothetically quotes a future prophet or visionary urging the worship of gods other than YHWH – the antidote to which is to view it as a test of loyalty to YHWH (13.4–5).

13.7: The narrator quotes Moses (continuing the speech he began at 5.1), who hypothetically quotes future Israelites' close relatives and friends urging the worship of gods other than YHWH – the antidote to which is to recall that those gods have nothing to do with Israel and in fact belong to other peoples (13.7–8).

13.14: The narrator quotes Moses (continuing the speech he began at 5.1), who hypothetically quotes a town of "certain base fellows" among future Israelites urging the worship of gods other than YHWH – the antidote to which is realize that such behavior brings retribution from YHWH, which may be forestalled by destroying the town (13.15–18).

15.9: The narrator quotes Moses (continuing the speech he began at 5.1), who hypothetically quotes a future Israelite intending to refuse to make a loan to a poorer Israelite because the septennial year of remission is near – the counter to which is the reassurance that YHWH will bless the giver of the loan (15.10).

29.18: The narrator quotes Moses (continuing the speech he began at 29.1), who hypothetically quotes a future Israelite[86] saying to himself that he will continue to prosper as he turns away from YHWH to worship the gods of other nations – the counter to which is the assertion that YHWH will not overlook the breach of loyalty but will in fact completely destroy the offender (29.19–20).

30.12–13: The narrator quotes Moses (continuing the speech he began at 29.1), who hypothetically quotes the Israelites doubting that the commandment they are receiving from Moses is meaningfully accessible to them – the counter to which is the reassurance that the commandment is both easily known and fully achievable (30.11, 12a, 13a, 14).

---

86. As 29.17 indicates, this voice may represent not just an individual but also a group of future Israelites.

Whom They Knew Not

The phrase "gods that they did not know" (אֱלֹהִים לֹא יְדָעוּם) in SoM 17b is the basis for another set of parallels and expansions in the rest of Deuteronomy. In context, these אֱלֹהִים are the gods (or idols) to whom Israel offers sacrificial service instead of to YHWH, when they have forgotten (SoM 18) who it was who provided them with the benefits listed in the elders' narrative in SoM 8–17. YHWH is the one whom the Israelites had reason to know, unlike these gods with whom even their ancestors were unfamiliar: לֹא שְׂעָרוּם אֲבֹתֵיכֶם (your ancestors did not dread them; SoM 17d).

The only parallels this phrase has outside of Deuteronomy occur not in the Pentateuch but in Jeremiah 7.9; 19.4; 44.3 and in Daniel 11.38, while in Deuteronomy there are six occurrences of this phrase or of a very close variant. In 29.25, part of the exilic frame identified by Levenson, the parallel is exact. The verse exhibits an additional strong parallel to the Song, which is the idea of YHWH's assignment of gods and nations to each other (אֱלֹהִים אֲשֶׁר לֹא חָלַק לָהֶם ... [gods whom ... he had not allotted to them]; cf. SoM 8–9), and its near context (29.21–27) shows many other points of similarity with the Song. In the other five occurrences within Deuteronomy (11.28; 13.3, 7, 14; 28.64), the verb לדעת 'to know' has a second-person subject (variously singular and plural) that in each case refers to Israel, while the noun אֱלֹהִים 'gods' is modified by the plural adjective אֲחֵרִים 'other'. Of these five, two also specify Israel's ancestors as part of the subject (13.7; 28.64), which would seem to be in parallel to אֲבֹתֵיכֶם 'your ancestors' in SoM 17d.

A slight elaboration of אֱלֹהִים לֹא יְדָעוּם (gods whom they did not know) may be found in 28.33, 36, where the object of the Israelites' knowing is not a divinity but a nation that YHWH will make superior to Israel: עַם/גּוֹי אֲשֶׁר לֹא־יָדַעְתָּ (a people/nation whom you have not known). While the syntactical resemblances are obvious enough, what may enable this particular elaboration is the reciprocity that YHWH inflicts on Israel in SoM 21: given that Israel replaced YHWH with gods that they had not known, YHWH will replace Israel with a nation that they had not known. The rest of Pentateuch contains nothing like this usage; it does appear in Jeremiah 9.15, Zechariah 7.14, and Ruth 2.11.[87]

The appearance of similar phrasing in Deuteronomy 8.3, 16, where manna is the object of the Israelites' knowing, represents a dubious parallel – that is, a parallel that may draw its wording but not its content from

---

87. Similar phrasing where אֶרֶץ 'land' replaces עַם 'people' or גּוֹי 'nation' may represent a further elaboration of this theme; see Jeremiah 16.13; 17.4; 22.28; and Ezekiel 32.9. Note that Ezekiel 32.9 uses גּוֹיִם 'nations' and אֲרָצוֹת 'lands' as parallel terms and that אֶרֶץ and עַם also appear closely linked in Ruth 2.11.

the Song. To begin with, although אֲשֶׁר לֹא־יָדַעְתָּ וְלֹא יְדָעוּן אֲבֹתֶיךָ (which you did not know, nor had your ancestors known [it]) in 8.3 and אֲשֶׁר לֹא־יָדְעוּן אֲבֹתֶיךָ (which your ancestors did not know) in 8.16 do show a striking resemblance to SoM 17b, d and to the passages in Deuteronomy discussed above, neither are they very far off from the relevant wording from the manna story in Exodus 16.15: וַיֹּאמְרוּ ... מָן הוּא כִּי לֹא יָדְעוּ מַה־הוּא (they said ... "what is it?," for they did not know what it was). Moreover, Deuteronomy 8.3, 16 have much more in common with the Exodus passage: the object of the Israelites' knowing has a positive function in the narrative, rather than being a god that the Israelites should not worship or a nation with which YHWH punishes the Israelites; the manna is a miraculous type of food, not simply a food that YHWH provides in abundance as in the Song; the manna is provided in the wilderness, not in the land. Therefore, while the wording of Deuteronomy 8.3, 16 may have been influenced by the Song (and/or by other texts in Deuteronomy influenced by it), the content of 8.3, 16 seems to be more closely related to the P source found in Exodus.

Deuteronomy 1.39; 11.2; and 31.13 may constitute a further elaboration of this wording and a combination of it with the theme of generational continuity/discontinuity. In these verses, the antecedent of the relative clause אֲשֶׁר לֹא־יָדְעוּ (who have not known) is the subject, not the object, of the verb לָדַעַת 'to know', and that subject is בְּנֵיכֶם 'your children', that is, not a preceding but a subsequent generation of Israelites. Compare Judges 2.10: וְגַם כָּל־הַדּוֹר הַהוּא נֶאֶסְפוּ אֶל־אֲבוֹתָיו וַיָּקָם דּוֹר אַחֵר אַחֲרֵיהֶם אֲשֶׁר לֹא־יָדְעוּ אֶת־יְהוָה וְגַם אֶת־הַמַּעֲשֶׂה אֲשֶׁר עָשָׂה לְיִשְׂרָאֵל (that whole generation too were gathered to their ancestors, and another generation arose after them who did not know YHWH or even the deeds he had done for Israel), which also 1) reapplies the adjective אַחֵר 'other' that figures prominently in Deuteronomy 11.28; 13.3, 7, 14; and 28.64, discussed above; 2) which explicitly invokes the concept of generational succession; 3) which is a narrative continuation of Deuteronomy 1.39; and 4) in which – as in Deuteronomy 11.2; 31.13 – the Israelites know something related to YHWH (his work, as in Judges 2.10; his discipline, greatness, hand, and arm, as in Deuteronomy 11.2; or simply how to fear YHWH, as in Deuteronomy 31.13).

End of Days

Levenson notes that the phrase בְּאַחֲרִית הַיָּמִים (in/at the end of days) occurs in both parts of Deuteronomy's exilic frame (at 4.30 and 31.29) and that, while it is common enough in prophetic texts (eight occurrences),[88] it appears no-

---

88. Levenson does not list the occurrences, which are: Isaiah 2.2; Jeremiah 23.20; 30.24;

where else in the Deuteronomistic History.[89] Genesis 49.1 and Numbers 24.14 also contain the phrase.

In Deuteronomy, the phrase indicates the time when evil and hardship will come on the Israelites. In 4.30, what happens in the end of days is that "these things" "find" (לִמְצֹא) the Israelites. "These things" presumably are the curses recounted in Deuteronomy 28 (see 28.69; 30.1).[90] In 31.29, it is "evil" that "happens" (לִקְרוֹת) to the Israelites. Note that language from both 4.30 and 31.29 appears together in 31.17, where "many evils – and hardships" "find" the Israelites (not at the end of days but בַּיּוֹם־הַהוּא [on that day]).

Now, the phrase בְּאַחֲרִית הַיָּמִים (in/at the end of days) is clearly not drawn directly from the Song, where it does not in fact occur. The word אַחֲרִית 'end' occurs in SoM 20 and 29, with an identical valence in both places, where there is talk of YHWH and of a people (characterized as non-wise, etc., whether Israel or another nation) seeing or understanding the outcome of events as it affects a people. In SoM 20, YHWH will see – or perhaps, given how active a role he takes in SoM 21–25, he will prove – how his people will fare without his help. In SoM 29 the nation in question fails to understand not just their אַחֲרִית but, as SoM 27cd and 30cd make clear, that it is dependent on YHWH's involvement. In particular, it is a question of the end result of human misattribution of human prosperity and success, whether attributing it to themselves (as in the case of the people spoken of in SoM 29) or attributing it (as in the case of Israel) to gods other than YHWH. This attribution is indicated by the Israelites offering sacrifices to those other gods, whether in thanks or in supplication.

Once sacrifice is understood as a form of recognizing the recipient's sovereignty over the sacrificer's situation, it becomes clear that the narratives in Deuteronomy 4 and 31 exhibit another parallel to the narrative in the Song. In 4.30, although the focus is on the particular practice of idol-making, the worship of other gods (or non-gods) is its basis (4.19). In Deuteronomy 31, the practice of idol-making is in the background, present only in the phrase מַעֲשֵׂה יְדֵיכֶם (the works of your hands; 31.29), while the turn to other gods receives the more extended treatment (31.16, 18, 20 – all part of Dtr₂'s original introduction to the Song).

Insofar as the word אַחֲרִית 'end' is concerned, then, the phrase בְּאַחֲרִית הַיָּמִים (in/at the end of days) can be seen as a natural outgrowth of the language of the Song. The same holds true for the other element of the phrase, the

---

48.47; 49.39; Ezekiel 38.16; Hosea 3.5; and Micah 4.1. It also occurs in Daniel 10.14. Cf. the phrase בְּאַחֲרִית הַשָּׁנִים in Ezekiel 38.8.

89. Levenson 1975:214.

90. "These lines [4.30; 31.17, 21] speak of the inevitable actualization of curses in very similar language" (Levenson 1975:214).

word יוֹם 'day', which likewise appears twice in the Song. The first occurrence (SoM 7a) is not pertinent, since it refers to days that lie in the past rather than in the future and that stand at the beginning rather than at the end of a sequence of actions. The other occurrence (SoM 35c), however, refers to a future time, a time of calamity (cf. the hardship and evil of 4.30 and 31.29), a time that is the result of earlier actions (as indicated by its serving as נָקָם 'recompense' for them). This is the same way that the phrase בְּאַחֲרִית הַיָּמִים functions in the exilic frame of Deuteronomy.

It is quite plausible, then, that this phrase was inspired by the language of the Song; at the very least, it is compatible with it.

Satiety and Apostasy

This theme appears in the Song only in SoM 15ab, in the verbs לשמן 'to be fat, to grow fat' (appearing twice) and לעבות 'to be thick, to grow thick'. In 31.20, the theme is represented by the verb לדשן 'to be fat, to grow fat'; as Levenson notes, nowhere else does this root have an association with apostasy, whether in Deuteronomy, in the rest of the Pentateuch, or elsewhere among biblical texts.[91] The full context of fatness in 31.20 is as follows: כִּי־אֲבִיאֶנּוּ אֶל־הָאֲדָמָה ... וְאָכַל וְשָׂבַע וְדָשֵׁן וּפָנָה אֶל־אֱלֹהִים אֲחֵרִים וַעֲבָדוּם וְנִאֲצוּנִי וְהֵפֵר אֶת־בְּרִיתִי ... (when I bring him [= the people Israel] into the land ... and he eats and is sated and becomes fat and turns to other gods and they serve[92] them and scorn me and he violates my covenant ...). This sequence roughly matches the order and nature of events in the Song – being brought by YHWH into the land, eating, becoming fat, apostatizing (SoM 12–19) – with the caveat that the Song does not use לשבע 'to be sated, to grow sated' (or a synonym) to say that the Israelites were sated after eating.[93] Given, however, the richness of the food and drink that YHWH provides in SoM 13–14, satiety is not an unreasonable inference. Further, satiety, like fatness, has this kind of negative valence almost exclusively in Deuteronomy.[94]

Now, as do some of the other themes that Levenson observes are shared between the Song of Moses and Deuteronomy's exilic frame, morally nega-

91. Levenson 1975:216.

92. Note that two of these verbs describing Israel's sequence of actions are plural.

93. Another difference is that the Song itself does not use the language of covenant in characterizing Israel's actions, as is done in 31.20, while nevertheless describing actions that would be understood in the context of Deuteronomy as constituting a violation of YHWH's covenant with the Israelites. Therefore, the appearance of להפר 'to violate' and of בְּרִית 'covenant' in 31.20 should also be understood as an elaboration – or even as a simple joining of one of Deuteronomy's main concerns with the contents of the Song.

94. Jeremiah 5.7 provides the sole instance of morally negative satiety outside of Deuteronomy.

tive fatness occurs only in the frame's second part, that is, in 31.20. Within the frame's first part, 4.25 makes the closest approach, and it has nothing to do with complacency of a specifically post-prandial nature. While both 4.25 and 31.20 concern Israel's initial positive experiences in the land that precede their apostasy, in 4.25 the sequence begins not with eating or with fatness but with producing children and growing old in the land – as if getting settled, so to speak, were a form of satiety – and moves on not to turning to other gods, serving them, scorning YHWH, and violating YHWH's covenant but to becoming corrupt, making an idol, and doing what YHWH considers evil, to his vexation.[95] If, therefore, these two passages can be considered outworkings of the same theme (which is the point I am arguing), then the theme in question connects apostasy not with fatness but with satiety and, in this case, operates at a schematic level, allowing for wide variation in details.

If we thus take satiety rather than fatness per se as the point of comparison, three passages outside of Deuteronomy's exilic frame offer parallels that are equally, if not more, striking than what is found in 31.20 (and 4.25): 6.10–12; 8.7–19; and 11.8–17. As do SoM 15; 4.25; and 31.20, these three passages address the potential for apostasy at a time when YHWH will have brought the Israelites into the land and when the Israelites will have come into possession of further benefits; credit for these benefits is explicitly given to YHWH in 11.8–17 and explicitly denied to the Israelites in 6.10–12 and 8.7–19.[96] Moreover, in these three passages (as well as in 31.20), the phrase וְאָכַלְתָּ וְשָׂבָעְתָּ (you will eat and be sated) signals the shift from prosperity to danger (6.11; 8.10;[97] 11.15).[98] Each of these passages exhibits other parallels to the Song, which I will discuss below in my more detailed treatment of them.

In Deuteronomy 6, after the notice of YHWH's bringing Israel into the land (6.10), there occurs a list of benefits that the Israelites will possess there without any action on their part: cities, houses, cisterns, vineyards, and olive trees (6.10–11). After the Israelites eat and become sated (6.11), the danger is of forgetting YHWH (לשׁכח 'to forget'; v. 12). Forgetting as an aspect of apostasy occurs also in the Song (SoM 18: [99]לשׁכח). Grapes and olives are also mentioned in the Song as produce of the land (SoM 12d, 14e); in 6.11

---

95. As I noted earlier in this chapter in the section on integrity and corruption, the language of corruption and of Israel vexing YHWH shows the influence of the Song.

96. Regarding 8.7–19, a degree of Israelite agency is assumed in 8.9, 12, 18, while it is explicitly denied in 8.17. YHWH's agency is highlighted in 8.7, 10, 14–16, 18.

97. Cf. פֶּן־תֹּאכַל וְשָׂבָעְתָּ (lest you eat and be sated) in 8.12.

98. As discussed above, the concept of satiety is also present in SoM 15 and 4.25, expressed in other vocabulary.

99. Cf. also the form תֵּשִׁי (you forgot) in SoM 18.

it is specifically said that the Israelites are not responsible for these crops, while the Song simply treats them as part of the natural abundance of the land (for which the Israelites also receive no credit).

In Deuteronomy 8, after the notice of YHWH's bringing Israel into the land (8.7), the land's various forms of richness are listed: sources of water, agricultural products, and metals (8.7–9). After the decisive moment of eating and satiety, the desired outcome is given: וּבֵרַכְתָּ אֶת־יְהוָה אֱלֹהֶיךָ (you will bless YHWH your god; 8.10). Next the possibility of apostasy is warned against, with similar elements occurring in reverse order: the non-desired outcome of forgetting YHWH (and not keeping his commands), eating and being sated, and possessing benefits (houses, domesticated animals, precious metals, and general abundance) that are related to the land (8.11–13). Then the act of apostasy is mentioned again, characterized not just as forgetting YHWH (8.14) but also as the Israelites' heart or mind being "lifted up" (8.14) to the point of thinking that they themselves were responsible for all the benefits they have been enjoying (8.17). The act of forgetting appears once more at the end of the passage (8.19), preceded by the commanded act of remembering that can prevent it from occurring (8.18).

This passage in Deuteronomy 8 has quite a few other features in common with the Song, besides the centrality of a moment of eating and of satiety. In addition to forgetting YHWH as an element of Israelite apostasy (SoM 18; 8.10, 12), the verb לרום 'to be high' also plays a key role in both. In the Song, YHWH fears that his enemies will claim credit for what he has done, saying that their hand is "lifted up": יָדֵינוּ רָמָה וְלֹא יְהוָה פָּעַל כָּל־זֹאת (our hand is exalted, it was not YHWH who accomplished all this; SoM 27cd). As discussed above, in 8.14, 17 Moses warns against the Israelites' "heart" or "mind" being "lifted up" (8.14: וְרָם לְבָבֶךָ) such that they should claim "in [their] heart" that their own hand has done what, in fact, YHWH is responsible for: וְאָמַרְתָּ בִּלְבָבֶךָ כֹּחִי וְעֹצֶם יָדִי עָשָׂה לִי אֶת־הַחַיִל הַזֶּה ([lest] you say in your heart, "my strength and the power of my hand has made for me this wealth"; 8.17). Both of these examples also use the device of quoting hypothetical speech that must be prevented. The turn of phrase [אֲשֶׁר] לֹא יָדְעוּ (whom/which they did not know) also appears in both (SoM 17b; 8.16), as does a description of the land that emphasizes plant and animal abundance (SoM 13–14; 8.7–8, 13).

In Deuteronomy 11, after a notice that obeying YHWH's commands will allow the Israelites to enter the land and prosper there (11.8–9, reprised in 11.13), there follows a long description of the land's various (good) features, highlighting its general fertility (11.9), its hilly terrain (11.11), the sufficiency of the rain it receives (11.11, 14), and its herbage that is suitable for cattle (11.15). Woven into this description is a continuous emphasis on YHWH's agency in the Israelites' possession of the land and in the land's fertility, which YHWH provides or withholds in response to the Israelites' obedience or disobedience: YHWH has promised them the land (11.9), and he cares for it (11.12), keeps his eyes on it (11.12), makes its various seasonal rains fall (11.14), and makes its grass grow (11.15). At the end of 11.15 finally comes the decisive moment of eating and satiety, followed by an invocation of the apostasy that is to be avoided, characterized here not as forgetting but as the Israelites' heart being deceived (rather than lifted up, as in ch. 8) and as the Israelites turning away to serve and bow down to other gods: פֶּן יִפְתֶּה לְבַבְכֶם וְסַרְתֶּם וַעֲבַדְתֶּם אֱלֹהִים אֲחֵרִים וְהִשְׁתַּחֲוִיתֶם לָהֶם (lest your heart be deceived and you turn away to serve other gods and bow down to them; 11.16).

This passage's other similarities to the Song, besides the pivotal role of satiety in introducing apostasy, are relatively slight compared to those of 8.7–17. For example, while this passage mentions the products of the land's fertility (11.9, 14b), as does the Song (SoM 13–14), it seems to emphasize features of the land itself, such as its topography, its meteorological source of water and the timeliness thereof, and the kind of plants that grow there, to which is added a contrast to the land of Egypt (11.10–12, 14a, 15). Further, while in both YHWH becomes (or will become) angry when the Israelites relate to other gods instead of to YHWH, the effects of YHWH's anger differ. In the Song, YHWH threatens plague, wild animals, and military defeat (SoM 24–25), while here the non-productivity of the land is the only deadly threat (11.17).

To summarize, then, if 31.20 – exhibiting a sequence of entry into the land, enjoyment of the land's gratuitous fertility, eating, satiety, and apostasy – can be said to draw on the Song, then so too can 6.10–12; 8.7–17; and 11.8–17. Further, 4.25 is not far off, even though it is not couched in terms of eating, satiety, and apostasy; rather, it is concerned with the possible corruption of successive generations and a turn to the making of idols.[100] All this is not to say that every instance of (eating and) satiety in Deuteronomy is associated with apostasy; indeed, satiety has a neutral or even positive valence in 14.29; 23.25; 26.12; and 33.23. It is noteworthy about even these occurrences, however, that in them there is no question of those who are being satisfied having any hand in the provision that is being made for them.

As a final piece of evidence, satiety is not used this way anywhere else in the Pentateuch, as can be shown by two examples, both of which involve

---

100. The law in 21.18–21 deserves mention here (despite its many divergences from the passages so far under discussion), due to the fact that it gives a negative moral valence to the actions of eating and drinking, insofar as the offender is labeled "a glutton and a drunk" (זוֹלֵל וְסֹבֵא; 21.20).

YHWH's provision of manna and quail to the Israelites in the wilderness. In Exodus 16 (from the Priestly source) – where the Israelites complain of hunger and then receive manna and quail – the root שׂבע 'be sated' appears three times (paired in each case with the concept of eating): as a noun in the Israelites' complaint in v. 3, as an infinitive in Moses's retort in v. 8, and as a finite verb in YHWH's pronouncement in v. 12. As in the passages from Deuteronomy just discussed, here too the recipients of the food are in no position to provide it for themselves. The similarities end here, however, for satiety functions completely differently in Exodus 16. Most significantly, Exodus 16 does not particularly link the Israelites' failure to their being satisfied. The moment when they have had enough to eat is not the turning point of the story, for they were at fault before YHWH fed them, and they continue to be at fault afterwards.[101] Further, the Israelites' failure in Exodus 16 is not apostasy, as is it in the passages in Deuteronomy; rather, they complain about YHWH's provision and refuse to follow YHWH's instructions regarding the manna and the Sabbath. In Numbers 11 (from the Elohistic source; the relevant narrative thread is found in vv. 4–10, 13, 18–24a, 31–35) – where the Israelites have already been eating manna, ask for meat, and receive quail in rather large quantities – although the root שׂבע is not used, the concept of satiety nonetheless operates in the background. The narrative raises the question of whether the Israelites should be satisfied by YHWH's provision of manna, which has already taken place when the account begins. The Israelites evidently are not satisfied with manna alone, while YHWH evidently thinks that they should be satisfied with it; ultimately, YHWH uses satiety to punish the Israelites. In any case, the Israelites' offense in Numbers 11, as in Exodus 16, is not linked to their being satisfied; the initial possibility of satisfaction based on manna is not clear enough in the narrative to function this way, and the (over-) satisfaction that comes at the end actually puts a stop to their offense rather than provoking it anew. Further, the offense in question here is not apostasy; although Numbers 11 lacks Exodus 16's emphasis on adherence to YHWH's instructions (Sabbath-related or otherwise) regarding the manner of gathering the sustenance he provided, in both of

101. On the other hand, the desire for satiety may be the essence of the Israelites' fault in Exodus 16, or perhaps more accurately, the failure to trust YHWH to provide for their satiety – and to do so in a way that also accommodates his instructions concerning the Sabbath. That is, it may be that they fail in trusting YHWH first by complaining about his provision in general (Exodus 16.3), then by trying to make what was provided last longer than it should have (Exodus 16.19–20), and lastly by looking for YHWH's provision at the wrong time (Exodus 16.27–28) and/or when they already have enough (Exodus 16.23–24, 29). Be that as it may, satiety itself is neither positive nor negative in this passage.

these passages the Israelites' primary fault is to complain about YHWH's provision.[102]

In summary, the sequence of land, satiety, and apostasy as it appears in Deuteronomy appears to have no likely precedents in the other Pentateuchal sources but can easily be seen as relying on or being inspired by the concepts and narrative sequence present in the Song.

Concluding Remarks

This chapter constitutes a catalog of ways in which the book of Deuteronomy shows the influence of the Song of Moses.[103] In some cases, the theme or motif in question is adopted in a more or less straightforward manner, used elsewhere as it is in the Song. The theme of satiety and apostasy is one such case. In other cases, the theme or motif is not only adopted but also extended in some way, as is the case, for example, for the noun אַחֲרִית 'end' and its reuse in the phrase בְּאַחֲרִית הַיָּמִים (at the end of days) as well as for the theme of YHWH's sovereignty over boundaries. In yet others – and most relevant to a performative approach – Deuteronomy seems to be acting out a particular aspect of the Song. Such is the case, for example, with Deuteronomy's use of layered quotations. Finally, with a motif such as וַאֲשֶׁר] לֹא יְדָעוּ] (whom/which they did not know), although adopted elsewhere in Deuteronomy both straightforwardly and with elaborations, its phrasing has also been taken over without any particular relationship to the content or context of the passage in the Song from which it is drawn. These examples demonstrate that the language and concepts of the Song, far from influencing only Deuteronomy's exilic frame, are recognizable throughout the book in one form

---

102. In Numbers 11 the Israelites' desire for satiety is placed in a more clearly problematic light, by contrast to Exodus 16. For example, the passage in Numbers is framed with the root אוה 'desire' (v. 4: הִתְאַוּוּ תַּאֲוָה [they desired exceedingly]; v. 34: וַיִּקְרָא אֶת־שֵׁם־הַמָּקוֹם הַהוּא קִבְרוֹת הַתַּאֲוָה כִּי־שָׁם קָבְרוּ אֶת־הָעָם הַמִּתְאַוִּים [that place has the name "graves of desire," for that is where they buried the people who felt desire]); note the opposed term זָרָא 'loathsome thing' that occurs more or less in the middle of the narrative (v. 20). YHWH punishes the Israelites by turning what they desire into something that disgusts them.

103. There are yet other themes and motifs present in the Song of Moses that Deuteronomy seems to be adopting or acting out, to which I have not given extended treatments for reasons of space, believing also that my thesis has been sufficiently demonstrated by the foregoing examples, e.g.: 1) forgetting YHWH (SoM 18) vs. remembering YHWH's past beneficent actions (SoM 7–14), for which see Deuteronomy 4.9, 23; 5.15; 6.12; 7.18; 8.2, 11, 14, 18, 19; 9.7; 15.15; 16.3; 24.9, 18; 26.13; 31.21 ; 2) foolishness (SoM 6b, 15, 21d) vs. wisdom (SoM 6b, 28–29), for which see Deuteronomy 4.6; and 3) a pretension of self-sufficiency (SoM 27cd) vs. recognizing YHWH's sovereignty (SoM 30, 39–40), for which see Deuteronomy 8.3, 17–18; 29.23–27.

or another, and provide support for the hypothesis that the Song was already established as a "classic," at least in Deuteronomic circles, prior to the point that its text was explicitly quoted within the book. Further, the fact that the Deuteronomic writers had a history of embodying the Song at least in their own written performances provides an actual, historical template by which to understand the future history of performance and re-enactment that they explicitly create for the Song of Moses in Deuteronomy 31.

Conclusions and Further Research

I SET OUT AT THE BEGINNING OF THIS PROJECT to examine the dynamics of performing the Song of Moses within the tradition described for it by Deuteronomy. This task is important both because it has been virtually unaddressed in previous research and also because it sheds light on Deuteronomy's rhetorical and educational strategies, as well as on its compositional influences, among which I have shown the Song itself to figure prominently. By comparison to other studies of the Song, this investigation has uniquely emphasized the performed Song's character as a poem embedded in a narrative context,[1] and by comparison to other performance-critical studies of biblical texts, it has uniquely emphasized the effect of performance on the performers themselves, rather than on, for example, an attending audience. Specifically, I have sought to answer the following two questions, corresponding to the observations presented in Chapters 3 and 4: Given that a performer of the Song re-enacts the characters within the Song as well as previous performers within the tradition, how does the persona of the performer interact in the moment of performance with these re-enacted personas? Does the text of Deuteronomy give any indications that its own writers participated in this tradition of performing the Song?

Regarding the first question, I found that the Song's performers accumulate within themselves the viewpoints of figures from all throughout Israelite history. Through the performance of the Song, the Israelites are made to embody YHWH first and foremost, both as the jealous and angry character within the Song, in the future of Israelite history, who promises to annihilate the Israelites in anger over their failure to reciprocate his parental affection and generous provision and who then turns that anger outward to Israel's enemies (enemies who, if YHWH allowed them to destroy the Israelites on his behalf, would themselves fail to understand that YHWH had

---

1. Two exceptions to the overwhelming tendency to study the Song as an independent composition are provided in Watts 1992 and Weitzman 1997. Although Watts mentions in passing that the Song is to be performed by all the Israelites, he focuses his investigation on the Song's contributions to the surrounding narrative in terms of plot, theme, and characterization. While characterization has been at issue in this investigation as well, I have highlighted instead the contributions of the surrounding narrative's characterizations (primarily of Moses) to the performance of the Song. Weitzman focuses entirely on the way the surrounding narrative portrays the Song of Moses as an instance of last-words literature, or a death-bed speech. Further, as I mentioned above in Chapter 1, Terry Giles and William Doan do observe some aspects of the performance history created for the Song by the surrounding narrative, but they refrain from giving it a detailed treatment since in its narrative context the Song is not sung per se but rather spoken or recited (Giles and Doan 2009:105).

been the agent of their success) and also as the knowledgeable composer of the Song, who foresees not only the Israelites' perverseness but also his own resulting anger, establishing the Song in advance as a witness to these facts. Deuteronomically-influenced Israelites are further made to embody: 1) their ancestors, as those who, within the Song, will pass down knowledge of YHWH's generosity and who also, according to Deuteronomy's version of Israelite history, pass down the witnessing Song itself; 2) the skies and the earth, who, within the Song, will declare YHWH's greatness and integrity and are, in Deuteronomy's external narrative, anticipated as witnesses against the Israelites; 3) enemies, who, both in the Song and in Deuteronomy's telling of history, will defeat the Israelites militarily and, in the Song alone, take credit to themselves for that victory; 4) other nations in general, who, both in the Song and without it, praise the unique relationship between YHWH and the Israelites; 5) the persona of a prophet, who, both within the Song and in Deuteronomy's framing account, speaks YHWH's words to the Israelites; and 6) Moses, who, according to Deuteronomy's narrative, is both prophet and ancestor, the first Israelite to embody the above-mentioned figures at the beginning of the tradition of performing the Song. Through the performance of the Song, therefore, the weight of their own history is brought to bear on the generation of Israelites to whom Deuteronomy is addressed.

In pursuing an answer to the second question, I observed that discrete elements found in the Song are recognizably adopted, elaborated, acted out, or even merely mimicked in diverse parts of Deuteronomy, including not only the Dtr$_2$ frame but also the material attributed to Dtr$_1$, the hortatory material introducing the law code, and the legal core itself. This includes themes and motifs such as transgenerational corruption/integrity, YHWH's sovereignty over boundaries, and satiety as a prelude to apostasy; rhetorical devices such as layered quotation and imagined intergenerational speech; and phrasings such as as יְדָעוּם לֹא [אֲשֶׁר] (whom/which they did not know) and בְּאַחֲרִית הַיָּמִים (in/at the end of days). It would seem, therefore, that Deuteronomy's various composers have on several levels drawn inspiration from the Song of Moses. As is to be expected for a poem that has had its place "in their mouth" for generations, the Song has evidently affected their preoccupations, manner of speaking and of imagining speech, and even their very words.

The observations presented above indicate directions for further research. The fact that the Song's influence is seen throughout Deuteronomy suggests that the dynamic of embodiment in traditional performance through which the Deuteronomists conceived of the Song may be present elsewhere in the book, if not also in the Deuteronomistic History. In support of such a hypothesis, at least for Deuteronomy, one could point to the commands for the Israelites to attach "these words" to their bodies (6.8; 11.18) and to write them on the places of their residence within the land (6.9; 11.20). Unsurprisingly, these two injunctions appear alongside the command to recite "these words" on a regular basis (6.7; 11.19); the Song too is to be recited over and over again. Not only are the Israelites to speak the words of the tradition continually, they are to live within them and to clothe themselves with them. To these points may be added the phenomenon that Hindy Najman labels "Mosaic Discourse," describing "the developing conceptions of the Mosaic Law and figure of Moses" that she traces from its beginning in Deuteronomy through the book of *Jubilees*, the Temple Scroll, and the writings of Philo of Alexandria.[2] According to Najman, the practice of Mosaic Discourse extends the tradition's authority to these successive works, in which the tradition is re-composed and which therefore represent the tradition's continuation(s). The features of texts that participate in this discourse are: 1) reworking and expansion of older traditions through interpretation; 2) a claim to be torah; 3) a claim to re-present the revelation at Sinai; and 4) a claimed association with Moses.[3] While Najman's concern is that the whole of Deuteronomy exhibits these features,[4] I would add that the Song of Moses, as a discrete text within Deuteronomy, does the same. I have already discussed above how Deuteronomy identifies the Song as torah (31.24–30) and associates it with Moses (31.16–22, 24–30; 32.44).[5] Concerning the third point, Najman cites Deuteronomy 31.28–30 as showing that the book as a whole re-presents Sinai;[6] indeed, but this passage is also an explicit introduction to the text of the Song, which immediately follows it. Further, the invocation of skies and earth in 31.29 also appears in the introduction to the Decalogue, at 4.26, which foreshadows the Song, and at 4.36, which foreshadows the immediately following narrative in Deuteronomy 5.[7] The Song is no less strongly associated with Sinai than is the entire book. As for the first point, it is only through comparison that one text can be shown to be a reworking or expansion of another, and no discernibly earlier version of the Song is currently known. Nonetheless, as previously discussed, the very fact that the Deuteronomists treat the Song as a discrete text and re-

2. Najman 2003:13.

3. Najman 2003:16–17.

4. Najman 2003:20–39.

5. See Chapter 2 above for the full discussion.

6. Najman 2003:33.

7. Najman also cites Deuteronomy 5.3 as evidence of Deuteronomy's re-presentation of Sinai (Najman 2003:32).

count its history demonstrates that they knew the Song as an independent text; thus, their setting of the Song within Deuteronomy already constitutes an adaptation and reinterpretation of its earlier function.[8] While I am not asserting that the Song is the kernel from which Mosaic Discourse sprang, Najman's observations have an obvious relevance for a performance-based analysis such as I have been pursuing here. This relevance is encapsulated in the following quotation, which employs the same language of re-enactment or embodiment as I have been using throughout this project: "when Deuteronomy 34 insists on the impossibility of another prophet like Moses, this means in effect that one crucial way of claiming authority within Second Temple Judaism will be to write in the name – indeed, in the voice – of Moses himself."[9] Overall, therefore, given that the Deuteronomists' conception of one's proper relationship to tradition seems to have a strong performative aspect, a more systematic tracing out of its manifestations in the Deuteronomic and Deuteronomistic corpora promises to be a fruitful avenue of investigation.[10]

The findings reported in Chapter 4 suggest that the Song of Moses exerted a greater influence on Deuteronomistic literature than has been appreciated heretofore. The dictum that the Song is a "compendium of prophetical theology" is well known in the secondary literature,[11] and examinations of allusions to the Song in the prophetic collections are not uncommon.[12] Research into signs of the Song's influence in Deuteronomistic literature (outside of Deuteronomy) has been relatively rare, however.[13] Yet

8. It seems particularly unlikely that the Song had an original association with the revelation at Sinai (whether or not the Deuteronomists were the first to make that association).

9. Najman 2003:40. Where Najman analyzes written performance within a tradition, however, I have been treating oral performance.

10. A corresponding line of inquiry would be to examine the Second Temple texts that participate in Najman's Mosaic Discourse for specific signs of the Song's influence beyond the associations with torah, Sinai, and Moses that the Song shares with Deuteronomy as a whole.

11. The phrase is Cornill's: "es ist gewissermassen ein Compendium der prophetischen Theologie" (Cornill 1891:71, as translated in Driver 1906:346).

12. For example: Soggin 1958; Holladay 1966; Holmyard 1992; Bergey 2003; Keiser 2005; Gile 2011; Groenewald 2011.

13. While Levenson pointed out correspondences between the Song and Deuteronomy's Dtr$_2$ frame as well as between that frame and parts of the Deuteronomistic History that Cross assigned to Dtr$_2$ (Levenson 1975:215–17, 219–20), he did not specifically investigate correspondences between the Song and Dtr$_2$ texts outside of Deuteronomy. Given that in Chapter 4 above I drew a connection between SoM 9 and Deuteronomy 9.26, 29 on the basis of the paired words עַם 'people' and נַחֲלָה 'inheritance', here I note that the same paired words occur in the first of Levenson's examples, Deuteronomy 4.20 and 1 Kings 8.51 (Levenson 1975:219); in fact, the phrasing עַמְּךָ וְנַחֲלָתְךָ (your people, your inheritance) appears identically in Deuteronomy 9.26, 29 and in 1 Kings 8.51. Lundbom has argued, on the basis both of Deuteronomy 31's identifica-

it would be a natural extension of this project to compare the adoption and adaptation of certain of the Song's motifs, rhetorical devices, and phrasings in Deuteronomy with their treatment in the Deuteronomistic History. The Deuteronomistic History's many speeches would seem to provide the most promising beginning point, given the emphasis on speech both in the Song and in Deuteronomy as a whole.

Even before this further research is undertaken, however, a few points have been established by the preceding study of the Song, which may be summarized as follows. First, the Song served as a considerable literary and theological resource for the Deuteronomic and Deuteronomistic circles that produced the Deuteronomy that we have today. They drew from it not only phrases, tropes, and themes but also – not to overdraw the distinction – some of Deuteronomy's characteristic theologoumena. Second, Deuteronomy is a performance-oriented composition whose rhetorical strategy is educational, operating at the level of transformation and reinforcement of identity. The goal of transformation itself may have arisen from a meditation on a conflict of metaphors within the Song: either the Israelites of the Song have failed to reciprocate because they are not really YHWH's children at all, a vine whose grapes are bitter by nature, or the crisis was an aberration, a momentary forgetting from which they can be called back through an act of remembrance, a rehearsal of the founding acts by which YHWH gave birth to them.

---

tion of the Song with torah as well as of putative parallels between the Song and the oracle of Huldah recounted in 2 Kings 22.16–17, that the Song of Moses was the law book found in the temple by the priest Hilkiah and then read to Josiah (2 Kings 22.8–13) (Lundbom 1976). I would counter that Huldah's oracle shows its closest parallels to the Song's introduction in Deuteronomy 31, rather than to the Song; however, as I have discussed extensively above, that introduction itself shows many parallels to the Song. Friedman has argued that לְהָסִיר מֵעַל פָּנָיו (to remove [them] from before his face) in 2 Kings 24.3, coming at the end of the Deuteronomistic History as redacted by Dtr₂, recalls the phrasing אַסְתִּירָה פָנַי מֵהֶם אֶרְאֶה מָה אַחֲרִיתָם (let me hide my face from them, let me see what their end will be) in SoM 20 (Friedman 1981:36–37).

Bibliography

Baden, Joel S. 2009. *J, E, and the Redaction of the Pentateuch*. Forschungen zum Alten Testament 68. Tübingen.

Bergey, Ronald. 2003. "The Song of Moses (Deuteronomy 32.1–43) and Isaianic Prophecies: A Case of Early Intertextuality?" *Journal for the Study of the Old Testament* 28:33–54.

Blenkinsopp, Joseph. 1999. "Deuteronomic Contribution to the Narrative in Genesis—Numbers: A Test Case." In *Those Elusive Deuteronomists: The Phenomenon of Pan-Deuteronomism*, edited by Linda S. Schearing and Steven L. McKenzie. JSOTSup 268:84–115. Sheffield, U.K..

Boston, James R. 1996. *The Song of Moses: Deuteronomy 32:1–43*. Th.D. Dissertation, Union Theological Seminary (New York).

Britt, Brian. 2000. "Deuteronomy 31–32 as a Textual Memorial." *Biblical Interpretation* 8:358–74.

Brooke, Alan E., and Norman McLean, eds. 1911. *Numbers and Deuteronomy*. Vol. 1.3 of *The Old Testament in Greek: According to the Text of Codex Vaticanus*. London.

Broyles, Craig C. 1999. *Psalms*. New International Biblical Commentary on the Old Testament 11. Peabody, Mass.

Brueggemann, Walter. 1968. "The Kerygma of the Deuteronomic Historian." *Interpretation* 22:387–402.

———. 1972. "The Kerygma of the Priestly Writers." *Zeitschrift für die alttestamentliche Wissenschaft* 84:397–413.

Brueggemann, Walter, and Hans Walter Wolff. 1982. *The Vitality of Old Testament Traditions*. 2nd ed. Atlanta, Ga.

Budde, Karl. 1920. *Das Lied Moses Deut 32*. Tübingen.

Burke, Kenneth. 1945. *Grammar of Motives*. New York.

Carillo Alday, Salvador. 1970. *El Cántico de Moisés (Dt.32)*. Bibliotheca Hispana Bíblica 3. Madrid.

Carr, David M. 2005. *Writing on the Tablet of the Heart: Origins of Scripture and Literature*. New York.

Clines, David J. A. 1997. *The Theme of the Pentateuch*. 2nd ed. JSOTSup 10. Sheffield, U.K.

Cornill, Carl Heinrich. 1891. *Einleitung in das alte Testament*. Grundriss der theologischen Wissenschaften 2.1. Freiburg.

Cross, Frank Moore. 1973. *Canaanite Myth and Hebrew Epic*. Cambridge, Mass.

Daniels, Dwight R. 1987. "Is There a 'Prophetic Lawsuit' Genre?" *Zeitschrift für die alttestamentlich Wissenschaft* 99:339–60.

Davies, Eryl W. 1995. *Numbers*. New Century Bible. Grand Rapids, Mich.

Davies, Philip R., ed. 2002. *First Person: Essays in Biblical Autobiography*. The Biblical Seminar 81. New York.

Doan, William, and Terry Giles. 2005. *Prophets, Performance, and Power: Performance Criticism of the Hebrew Bible*. New York.

Driver, Samuel R. 1906. *A Critical and Exegetical Commentary on Deuteronomy*. International Critical Commentary 5. New York.

Elliger, Karl, et al., eds. 1997. *Biblia Hebraica Stuttgartensia*. 5th ed. Stuttgart.

Fokkelman, Jan P. 1981–1993. *Narrative Art and Poetry in the Books of Samuel: A Full Interpretation Based on Stylistic and Structural Analyses*. Studia Semitica Neerlandica 20, 23, 27, 31. 4 vols. Assen, Netherlands.

———. 1998. *Major poems of the Hebrew Bible: At the Interface of Hermeneutics and Structural Analysis: Ex. 15, Deut. 32, and Job 3*. Studia Semitica Neerlandica 37. Assen, Netherlands.

Friedman, Richard Elliott. 1981. *The Exile and Biblical Narrative: The Formation of the Deuteronomistic and Priestly Works*. Harvard Semitic Monographs 22. Chico, Calif.

Geertz, Clifford. 1980. "Blurred Genres: The Refiguration of Social Thought." *The American Scholar* 49:165–79.

Geoghegan, Jeffrey C. 2003. " 'Until This Day' and the Preexilic Redaction of the Deuteronomistic History." *Journal of Biblical Literature* 122:201–27.

Gile, Jason. 2011. "Ezekiel 16 and the Song of Moses: A Prophetic Transformation?" *Journal of Biblical Literature* 130:87–108.

Giles, Terry, and William J. Doan. 2008. "The Song of Asaph: A Performance-Critical Analysis of 1 Chronicles 16:8–36." *Catholic Biblical Quarterly* 70:29–43.

———. 2009. *Twice-Used Songs: Performance Criticism of the Songs of Ancient Israel*. Peabody, Mass.

Goffman, Erving. 1959. *The Presentation of Self in Everyday Life*. Doubleday Anchor Books A174; Garden City, N.Y.

Groenewald, Alphonso. 2001. "Isaiah 1:2–3, ethics and wisdom. Isaiah 1:2–3 and the Song of Moses (Dt 32): Is Isaiah a Prophet Like Moses?" *HTS: Theological Studies* 67:1–6.

Gunkel, Hermann, and Joachim Begrich. 1933. *Einleitung in die Psalmen: Die Gattungen der religiösen Lyrik Israels*. Göttinger Handkommentar zum alten Testament. 4th ed. Göttingen. Translated 1998. *Introduction to the Psalms: The Genres of the Religious Lyric of Israel*. Translated by James D. Nogalski. Macon, Ga.

Holladay, William L. 1966. "Jeremiah and Moses: Further Observations." *Journal of Biblical Literature* 85:17–27.

———. 2004. "Elusive Deuteronomists, Jeremiah, and Proto-Deuteronomy." *Catholic Biblical Quarterly* 66:55–77.

Holmyard, Harold Roy, III. 1992. *Mosaic Eschatology in Isaiah, Especially Chapters 1, 28-33*. Th.D. diss., Dallas Theological Seminary.

Huffmon, Herbert B. 1959. "The Covenant Lawsuit in the Prophets." *Journal of Biblical Literature* 78:285-95.

Hyatt, J. Philip. 1971. *Commentary on Exodus*. New Century Bible. London.

Johnson, Vivian L. 2009. *David in Distress: His Portrait through the Historical Psalms*. Library of Hebrew Bible / Old Testament Studies 505. New York.

Keiser, Thomas A. 2005. "The Song of Moses: A Basis for Isaiah's Prophecy." *Vetus Testamentum* 55:486-500.

Knowles, Michael P. 1989. " 'The Rock, His Work Is Perfect': Unusual Imagery for God in Deuteronomy 32." *Vetus Testamentum* 39:307-22.

Koch, Klaus. 1969. *The Growth of the Biblical Tradition: The Form-Critical Method*. Translated by S. M. Cupitt. Scribner Studies in Biblical Interpretation. New York.

Leuchter, Mark. 2007. "Why Is The Song of Moses in the Book of Deuteronomy?" *Vetus Testamentum* 57:295-317.

Levenson, Jon D. 1975. "Who Inserted the Book of the Torah?" *Harvard Theological Review* 68:203-33.

Levinson, Bernard M. 2000. "The Hermeneutics of Tradition: A Response to J. G. McConville." *Journal of Biblical Literature* 119:269-86.

Levy, Abraham J. 1930. *The Song of Moses (Deuteronomy 32)*. Scientific Series of *Oriens—The Oriental Reivew* 1. Baltimore.

Lohfink, Norbert. 1964. "Auslegung deuteronomischer Texte, IV." *Bibel und Leben* 5:247-56.

Lord, Albert B. 2000. *The Singer of Tales*. Edited by Stephen Mitchell and Gregory Nagy. 2nd ed. Harvard Studies in Comparative Literature 24. Cambridge, Mass. 1st ed. 1960.

Lundbom, Jack R. 1976. "The Lawbook of the Josianic Reform." *Catholic Biblical Quarterly* 38:293-302.

MacDonald, Nathan. 2006. "The Literary Criticism and Rhetorical Logic of Deuteronomy I–IV." *Vetus Testamentum* 56:203-24.

Martin, Richard P. 1989. *The Language of Heroes: Speech and Performance in the Iliad*. Myth and Poetics 1. Ithaca, N.Y.

Mayes, Andrew D. H. 1979. *Deuteronomy*. New Century Bible. London.

McGarry, Eugene P. 2005. "The Ambidextrous Angel (Daniel 12:7 and Deuteronomy 32:40): Inner-Biblical Exegesis and Textual Criticism in Counterpoint." *Journal of Biblical Literature* 124:211-28.

McKenzie, Jon. 2005. "Performance Studies." In *The Johns Hopkins Guide to Literary Theory and Criticism*, edited by Michael Groden, Martin Kreiswirth, and Imre Szeman. 2nd ed. Baltimore.

Mendenhall, George E. 1975. "Samuel's 'Broken *Rîb*': Deuteronomy 32." In

No Famine in the Land: Studies in Honor of J. L. McKenzie, edited by J. W. Flanagan and A. W. Robinson. 63–74. Missoula, Mont. Reprinted 1993. In *A Song of Power and the Power of Song: Essays on the Book of Deuteronomy*, edited by Duane L. Christensen. Sources for Biblical and Theological Study 3. 169–80. Winona Lake, Ind.

Miller, Patrick D. 1990. *Deuteronomy*. Interpretation. Louisville, Ky.

Mowinckel, Sigmund. 1962. *The Psalms in Israel's Worship*. Translated by D. R. Ap-Thomas. 2 vols. Oxford. Reprinted 2004. Grand Rapids, Mich.

Nagy, Gregory. 1990. *Pindar's Homer: The Lyric Possession of an Epic Past*. Rev. ed. Baltimore. http://nrs.harvard.edu/urn-3:hul.ebook:CHS_Nagy. Pindars_Homer.1990.

———. 1996. *Poetry as Performance: Homer and Beyond*. Cambridge, U.K. http://nrs.harvard.edu/urn-3:hul.ebook:CHS_Nagy.Poetry_as_Performance.1996.

———. 2007. "Did Sappho and Alcaeus Ever Meet? Symmetries of Myth and Ritual in Performing the Songs of Ancient Lesbos." *Literatur und Religion 1: Wege zu einer mythisch-rituellen Poetik bei den Griechen*, edited by Anton Bierl, Rebecca Lämmle, and Katharina Wesselmann. MythosEikon-Poiesis 1.1. 211–69. New York. http://nrs.harvard.edu/urn-3:hlnc. essay:Nagy.Did_Sappho_and_Alcaeus_Ever_Meet.2007.

Najman, Hindy. 2003. *Seconding Sinai: The Development of Mosaic Discourse in Second Temple Judaism*. JSJSup 77. Boston.

Nelson, Richard D. 2002. *Deuteronomy: A Commentary*. Old Testament Library. Louisville, Ky.

Nigosian, Solomon A. 1996. "The Song of Moses (Dt 32): A Structural Analysis." *Ephemerides Theologicae Lovanienses* 72:5–22.

———. 1997. "Linguistic Patterns of Deuteronomy 32." *Biblica* 78:206–24.

———. 2002. "Images of Moses: A Comparative Inquiry." *Theological Review* 23:27–46.

———. 2003. "Historical Allusions for Dating Deut 32." *Biblische Notizen* 119–120:30–34.

Noth, Martin. 1948. *Überlieferungsgeschichte des Pentateuch*. Stuttgart. Translated 1981. *A History of Pentateuchal Traditions*. Translated by Bernhard W. Anderson. Scholars Press Reprint Series 5. Chico, Calif.

Propp, William H. C. 2006. *Exodus 19-40: A New Translation with Introduction and Commentary*. Anchor Bible 2A. New York.

von Rad, Gerhard. 1996. *Deuteronomy: A Commentary*. Translated by Dorothea Barton. Old Testament Library. Philadelphia.

Sanders, Paul. 1996. *The Provenance of Deuteronomy 32*. Oudtestamentische Studiën 37. New York.

Schechner, Richard. 1985. *Between Theater and Anthropology*. Philadelphia.

——. 2003. *Performance Theory.* Rev. ed. New York.

Skehan, Patrick W. 1959. "Qumran and the Present State of Old Testament Text Studies: The Masoretic Text." *Journal of Biblical Literature* 78:21–25.

Soggin, J. Alberto. 1958. "Jeremías XII 10a: Eine Parallelstelle zu Deut. XXXII 8/LXX?" *Vetus Testamentum* 8:304–5.

Thiessen, Matthew. 2004. "The Form and Function of the Song of Moses (Deuteronomy 32:1–43)." *Journal of Biblical Literature* 123:401–24.

Turner, Victor W. 1957. *Schism and Continuity in an African Society: A Study of Ndembu Village Life.* Manchester, U.K.

Vogel, Dan. 2003. "Moses as Poet: Ha'azinu as Poem." *Jewish Bible Quarterly* 31:211–18.

Watts, James W. 1992. *Psalm and Story: Inset Hymns in Hebrew Narrative.* JSOTSup 139. Sheffield, U.K.

——. 1993. " 'This Song': Conspicuous Poetry in Hebrew Prose." In *Verse in Ancient Near Eastern Prose*, edited by Johannes C. de Moor and Wilfred G. E. Watson. Alter Orient und Altes Testament 42. 345–58. Neukirchen-Vluyn.

Weitzman, Steven. 1994. "Lessons From the Dying: The Narrative Role of Deuteronomy 32." *Harvard Theological Review* 87:377–93.

——. 1997. *Song and Story in Biblical Narrative: The History of a Literary Convention in Ancient Israel.* Bloomington, Ind.

Wettstein, Howard. 1998. "Ritual." In *Routledge Encyclopedia of Philosophy*, edited by E. Craig. London. http://www.rep.routledge.com/article/K090.

Wevers, John William. 1995. *Notes on the Greek Text of Deuteronomy.* SBL Septuagint and Cognate Studies 39. Atlanta, Ga.

Wolff, Hans Walter. 1961. "Das Kerygma des deuteronomistischen Geschichtswerks." *Zeitschrift für die alttestamentliche Wissenschaft* 73:171–86.

——. 1964. "Das Kerygma des Jahwisten." *Evangelische Theologie* 24 (1964) 70–98. Translated 1966. "The Kerygma of the Yahwist." Translated by Wilbur A. Benware. *Interpretation* 22:131–58.

——. 1969. "Zur Thematik der elohistischen Fragmente im Pentateuch." *Evangelische Theologie* 29:59–72. Translated 1972. "The Elohistic Fragments in the Pentateuch." Translated by Keith R. Crim. *Interpretation* 26:158–73.

Wright, G. Ernest. 1962. "The Lawsuit of God: A Form-critical Study of Deuteronomy 32." In *Israel's Prophetic Heritage: Essays in Honor of James Muilenburg*, edited by Bernhard W. Anderson and Walter Harrelson. 26–67. New York.

Index Locorum

Index Rerum et Nominum